CORE OF CONVICTION

CORE OF
CONVICTION

MY STORY

MICHELE BACHMANN

Sentinel

SENTINEL
Published by the Penguin Group
Penguin Group (USA) Inc., 375 Hudson Street,
New York, New York 10014, U.S.A.
Penguin Group (Canada), 90 Eglinton Avenue East, Suite 700,
Toronto, Ontario, Canada M4P 2Y3
(a division of Pearson Penguin Canada Inc.)
Penguin Books Ltd, 80 Strand, London WC2R 0RL, England
Penguin Ireland, 25 St. Stephen's Green, Dublin 2, Ireland
(a division of Penguin Books Ltd)
Penguin Books Australia Ltd, 250 Camberwell Road, Camberwell,
Victoria 3124, Australia
(a division of Pearson Australia Group Pty Ltd)
Penguin Books India Pvt Ltd, 11 Community Centre, Panchsheel Park,
New Delhi – 110 017, India
Penguin Group (NZ), 67 Apollo Drive, Rosedale, Auckland 0632,
New Zealand (a division of Pearson New Zealand Ltd)
Penguin Books (South Africa) (Pty) Ltd, 24 Sturdee Avenue,
Rosebank, Johannesburg 2196, South Africa

Penguin Books Ltd, Registered Offices:
80 Strand, London WC2R 0RL, England

First published in 2011 by Sentinel,
a member of Penguin Group (USA) Inc.

1   3   5   7   9   10   8   6   4   2

LIBRARY OF CONGRESS CATALOGING IN PUBLICATION DATA

Bachmann, Michele.
Core of conviction : my story / Michele Bachmann.
p.   cm.
ISBN 978-1-59523-090-4
1. Bachmann, Michele.   2. Women legislators—United States—Biography.   3. Legislators—United States—
Biography.   4. Legislators—MinnesotaBiography.   5. United States. Congress. House—Biography.   I. Title.
E901.1.B33A3   2011
328.73'092—dc23
[B]
2011035631

Printed in the United States of America
Set in Bulmer MT
Designed by Spring Hoteling

Penguin is committed to publishing works of quality and integrity. In that spirit, we are proud to offer this book to our readers; however, the story, the experiences, and the words are the author's alone.

*To the loves of my life: Marcus, Lucas, Harrison, Elisa, Caroline,
Sophia, twenty-three wonderful foster children, our parents.*

CONTENTS

CHAPTER ONE

A Middle-American Mom

IT was April Fools' Day 2000. I started out that morning thinking that I was headed for a joyful wedding. Then, instead, I found myself embroiled in a pitched political battle. So rather than witnessing a young couple start their new life together, I ended up finding a new political career. Yes, it was April Fools' Day, but it was no joke.

April 1, 2000, was the date of the Republican convention for the 56th Minnesota state senate district. The gathering was held in the beautiful little town of Mahtomedi, just east of St. Paul. The Bachmanns—my husband Marcus, our children, and I—were residents of that district, living in the nearby town of Stillwater.

It was also the day the Bachmann family was planning to attend a wedding in Brainerd, a town in the northern part of the state, a two- or three-hour drive away. My own wedding, back in 1978, has always been precious to me—a covenant that Marcus and I treasure for eternity. And I just love weddings. I love the ceremony, the music, the exchange of vows, the sense of a new joint destiny for the newlyweds, even the cake and the celebration afterward.

But on this one morning, I had second thoughts about going. I said to my husband, "Honey, do you mind if I don't go with you this time?" I had woken up thinking I really ought to go instead to the Republican district convention. Someone, I thought, should send a message to those entrenched insiders, reminding them that we didn't like what they were doing in the capital, St. Paul—that we didn't like what they were doing to us and our children.

Marcus knew I was especially concerned about a new left-leaning, state-mandated education curriculum. That new initiative, short on academic excellence, was the so-called Profile of Learning—a federal government program that our state legislators, following orders from Washington, D.C., had begun imposing on children across the state.

Indeed, Marcus shared my concerns about these and other top-down liberal policies. In his Christian counseling practice, he was constantly seeing, up close, the damage done to young people by wrongheaded ideas—ideas that led to poor educational experiences and poor outcomes. Yet at the same time, Marcus had to concern himself with the practicalities of running our ongoing business and being a father. I was the political activist, not my husband.

Marcus was serious about his work and his mission, and yet he was always loving and understanding. "Okay," he said. And so the Bachmann family changed its plans. He and our younger kids drove off to Brainerd for the wedding, and I made my way to the local GOP convention.

Poor Marcus; he had no idea what would happen next. And frankly, neither did I.

Because this was a last-minute decision and I was worried about being late, I simply flew out the door. Only when I was in the car did I realize what a mess I was. I had on jeans—and I never wear jeans if I can help it. I also wore some white moccasins worn to a dingy gray beige; my sweatshirt had a hole in it. I had no makeup on—and every woman knows what that means. And my hair was a fright.

But it was too late to turn back. I had to get to the convention before the registration table closed. Arriving in a flurry, I paid my twenty-dollar party registration fee, and I was in, along with some two hundred other Republicans. We were gathered in an auditorium at Mahtomedi High School, just west of Stillwater, and we were engaging in grassroots politics at its rootsiest.

It seemed likely that the convention would, without a hitch, endorse the incumbent senator yet again.

Or maybe there would be a hitch. Some of us began talking about why we were there. Why had we pulled ourselves away from other responsibilities on this Saturday morning? Was it just to sit and listen to political speeches? Was it simply to rubber-stamp our state senator?

Actually, we wanted to do more than that—we wanted to be heard. We all asked: *Why are we Republicans nominating this guy once again, when we can't trust him to represent us when he goes to St. Paul?*

This senator had fought for his country as a Marine in Vietnam; I will always honor him for that service. And because so many others honored him too, he had been elected to the Minnesota State House of Representatives in 1972; he had moved up to the state senate in 1982. By the time of the district 56 convention, he had been in the state legislature for nearly three decades. Yet during that time, his voting record had changed. And we, the people, his constituents, wanted now to make our voices heard. His twenty-eight years in power seemed long enough.

The problem was that the senator had come to embrace a "go-along, get-along" mentality in the legislature, and he took the same attitude toward the growth of our state government. The Democrats were large and in charge in St. Paul, and the senator seemed a little too willing to accept his lesser status as part of the Republican minority. Not only that, but he had also become known as a safe vote for crucial legislation that the Democrats wanted to push; by gaining his token Republican vote, they could say that their bill was bipartisan. That veneer of bipartisanship put a "Minnesota nice" front on the hard-edged leftism emanating from the Twin Cities. And St. Paul and Minneapolis were then happy, of course, to take their orders from the even more distant bureaucrats in Washington, D.C.

Our senator supported the Profile of Learning curriculum, brushing aside repeated attempts by parents like me to speak to him about our concerns. We phoned; we wrote letters; we made personal visits. When he would agree to see us, we showed him example after example of the faulty curriculum, including the dumbed-down tests and the politically correct guideline documents produced in St. Paul. We told him that parents, teachers, and taxpayers in his district were concerned that our kids needed rigorous academics—not liberal and secular values, attitudes, and beliefs imposed by the state.

In addition, the senator had changed his voting record on important social issues. He had once taken a pro-life stance, but not anymore. He had even proposed a bill to install a bust of former Supreme Court justice Harry Blackmun in the state capitol; Blackmun was a famous Minnesotan, to be sure, but he was particularly beloved by liberals because he had authored the Supreme Court's infamous 1973 *Roe v. Wade* decision, trampling state laws and legalizing abortion nationwide. And that was an unprecedented decree lacking constitutional substance. Blackmun absurdly declared that the basis for the *Roe v. Wade* decision could be found in the "penumbras," or shadows, of the Constitution. In other words, Blackmun's justification for legalizing abortion was made out of thin air. So why was the senator supporting a special honor for Blackmun? Why was he lionizing the champion of abortion on demand? Indeed, on all the big issues that my friends and I cared about, the senator was 100 percent wrong.

In the meantime, being the Democrats' favorite Republican, the senator had a cushy deal in the state legislature. In fact, there was just one possible obstacle to this symbiotic relationship's going on forever: He had to win reelection in his Republican district, and that meant he had to survive Republican nominating conventions, such as this one in Mahtomedi, every election year. So that had been his challenge: how to vote reliably "left" in St. Paul to keep his power-broker friends there happy, and then how to double-talk "right" back home to win the votes of local citizens.

As my friends and I caucused in the back of the auditorium, we thought: *Well, let's figure out a way to let the senator know we're not happy with his voting record. We need to make him realize he has to pay more attention to the folks back home, and to their views, than to the wishes of his liberal Democratic overlords in St. Paul. We need to ask him some tough questions, get him on record, and make him commit to some conservative stances. We need to turn up the heat, as they say, and hope that he sees the light.*

But then a friend pointed out that the only sure way to capture his attention—to convince him we weren't just a small speed bump on his path to another term—was actually to run against him. We'd have to put up a candidate to challenge him on the floor of the district convention; we'd have to present an alternative candidate to the Republican conventioneers. After all, most of the folks in the auditorium were far more conservative than the senator.

But who would step up? Who would send that signal? Eyes turned to me. I had been vocal on issues, including the Profile of Learning, for years. "Michele, will you do it? Will you put your name out there?" Folks were insistent: Someone had to do it. And apparently, that someone should be me.

I was thinking to myself: *Oh my, I look like a mess. I wasn't prepared for this. I'll look like a fool.* And I thought too that if I had any political ambitions for the future—which, at the time, I didn't—surely a sudden, last-minute move such as this would end them. Plus, I didn't know many people in the room; why would I want to introduce myself to them and look foolish at the same time?

But then I told myself: *Michele, sometimes you have to risk it. After all, others have taken far bigger risks for what they believed in. Now your turn has come.* And one issue in particular—insisting on academic excellence rather than dumbing down the curriculum and imposing a liberal scholastic agenda—was simply too important to ignore. And other issues too needed to be addressed, including the right to life, high taxes, excess spending, and improving the overall business climate of Minnesota.

For all those reasons, I agreed to go for it. I would make the challenge. At least we would get the senator's attention. Maybe he would even actually listen to us for a change.

The consensus among my friends was clear: The person to take on the senator was Michele. And when your friends ask you to do something— and you know it's a good idea and the right thing to do—well, you have to pay heed. In Christianity, it's called servant leadership. This was my moment to serve.

"So what do I do?" I asked. The answer came back: "You write your name on a sheet of paper, and you go up and tell them that you want to run for the Republican endorsement—easy!" *Oh, okay,* I thought to myself, *that doesn't sound too hard.*

So being encouraged by my friends yet having no idea what to expect next, I walked up to the table at the front of the room. I approached the chairman and handed him that fateful slip of paper. He looked down at the writing, and his jaw dropped: "You're challenging his endorsement?" Yes, I was. Technically, I was saying that this party convention should not endorse the incumbent senator for renomination.

I paused and asked: "So what do I do now?" That's how naive I was about what I was getting into.

He stared me up and down. He obviously didn't like what I was doing—that is, trying to block the senator's bandwagon. Yet I had a right to do it. Indeed, anyone in the room could have done the same thing. But I was the one who stepped up. "Well," he sighed, pointing to the podium, "you have to go up there and give a five-minute speech."

"Okay." Yikes. An actual campaign speech. And not just speaking about the issues but also taking on an entrenched incumbent.

Over the years, I'd done a lot of speaking—but never as a political challenger. I'd spoken to small groups, mostly concerning the obnoxious Profile of Learning. But in those instances I'd had plenty of time to prepare, to put myself together. Indeed, going back to my days of arguing tax cases, I'd known I always wanted to be the best-prepared person in the courtroom. But today, when I really needed some preparation, I didn't have it. In my old jeans and torn sweatshirt, I looked as if I were dressed for a garage sale. The April Fools' Day joke was on me.

Yet I knew what I wanted to say. I was nothing more than a concerned parent—one of many in the room—but I was fully aware of what was right and what was wrong. I wanted to speak from my heart, and yet my head was also ready.

So a calm and a confidence passing all understanding came over me. I thought of my sweet husband, Marcus, our five biological children, and the twenty-three foster children to whom we had also opened our home and our hearts. I was proud of the values we had been able to instill in them. It hadn't always been easy. And the liberal meddlers in the state education bureaucracy hadn't made it any easier. So we were fighting for our kids and our values, and we needed one fighter out front. That was my job. I had accepted the mission, and now I had to fulfill it. It was as simple as that.

I was just doing my duty as a citizen, speaking out. It was like that wonderful Norman Rockwell painting from the forties, *Freedom of Speech*, in which an earnest man speaks out at the town meeting, politely but firmly.

Finally, I thought of Philippians 4:13, "I can do all things through Christ which strengthens me," and I said a prayer. Now I was ready.

I got up to the stage and delivered a speech that came straight from the heart. It was about freedom, and what freedom means in the hearts of Minnesotans and of all Americans. I declared that freedom is connected to the issues we should care about: life, taxes, education. That is, the issues on which the state senator had once stood with us but now stood against us.

And when I saw the faces of all those folks listening to me, following with warm attention, I felt confident enough to speak truthfully and forcefully. I was among people who shared the same vision, and they gave me strength and confidence. My neighbors and fellow Republicans were happy to hear someone speak clear words, words that expressed their own faith and beliefs. I had entered the room as just a name to most of those folks, but after a few minutes we had all become friends. They could look into my heart as I spoke, and even as I was speaking, I could look into their hearts. That's a sacred feeling. So it was their support—and maybe their quiet prayers—that helped to sustain me in my partisan-politics debut.

My five minutes were up. I sat down, and the incumbent senator said gruffly: "You paid your twenty dollars, and now you just had your entertainment."

Your "entertainment"? Did he really say that? The "entertainment," in his reckoning, was me—as if I were a sideshow. Chilly silence hung in the room. Nobody could believe that the senator had just said something so demeaning. After all, even people who weren't planning on voting for me had seen that I was sincere. At age forty-four, I had lived, worked, and raised a family in the area for a long time. Why was he so publicly condescending?

The folks in the room now began to see the senator with new eyes. Maybe, they thought, he had been in the legislature too long. Maybe he had a bad case of "incumbent-itis"—or "RINO-itis." And if he was capable of throwing such cutting words at one of his constituents, what had he been thinking, really, about *all* of his constituents? In a single instant, his tongue had revealed what appeared to be in his heart. We had gotten a glimpse too of what he was like when he was making deals and clinking glasses with the Democrats in St. Paul. We Republican voters back in the boonies had finally gotten the message—right between the eyes. We were now saying to ourselves, *That's a pretty high horse you're riding, Senator, looking down on us, and now we're going to take you down.*

Other than that gruff opening line, I don't think anyone remembered anything he said. Having finished his talk, he sat down. But the chill remained. He had frozen—and snapped—his connection to his voters.

Meanwhile, outside the auditorium, a political crisis was heating up. I found out later that his political operatives in the room had realized immediately that their man had messed up, and so they had gone into instant damage-control mode. They had picked up their cell phones and called the leading state senate Republicans, telling the big bosses that one of their members was down—and wasn't going to get up without a lot of political help. So GOP apparatchiks jumped in their cars and hightailed it to Mahtomedi, hoping somehow to save their man.

Inside the auditorium, it was time to vote: the incumbent versus Mrs. Bachmann. Each person handwrote his or her choice on a white slip of paper and handed it to his or her precinct leader. Then the convention chairman requested that representatives from the two campaigns come to a back room and witness the ballot counting. "Could someone from the Bachmann campaign come to the counting room?" he asked.

Sitting in the audience, I thought to myself, *What Bachmann campaign?* So far, at least, I was it—I was the whole campaign. So I turned to the woman seated to my right and asked, "Would you be willing to be my representative?" That was Barbara Harper, one brave lady.

Barbara immediately agreed to act as witness. And when she got to the back room, she found it swarming with political operatives, all eager to "help" with the counting. For well over an hour, Barbara was in there with them, and it's a good thing she was. When one politico "discovered" an envelope full of "ballots," Barbara challenged them on the spot—and won. A few operatives seemed to wish to try "creative balloting," but the Republicans of district 56—even if they didn't support me—wanted an honest count. This was Minnesota, not Chicago.

In the meantime, out in the auditorium, folks were growing impatient. They would walk up to the microphone and ask, "Mr. Chairman, why is it taking so long to count a few hundred ballots?" The Republican operatives, meanwhile, could be seen chatting on their cell phones—and yet it wasn't us local Republicans they were talking to; they were talking instead *about* us to their wheeler-dealer pals in St. Paul. They were trying to figure out how to use the convention rules to invalidate the voting.

As for me, I sat in my seat. There was nothing I could do. I went to find a pay phone—I didn't have a cell phone in those days—and I called my sweet, nonpolitical friend, Ann, the greatest walking partner I ever had. I explained to her what was happening and implored her, "I really want you to come over. I am sure to lose this thing, and I need you, please, to be with me." Ann was doing the dishes with her husband, but, kind as always, she drove over to offer moral support. I felt better, and yet I still had no inkling that my life was about to change.

Finally, after an hour and twenty minutes, Barbara came bursting out of the back room, running toward me in my seat in the auditorium. She had written the results in blue ink on the palm of her hand. "You won!" she exclaimed, waving her hand in front of my face. "And you won with a supermajority." That is, over 60 percent of the vote! So I had just become the officially endorsed Republican candidate; the longtime incumbent had lost the mandate of Republicans in his district. As I said, this was grass-roots politics at its rootsiest—the people had spoken. Decisively.

The senator, a sheaf of papers in his hand, then tried to disqualify the balloting. But now there wasn't just a chill in the auditorium; there were boos and shouts. We, the spontaneous insurgents, had done everything by the book, and now, at the end of a long count, we had won—and nobody wanted to hear gripes from the senator.

Eventually, the chairman had to announce the obvious. He climbed to the podium, moved toward the microphone with obvious reluctance, and then, speaking in a pained voice, said: "I guess we've got a result." Pause. "And, uh, I guess it's Michele Bachmann."

The audience—most of it—cheered. Nobody in that auditorium was more surprised than me. Amid the tumult, someone said, "You have to go back up onstage and thank the delegates." And so I did. Those delegates were now my supporters, and I needed to thank them.

In that moment, I felt honored, humbled, blessed, and challenged all at the same time. I thanked everyone, reiterated the critical issues, and then reminded the audience that the bigger electoral battle lay ahead. And as it turned out, I faced two elections. Not only would I have to confront a Democrat in November, but the incumbent senator had not conceded his defeat at the Mahtomedi convention; he eventually chose to run against me in the September Republican primary, as he had a perfectly legal right to do.

In that auditorium, I had become an accidental politician. I hadn't planned on going to the convention, hadn't planned on running for anything, hadn't planned on speaking—and certainly hadn't planned on winning. And yet there I was. My friends joked that our slogan for the upcoming campaign would be "We know nothing about campaigning, and we can prove it."

Ann and I drove back home to Stillwater, and then, to catch our breath, we sat on a bench in a park overlooking the St. Croix River. We looked at the beautiful flowing water, then at each other. I said, "Ann, we had better pray." We prayed together, giving this remarkable turn of events over to the Lord. We both asked for guidance, and I asked one more thing: How would I tell Marcus?

It was April 1, and this poor man was in northern Minnesota, along with the girls, Elisa, Caroline, and Sophia. Attending a wedding, fulfilling obligations, looking out for his family, he had no idea what his wife had just done.

There was no way for me to contact him; neither of us had a cell phone then. How should I break the news that I had left the house in the morning as a full-time mom, a homemaker, and a retired tax lawyer—and was coming back in the afternoon as the Republican-endorsed candidate for the state senate? And that I was facing an uncertain future in the coming election, to say nothing of an uncertain future if I ended up sitting in the Minnesota legislature?

I got home, and the house was empty. I could see that the answering machine was filled up but didn't have the heart to listen to the messages. Marcus and I had always worked as a team; it's the only way we could get through graduate school, raise our twenty-eight biological and foster children, and work in business. I knew I had stepped outside our long-established norm. It was one thing to go to a political convention; it was quite another to launch a political career. My husband would have told me if he'd been thinking about starting up a new clinic, so why hadn't I told him that I was starting up a new career? It was an accident, of course, albeit a happy, challenging accident. Still, I knew that the first thing I needed to do was make things right with Marcus and my family.

So I went upstairs and waited in the bedroom. Actually, the bathroom. And I thought about how I would tell him the news.

After a while, I heard the garage door open. The Bachmanns were back, even if Mom hadn't made the trip. I was always elated to hear everyone come home; the familiar sounds were like music to me: the jingling of keys, the tramping of feet, the whoosh of coats being taken off and put away—or flung on the couch. All the happy sounds of a homecoming. But this time it was different. Marcus thought I was asleep, and so, always thoughtful, he didn't come bounding up the stairs.

But I was awake, of course. I was just dreading the moment of truth.

Downstairs, I could hear Marcus clicking on the answering machine. "Congratulations, Michele!" the first message rang out. "Congratulations on your victory!" I thought to myself that Marcus must be assuming this was all some sort of elaborate April Fools' joke—on me, on him, on all of us. Yet after the second or third congratulatory message, I could sense that he knew something real was up.

Marcus called up to the second floor: "Michele?"

"Yes?" I was trying to sound as innocent as possible.

"Is there something you'd like to tell me?" It was one of those moments we've all seen on TV—a Lucy and Ricky Ricardo moment from the old *I Love Lucy* show. All that was missing was Marcus-as-Ricky saying to his wide-eyed wife, "Lucy! You've got some 'splaining to do!"

"Well," I answered, "I am the endorsed candidate for state senator. I made a speech at the convention . . . and . . . I won the balloting."

"No!" Marcus said. He wasn't being harsh—he is never harsh. He really thought this was some sort of April Fools' joke.

"You did *what*?" My victory was not an overly happy piece of news for Marcus. After a lot of hard work, having gone through much sacrifice and deferred gratification, we had built a wonderful family and successful careers. And yet unilaterally I had just moved forward into a new endeavor that he had had nothing to say about. We had always planned everything together, but not this. His life, the kids' lives, all would be affected, and he hadn't received the courtesy of being consulted. Now I would have to be off campaigning—and then, if I won, legislating. Inevitably an extra burden would be on all of us, but mostly on him.

However, being the wonderful man that he is, he took three days to think these things through. He knew that issues such as improving education, protecting life, and lowering taxes were important. They were important to me, and they were important to him. He just needed a few moments to recalibrate his already strenuous schedule. Now it would be even more strenuous.

"You know," he warned, "you can't take this back." And he was right. I was in. And when I am in, I am 100 percent in. All the way.

But for my part, I made a commitment to Marcus and to my family: Every next step in politics, whatever it might be, would be made in full and prayerful consultation with the family. I would only proceed with their full agreement—and, of course, asking for the Lord's blessing.

So how had I gotten this far? How had I been so fortunate as to have Marcus and all our kids? And to be at that podium in a little corner of eastern Minnesota? And then, later, to see a new future in politics—the state legislature, the U.S. Congress, and the national stage?

Well, that's a long story.

The personal story begins in Iowa, but before I tell it, I should make this point as clear as the Stillwater night sky: At every step of my life's journey, I believe that God has been with me. He has prepared me for the next challenge, lesson by lesson. God gently prepares all of us, if we want His help, for our small struggles—and our big battles. I learned back in Sunday school the story of David, how he was a shepherd boy and how, as he grew toward manhood, he learned to kill the lion and the bear. Only then was he ready for his epic confrontation with Goliath. One thing led to another, but only God planned the full story in advance.

So I didn't have a plan when I went into that convention in Mahtomedi. But I did have experience and the strength of core principles. I had the strength, in fact, of a movement of liberty-loving people, all the concerned voters whom I had met across the state of Minnesota. They were all reasonable, fair-minded citizens, living carefully and conservatively. And they were folks who wanted for the next generation what every American has wanted—a better life and a brighter hope. Movements can create their own energy. And they can produce new candidates, one of whom was me.

So that was the first political lesson: With the right kind of popular energy, ordinary people can make a difference. You can fight city hall. That is, you can take on the establishment and win. The political waters back home in Stillwater have not been still since.

But a second lesson was even more important: Nothing can succeed without faith. Faith is being sure of what we hope for, even as it provides assurance of what we do not see. I took a leap of faith that Saturday, and yet I always knew that if I failed in my political bid, God would still catch me.

Third, I was reminded that I would be lost without my family. Even if I am in a faraway place, they will always be right there with me, heart and soul. Marcus, our children—they have all been so good to me. And while I have tried to do right by them, I am blessed to have their solid support in my career, and I never want to take them for granted. So someday, I promise, we'll all take that long vacation!

And here's a fourth lesson, gained from that political battle in a little corner of Minnesota eleven years ago: Principle is more important than partisanship. I am a proud Republican, fully committed to the profamily, pro–free enterprise, prodefense policies of my party, but if I see a GOP leader failing to fight for our party's principles, I will not hesitate to speak out—and, if necessary, stand up.

As John F. Kennedy once said, sometimes political parties ask too much. The Minnesota Republican hierarchy didn't want me to run against their incumbent in 2000; they didn't know who I was. And once many party bigwigs did get to know me, they weren't sure that I could win the seat. But I did. And I did it again two years later. Even then, many of them never warmed up to me, because I always spoke up for what I believed were our core principles. I didn't get into politics to please men and women who had grasped for power—just the opposite, in fact.

I have always seen myself as a champion of the values I grew up with— the values that have grown even stronger in my heart in the decades since. So I felt called to serve on April 1, 2000, and I have sensed that call ever since.

Armed with values and faith, supported by family and fellow citizens, together we can do much. We can secure what people are yearning for—the chance to take our country back. Just watch.

CHAPTER TWO

The River That Finds Its Way: From the Sogne Fjord to Waterloo

I was born Michele Marie Amble on April 6, 1956, at Allen Memorial Hospital in Waterloo, Iowa.

But first let me tell you about those who came before me. I owe everything to them, and to the faith and values that they passed on to me. I often say that everything I need to know I learned in Iowa, but in fact the essentials of my life are rooted even further back in time.

My people were Norwegians; family names include "Johnson," "Munson," and "Thompson," as well as "Amble."

Norway is a beautiful country boasting many scenic fjords—long, narrow inlets of water surrounded by rocky cliffs and hills. Fjords are wonderful to look at, although they are hard to make a living from. As a result, only about 3 percent of the land can be farmed, and those farms suffer from a short growing season and rocky soil. The Munson ancestral home was a modest farm called Ronnei; the family grew mostly potatoes, supplementing its meager food supply with fish caught from the nearby Jostedal River.

A few miles downriver from Ronnei is the village of Sogndal, looking out on the Sogne Fjord. "Sogndal" means a river that seeks its way.

Seeking the way. That was our story.

Norwegians had been coming to America since the seventeenth century, but organized emigration from Norway began in 1825, when fifty or so Norwegians arrived in New York City aboard the *Restauration*—a sloop my people remember as the Norwegian *Mayflower*. These history-making "sloopers," as the early pioneers were called, settled in upstate New York, but most Norwegians chose to go farther west, where the land was cheaper and the horizon seemed wider.

In 1845 a group of eighty Norwegian Americans, living in what was then called the Muskego Settlement—near present-day Norway, Wisconsin—wrote an open letter to the people back home in the old country, extolling life in America and urging more Norwegians to join them in coming to the new realm, where the growing season was longer and the soil was richer. The signers proclaimed, "We live under a generous government in a fertile land, where freedom and equality prevail in civil and religious affairs, and without any special permission we can enter almost any profession and make an honest living. This we consider more wonderful than riches." Freedom! What a wonderful word, brightening the hearts of people all over the world.

One of those who learned of the Muskego manifesto was my great-great-great-grandfather, Melchior Monsson. He was born in 1812 into a family too poor to afford any education; he learned to read only late in life. As a young man, Melchior enlisted in the army; because he was tall, he was picked for the King's Guard. But lifelong military service was not for him, and he went back home to be a farmer. When the exciting news of the Muskego Manifesto rippled through Norway, Melchior was already well into middle age. This was at a time, of course, when the average life expectancy was perhaps half of what it is now. So in terms of the likely number of years left to him, there wasn't much reason for him or his wife, Martha, born in 1815, to leave Norway and start over.

Still, the celestial fire of freedom was sparked within Melchior. He and Martha agreed that they wanted a better life for their five children; that was the most important thing. And if that meant crossing the ocean, traveling to what Norwegians were to call *Vesterheim*—the western home—well, that's what they would do.

Indeed, all across Europe, striving people—the "huddled masses, yearning to breathe free," in the immortal words inscribed on the base of the Statue of Liberty—had the same idea of seeking a better life. They were coming to America.

In 1857 Melchior sold the farm, along with everything else the family owned, to buy passage on a ship to journey across the Atlantic. There were five children: Gjertru, Halvor, Elin, Monsine, and Ingeborg Marie. But when the Monssons arrived at the dock, the captain looked at Halvor—my great-great-grandfather—and declared that he was an adult and would have to pay full fare. Halvor was only eleven, but, taking after his father, he was tall and looked much older. The Monssons didn't have any extra money for the additional fare; they had spent everything they had on the tickets.

It was a heart-wrenching dilemma. The farm had been sold; there was nothing anywhere in the Sogn region for the family to go back to. So Melchior made a painful decision. He told Halvor that he would have to walk back to the old village, hoping that someone would take him in so he wouldn't starve. Someday, the father pledged, they would earn enough money to bring him to America. But not now.

As a mother of five, I pause over that story, because it's impossible for me to imagine being cruelly separated from one of our sons like that. The pain that Martha Monsson must have felt at that moment still lingers in my soul.

But then, just at the moment when the ship was about to push off, the heart of the captain softened and he took pity on the Monssons, saying, "Oh, I guess the boat won't sink if there's one more on board. Hop on!" The boy-man scrambled onto the ship like a jackrabbit. Hallelujah! The family was reunited.

Yet the Monssons' arduous journey was just beginning. In those days, a passage across the Atlantic Ocean took at least two months. Arriving in Canada, the Monssons next had to spend six weeks traveling overland, carrying their belongings from Quebec all the way to Dane County, Wisconsin, where a Norwegian family was waiting to host them. When the Monsson family finally arrived, they dropped down in front of the house in sheer exhaustion. The welcoming family rushed out to give them milk and bread. Thinking back on this kindness, I recall the biblical injunction: Love the stranger, because you were once a stranger yourself. Miraculously, all seven Monssons had survived the long trip from Norway.

Soon these strangers—or rather, these new Americans—were back on their feet, although fully aware that their trek was not over. They then chopped wood and built a simple wagon that could also be used as a raft to take them across the mighty Mississippi River. From De Soto, Wisconsin, they crossed the Father of Waters into Lansing, Iowa, where they looked forward to a homestead of their own. Soon the new "Iowegians"— that is, Iowans from Norway—had simplified their name to "Munson."

My goal here is not to tell the whole story of their remarkable lives, nor those of all my other ancestors. The saga of the Norwegian Americans was better told by the novelist Ole Edvart Rölvaag. In his many works, the most famous of which is *Giants in the Earth,* Rölvaag describes the heroism of those early pioneers, who survived snow, drought, hunger, and loneliness to achieve the upper-midwestern version of the American Dream.

I am proud of my sturdy forebears. I took Norwegian in college but never had the time really to gain proficiency in the language; to this day, that's a regret. One legacy, though, is the way I pronounce my vowels, like the *O* and *A* in "Minnesota," which comes out as "Minne-so-oh-tuh-uh." But to my mother, who sang Norwegian folk songs to us as kids way back when, I sound just fine.

Of course, I realize that few people anywhere had it easy when they first came to America. Every family has great stories like mine—because back then, you didn't make it if you couldn't overcome adversity. Whether in a rural area, a small town, or a big city, every American can take pride in ancestors who possessed the grit and ambition to sacrifice much and to achieve much.

One great source of strength for many of the early pioneers was faith. As the psalmist tells us, "Many are the afflictions of the righteous, but the Lord delivereth him out of them all." Most of the Norwegians were Lutherans; their faith in God was indeed a mighty fortress. Bolstered by their beliefs, the Munsons, Ambles, Johnsons, and Thompsons smoothed the path for those that followed.

Through the hard times and the good, those early Iowans always worked purposefully. They planned for success, never for failure, and that faith in success kept them going. The first permanent settlement in what is now Black Hawk County began in 1845. The early settlers grew corn and wheat; they also harvested honey and syrup. The very next year, they built a school, because they knew that education was important for their young people. No bureaucrat in Des Moines or Washington, D.C., had to tell them that truth; they simply knew the value not only of reading, writing, and arithmetic but also of learning civic republicanism. And of course, they knew the supreme importance of reading and knowing the Bible.

Indeed, within a few years, the pioneers had created a functioning government. The first taxes were levied in 1853; the county collected a grand total of $873.08. As a former tax lawyer—and always a thrifty tax-payer—I appreciate that sort of precision when it comes to using other people's money, down to the penny. By contrast, in today's Washington, a billion dollars is counted as a mere rounding error. Good government should be a closely monitored tool for the people, of course, not a play-thing for the powerful elite. Two years later, in 1855, Waterloo was designated the Black Hawk County seat, the home of courts and public administration.

These details of self-government are important, because we should understand that the early settlers were seeking freedom and order, not anarchy. As soon as they could, they established representative institutions to provide the responsible order that promotes both liberty and prosperity. They knew that they needed *some* government out there on the frontier, just not too much. And in their desire to keep government limited, they insisted that it be kept close to them, so that the humblest citizen could know that public servants were truly serving the public.

Yes, these new Americans loved their new country and were eager to be part of its institutions. Indeed, as the Frenchman Alexis de Tocqueville observed in the early nineteenth century, Americans were not only joiners but also builders and creators. Every little Iowa town soon had not only schools but also libraries, auditoriums, and civic associations. Back in places such as Sogndal, people had been regarded by their rulers as merely peasants. Here in America, they were independent and proud citizens.

And that pride manifested itself in patriotism. When the bugle sounded, Iowans answered the call. That same great-great-grandfather Halvor Munson—the tall one who almost didn't get to leave Norway—was fifteen when the Civil War broke out. Halvor rushed to enlist, and because he was big, it was easy for him to join the army. The young soldier was sent west, spending the war years guarding U.S. forts out on the frontier.

After the war, Halvor was demobilized and ended up coming home on a river raft. And who else was on the raft? None other than Jesse James and his gang. That notorious criminal crew, in fact, invited Halvor to join them; he declined. Yet he did agree to play poker with James and his gang, and he won, of all things, a farm in Iola, Kansas. Who knew that you could win at poker with Jesse James and live? For a while, Halvor traveled back and forth between Kansas and Iowa, but Iowa was always his home. A true patriot, rightly proud of his military service, Halvor carried Old Glory in Fourth of July parades for many years thereafter. Once I counted two dozen Munsons who served during the Civil War—I claim them all!

They were good people, these folks—the Munsons, Ambles, Johnsons, and Thompsons—but they were never rich. That's what Waterloo was like: a town of workers. Iowa started out as a farm state where people mostly grew and ate their own food, but in the late nineteenth century, a new kind of economy was emerging. The big cities in the East were filling up with immigrant workers and their families, and all were hungry for food grown in the Midwest.

So as America grew, Iowa and the Midwest became export oriented, and the region prospered along with the nation as a whole. Rail lines snaked through the land, carrying foodstuffs back to the East and returning with consumer products from, perhaps, the Sears Roebuck catalog.

Indeed, my mother taught us that Iowa was the proud breadbasket of the world. Our whole family loved the Hawkeye State; we were schooled in the virtues of our hardworking heritage and equally determined, in our own time, to make future generations proud of us.

But first the crops and the livestock had to be processed—transformed into bread and meat. Iowans raised millions of hogs on their farms; the animals were then taken by rail to slaughterhouses in cities such as Waterloo. And there, on the banks of the Cedar River, the Rath Packing Company stood guard over the growing metropolis. Rath, founded in 1891, grew into a huge complex, a maze of red-brick buildings running a half mile along the waterfront; it was said to be the largest single meatpacker in the world.

It was rough work—dangerous, heavy machinery clanking and whirling around as workers cut the carcasses into ham, sausage, bacon, and lard. Nothing was wasted. They used the hides for leather and the hair for upholstery or insulation; the bones, hooves, and horns were boiled down into gelatin. They used, according to the old joke, "everything but the squeal." And then from that food factory, the Illinois Central Railroad carried these pork products to Chicago and beyond.

Yes, it was rough work, but it provided a living for thousands. In its heyday, Rath was a place where men could work for a lifetime and support a large family. One of my grandfathers, my mother's father, worked at Rath for years. In fact, he died inside the plant of a heart attack, just as he was pulling on his boots at the beginning of a shift.

Women worked there too. My grandfather's widow labored at the same plant for many years after his death. It's hard for me to imagine what it must have been like to go work every morning in the place where her husband had passed away. My grandmother was a tiny little woman, but she moved around huge trays of bacon—that was her job, and she did it.

In 1948 a major strike changed everything, and in the next few decades the plant began to decline. In 1980 the company, in desperation, turned the factory over to the union; in 1985, after a few more faltering years, the plant closed for good. At present, the city of Waterloo owns the plant, which is included on the National Register of Historic Places. Today there is no bustle and no jobs—just empty buildings holding powerful memories within their age-stained walls. Indeed, across America, we now see far too many sad and forlorn sites, all of which could tell similar tales of faded industrial greatness. Very sad.

In those meatpacking days, Waterloo was a tough town full of tough men. Tough men who never ran from a fight. And when the *real* fight came, Waterloo men were ready.

So we come to the legendary Sullivan brothers, Waterloo men whose heroic spirit abides with us to this day. My father always spoke with pride when he told us the story of the courage and sacrifice of this marvelous family.

Back in the 1930s, many members of the Sullivan clan worked at Rath. But when a friend of the family's died at Pearl Harbor on December 7, 1941, the five Sullivan brothers—Albert, Francis, George, Joseph, and Madison—all enlisted in the navy. But they joined under one condition: that they be allowed to serve together. One of the brothers wrote, "We will make a team together that can't be beat."

So they all served on the USS *Juneau*, a light cruiser fighting in the Pacific. In November 1942, a Japanese torpedo struck their ship. Almost the entire crew died, including all five Sullivans.

Hollywood made a movie about their lives, including scenes in Waterloo as the five sons were growing to manhood. Watching the film on TV years later, I still remember the scene inside the Sullivan household, as a little flag featuring five blue stars rests in the window, signifying the five sons away in military service. Then comes the fateful knock on the door. The women at home know what it means—bad news from Uncle Sam. "Which one?" they ask. And the representative from the Navy Department answers grimly, "All of them." At the end of the movie, we see the five Sullivans striding into heaven, trailing clouds of glory on their path to the Almighty. The Sullivans were home.

Most remarkably, the rest of the Sullivan family—their five blue stars now turned to gold—became active in war-bond drives, raising money for the ships and other weaponry needed to avenge their sons' deaths and win the war. Two navy ships since then have been named *The Sullivans*; in Waterloo today, the Five Sullivan Brothers Convention Center dominates the downtown.

Five children taken away. It's hard enough for me to picture Martha Monsson thinking she would be separated from one child, Halvor, on that dock in Norway. Now to think of all five gone. As the mother of five healthy biological children, I have had occasion to reflect on what it would mean to lose any one of them, let alone five. Others have faced that same sort of painful reality, of course, and sought to make sense of such loss.

I learned of a letter written by Abraham Lincoln to a Mrs. Bixby in 1864, after the president saw a military report that all five of her sons had died fighting in the Civil War. "I pray," Lincoln wrote, "that our Heavenly Father may assuage the anguish of your bereavement, and leave you only the cherished memory of the loved and lost, and the solemn pride that must be yours to have laid so costly a sacrifice upon the altar of freedom."

Later it was discovered that three of Mrs. Bixby's sons were only missing, not dead. But the Sullivans were real. All five gone. Their sacrifice was a demonstration of the Holy Scriptures: "Greater love hath no man than this, that he lay down his life for his friends." Sometimes, I have realized, no matter what the risk, no matter what the odds, it is necessary to fight. And to take comfort in the faith that a grateful nation, and a Heavenly Father, judges our sacrifice worthy.

As a kid in the living room listening to the grownups talk about World War II, I heard nightmarish tales of death camps in Europe, where millions of Jews had been killed. I remember thinking to myself, How could people be so cruel, so horrible? In my young mind, I could not plumb the depths of absolute evil; only years later could I fathom the full extent of the Holocaust. Then and now, we must ask ourselves: Are we ready to confront evil? Will we seek to look the other way, or will we stand up and fight? These are enduring questions for Americans to answer.

In the fifties and sixties, every adult had a World War II memory. Some were tragic, but others were poignant and sweet. My grandmother recalled receiving a Western Union telegram telling her that her son would soon be in New York City, as he was being shipped overseas to the battlefront. She always kept her spare change in a big glass jar, and when she received the telegram, she scraped together nickels and dimes to buy a train ticket to New York, fearful that it might be the last time she would see him. Happily, her son came back home.

World War II was only history to me, but my parents lived through it.

My mother was born in Mason City, Iowa, in 1931. Yes, that was the hometown of Meredith Willson, the creator of *The Music Man*, who modeled his fictional "River City" after Mason City. And yes, one of my aunts was named Marian and worked as a librarian, just like the famous character in the famous musical. But for the family, Mason City was a hardscrabble place. Marian's father, my grandfather, was an alcoholic who lost his butcher shop during the Depression; for a time his wife, my grandmother, worked as a cleaning lady for that same library. Indeed, back then, the Johnson family survived on food scraps such as neck-bone soup. That was the way it was back then.

And that's how my mother, Arlene Jean Johnson, the seventh and youngest child, grew up. When she was still in elementary school, the Johnsons moved to Waterloo, where things were a little better—but only a little. Jean, as she was called, grew up in a one-bedroom house with no indoor plumbing. The boys in the family, my uncles, had no choice but to leave home at age twelve or so, dropping out of school and looking for work. My mom and her two sisters, Marian and Bonnie, had to share a double bed, even as late as high school. They would steal each other's bobby pins so they could pin their hair up nicely to look pretty for class.

My mother got a big break in life when a Lutheran couple, O. K. and Malina Story, who did not themselves have children, fell in love with her. And why not? Jean was sweet and demure, a good little Norwegian girl, all blue eyes and yellow hair. So she stayed with them on their farm during summers, becoming an unofficial foster child. Jean helped out by working in the family's kitchen, but then she was given a special opportunity: The Storys arranged for her to attend Luther College in Decorah, Iowa. Thanks to their Christian love and good-hearted charity—the Storys were a blessing, a true "point of light"—Jean was assured a better future.

If little Jean was adorable, teenage Jean was beautiful—slim and cute, like a model or a movie star. Boys at East High School liked her; she always had dates. But there was one boy she really liked.

That was David John Amble, born on a Minnesota farm in 1929, just days before the stock-market crash and the beginning of the Depression. When he was a baby, the family house burned down and the Ambles lost everything. These were hard times; nobody had much to spare. So the Ambles moved to Waterloo, where David's father got a job at the Illinois Central rail yard, while his mother found work as a commercial seamstress sewing upholstery. I grew up visiting that old house they lived in, over on Lafayette Street; to say it was modest would be an understatement. The Ambles always had to scrimp, living on the first floor of their house with its one bedroom; they rented out the second floor. My dad too went to East High School, and he and Jean were soon an item.

As David was going into the Air Force, he and Jean married. Mom earned a one-year teaching certificate from Luther College and then left school, following David to Lowry Air Force Base, near Denver. Dad was only in his early twenties, but he was smart; he taught electronics on the base. Mom got a job as a secretary at a nearby company called Red Comet, which made fire extinguishers. One time, President Eisenhower came to visit the corporate headquarters, and Mom had the opportunity to shake his hand. She was a Democrat, but she was thrilled to meet a great hero of World War II, now the leader of the free world.

My older brother, David Jr., was born at nearby Fitzsimons Army Hospital, in 1953. After Dad's military service, the three Ambles ambled back to Waterloo. Dad took a full-time factory job at Chamberlain Manufacturing, an ordnance maker for the Pentagon, working a lathe to pay the bills. Meanwhile, he used his GI Bill benefits to attend Iowa State Teachers College, now the University of Northern Iowa. The first in his family to go to college, he studied engineering, aiming for a white-collar career.

The family moved into a tiny house at 210 East Ninth Street. As a piece of real estate, it wasn't much, but it was their own little piece of the American Dream. Like my grandparents, my parents lived on the first floor and rented out the second floor; they even rented out the attic. On a bright spring morning in 1956, my mother was planting tulips and went into labor. My dad was at school taking a test, so a distant relative, Elmer, who was renting upstairs, drove Mom to the hospital. Dad was at the hospital by the time I was born; he was the first to tell my mother, "Honey, we have a little baby girl!"

My first memories are of that house, sitting in the kitchen, watching my mother as she canned tomatoes. We had a black-and-white TV, and I remember watching President Eisenhower and thinking to myself, *Mommy knows him!*

But we didn't watch much TV, because Mom was a reader, and she wanted all her children too to be readers. She was—and still is!—a classic 1950s/1960s mother. She has always been feminine, gracious, ladylike, and totally devoted to her children. Soon there were four of us; Davey and I were joined by little brothers Gary in 1960 and Paul in 1962. Yes, I had the privilege, if that's the way to say it, of growing up with three rambunctious brothers, and I knew what it was like to compete with the boys; I learned what you have to do to fight back. In other words, it was great training for politics.

The six of us lived near a Dairy Queen, but it was a rare treat to go there. The more usual food was a Wonder Bread sandwich with a slice of lettuce and a layer of mayonnaise. We never ate fancy, but we were happy and we had freedom to play outside without the need for adult supervision—and that was the greatest wealth.

In addition, we had our extended family. It seemed that just about every weekend we would drive out somewhere to visit with grandparents, aunts, uncles, cousins, or close family friends. We would sometimes cook out, but I don't really remember food being the focus of our lives; the focus was our family and friends. We would go to church together, then maybe go for a drive to visit relatives; we did everything together. When I needed a new dress, my mother or grandmother would sew one for me. It wasn't the posh life, but it was the good life.

We also listened to the adults talk politics.

Let me tell you about my grandmothers. My mother's mother was named Laura, and she was a New Deal–style Democrat. She had worked hard all her life, but she also believed that FDR was a great president, that he had saved the country back in the thirties. She loved me and all of her other grandkids, and she let us know that she did. In my heart, she will always be just one thing: pure love.

My father's mother, Anna, was the Republican in the family. She would read *Time* magazine cover to cover—it was Republican back then—and she would devour too the *Wall Street Journal* every weekday. Then she would be ready for a lively discussion and, if need be, a spirited debate. She was a thorough reader, an intent listener, and a terrific conversationalist, although she always argued from principle. She loved to talk, and she loved to put pepper on food, and so on weekends she'd do both. I'd listen to her as she talked, added some pepper, then talked some more, then added more pepper. Her dishes had a *lot* of pepper. To this day, I like pepper so much that I usually remove the top of the shaker!

One day, sometime in the mid-1960s, I stood in my grandmother's kitchen on Lafayette Street, listening to my dad and my grandmother argue politics. Dad, always a Democrat, was talking to his mother, the family Republican, about what was happening in Washington, D.C. Dad said that President Lyndon Johnson was doing a good job pushing Great Society social-welfare programs. And my grandmother said, "David, it won't be you who pays for all these programs, it will be Davey and Michele."

At the age of eight or nine, I knew more about Barbie dolls than about fiscal issues, but that scene has stuck with me ever since. Government programs with nice-sounding names may seem like a good idea, but someone has to pay for them. And as we have learned in the decades since, Grandma Anna's prediction has come true. Indeed, I don't think that even Grandma Laura, the staunch Democrat, if she were with us today, would believe that the welfare state still works for working people—or anyone else. Indeed, I am sure she would be shocked and troubled by the degree to which governmental "help" has become, instead, a crushing burden on all of us.

Moreover, I know both grandmothers would say that all of us must be restrained and prudent in our spending. That's the way they got through their own lives; why should it be any different for the nation as a whole? Reckless people don't survive; neither do reckless countries.

Yet for all the spice of the food, and the spice of the argument, things never got too hot for us back in Waterloo. We were family. And that was everything to all of us, no matter which party we identified with.

I thank God for the loving framework that nurtured me. Faith, family, friends—we all need those. On Saturday night, we would take our weekly bath, put on our jammies, watch dinosaur cartoons on TV, and then go to bed early. The next morning, we would go to the early service at First

Lutheran Church of Waterloo; later we went to the Nazareth Evangelical Lutheran Church in Cedar Falls. My father's mother was an adult Sunday school teacher at the church, where she taught the Bethel Bible Series. And every summer, we went to two weeks of vacation Bible school. It was a life of comforting routine and simplicity, and it was all we wanted. To me, growing up, those familiar rhythms meant that I had everything.

It's a shame now, especially for children, that in the 1960s we started to lose those protective frameworks for families. It's vital that children be allowed to grow up in an environment of innocence, protected from inappropriate adult situations. How foolish it is to hurry children into premature crisis by exposing them to mature themes. Kids need to master the basics as they grow up; they need book learning, plus, of course, strong values. If kids are prematurely pushed into adulthood, oftentimes adult problems will ensue.

So some things should just wait—or never be seen at all.

For example, I went to kindergarten at Hawthorne Elementary School on Franklin Street, just a few blocks from my house. The neighborhood was definitely on the wrong side of the tracks, but back then, nobody worried for my physical safety. I walked to and from school, and the worst I'd see was beat-down old houses and beat-down old cars and rowdy taverns.

Today, it would be different. A neighborhood on the wrong side of the tracks nowadays isn't just physically beaten down; it's morally beaten down. Kids can handle scarcity, but they can't handle depravity. If our failed institutions produce young people, and then adults, who lack values and a moral compass, no neighborhood will ever be safe. And if those same failed institutions are also revolving doors of recidivism, then inevitably some neighborhoods will become war zones. No American child ought to live like that.

When I was in kindergarten, my parents moved out to the suburbs, to Cedar Falls. It was a three-bedroom rambler, as they called it, but you couldn't ramble very far, because it was no more than eight hundred square feet for the six of us. Still, compared with the old house, it felt like a palace.

My dad worked, and my mom took care of us at home full time. We walked to school, came home for lunch, then walked back to school, then came back home at three thirty. Or back *toward* home, I should say, because mostly we played outside after school.

I always liked school. I loved learning about words and numbers and holidays and music. Once, in third grade, the teacher asked us who didn't know how to tell time. I was the only kid who raised my hand. My teacher sent a note home to my mother, who had just assumed that I knew. But the teacher was nice; she gave me a clock to study, and soon I mastered it. I will always be grateful to her for that extra bit of kindness.

I learned of larger events too, along with my fellow students. All of us in the postwar generation—packed, as we were, thirty-five or more to a classroom—shared experiences, especially those brought to us by television. I happily remember, for example, sitting in the school gymnasium, watching the NASA Gemini program, as the rockets launched and the astronauts spacewalked—all on a single little black-and-white TV.

One day in school, I looked up from my second-grade schoolwork to see that my teacher, Mrs. Whitmeyer, had stepped out of the classroom and into the hall, speaking in serious but hushed tones with another teacher. I could tell immediately that something important was happening. Probably something bad, because both women were crying. Without saying a word, Mrs. Whitmeyer walked back into the classroom and wrote on the blackboard: "Ask not what your country can do for you—ask what you can do for your country." Then she turned to face the class, tears in her eyes, and said, "Children, the president of the United States, John F. Kennedy, has been killed."

Mrs. Whitmeyer continued, "Now I want you each to pull out a piece of paper and write down these words and remember them, in honor of our late president." Then she dismissed us, and we went home for days of national grief and mourning. That was November 22, 1963. The news made us little six- and seven-year-olds sad—and sadder when we came home and saw that our parents too were crying. Indeed, the whole world was shocked and stunned by the terrible loss of the dashing young leader.

And yet the powerful images of ceremony, duty, and grace stay with me, even now. The riderless horse. The little boy, John-John, raising his tiny hand to salute his father as the funeral caisson passed by. And Jackie Kennedy, regal in her gauzy black, demonstrating dignity and essential decency as she led her children, and the nation, through the proper rituals of honor and respect for her late husband.

Overall, my Iowa childhood was happy. As I grew older, I read more and more, the Nancy Drew and Trixie Belden mysteries being favorites; even then, in my own adolescent way, I loved piecing together forensic and legal puzzles. That was my idea of an extracurricular activity in grade school—to be curled up with a book. Yet most of the time, I was playing with my brothers or the neighbor kids. For fun we might play tag or hide-and-seek or run through the sprinkler. Eventually, I even figured out how to ride a bike; I've never been much of an athlete.

On a rare occasion, we would see a movie. Our parents took us to see two Disney movies, *Flubber* and *Son of Flubber*. That was a big deal, such a big deal that Mom sewed new outfits for me to wear. Just so we could go to a movie! Once a year we would go to the Cattle Congress, a combination amusement park and state fair at Waterloo.

My parents bought a 1959 Edsel station wagon; I remember it as two-toned white and lime green, with a powerful V-8 engine. To a little girl all that machinery was impressive, powerful, and shiny. My brothers were proud of our big, fast station wagon; from the backseat, we would beg Dad to drive it faster.

When I was in sixth grade, Dad took us on vacation and drove us up to Rainy Lake, Canada, for two weeks of fishing. He loved the sport, and from him I too learned to love fishing.

Our family of six piled into our new car, a tiny little Volkswagen Beetle, packed with all our luggage, gear, food, and even a boat motor. My older brother David and I, plus heaps of stuff, squeezed into the backseat. And my two little brothers, Gary and Paul, wedged even more tightly into the tiny cubby slot behind us; that slot was better suited for maps than for children, but it was all the room that we had. From Iowa all the way to Canada! On that trip we were an exceptionally close family, and not by the kids' choice!

Sometime during the sixties, I heard that wonderful Beatles love song, "Michelle." But it always confused me that the song title was spelled "M-i-c-h-e-l-l-e," with that double *L*. Why the two letters? Both ways of spelling are accepted, of course, but when I was little my mother teased me, saying that my father had given me my name and had not known how to spell it!

I was one of the seventy-six million or so baby boomers, the generation born between 1946 and 1964, when classes were big, cars had high tail fins, and national hopes were even higher. Thanks to the ingenuity and sacrifices of our parents, we boomers grew accustomed to a better life—yet a life all too often defined, unfortunately, as simply having more things. In fact, some of my generation felt increasingly entitled to more things, and then *demanded* more things.

Of course, there was much that was wrong with America in the sixties, but there was more that was wrong with the world. America could always be better, but the United States has always been a force for good. Yet by the end of the sixties, the American framework that had nurtured me had been shattered, ripped apart by the Vietnam war and its protesters, several tragic assassinations, racial concerns, crime and strife in the big cities, and, strangely, sometimes-violent protests staged by some of our most privileged young people. I can remember puzzling over some of those protests at universities. How did they think it would help to throw insults and rocks at the police?

When I think about America, I think about making it better. And I think of Melchior and Martha Monsson, who led their family to a new promise in a new land. Or of Halvor Munson, who volunteered to fight in what is still the bloodiest war in our history. Or the Sullivan brothers. Or my grandparents, who worked hard all their lives, gave a lot more than they received, and yet never complained.

I don't mean to sugarcoat this history. None of these folks were perfect; they had foibles and flaws. But if it's adversity that reveals character, then they all look pretty good. They never gave up, and the proof of their work remains with us to this day. My grandparents—Oscar and Laura, Jesse and Anna—are all buried in Iowa. My roots are with them. There could be no other way. Wherever I go, my Iowa childhood will always be a secure grounding for me.

And the same is true for my three brothers: David has had a great career in corporate finance; Gary is currently a television meteorologist for KCTV5 in Kansas City, Kansas; and Paul, having earned his MD, is now a forensic psychiatrist in Connecticut.

But please don't mistake my happy memories of growing up in Waterloo for a pining for the past. I know it's impossible to turn the clock back. Always mindful and respectful of the past, I want to move forward, maintaining trusted principles while reaching out for new possibilities.

The official state motto of Iowa is "Our liberties we prize and our rights we will maintain." Those words are always worth hearing, and yes, the principles they embody are worth fighting for. But a newer slogan for the Hawkeye State is worth hearing too: "A state of minds." Those words are a tribute not only to such great Iowa scientists and inventors as Norman Borlaug and Lee De Forest but also to such wonderful artists as Grant Wood and Glenn Miller. Those great Hawkeyes and their achievements are an inspiration to the next generation of Hawkeye achievers. The meat-packing jobs may never come back to Waterloo, but there's something new and even better in my hometown's future. I am sure of it—if we continue to encourage innovation and transformation.

We can do it. It just won't be easy, that's all. The American Dream is not a sure thing; it is a well-founded hope. Yet I believe that if we are mindful of all the hard work and sacrifice of our ancestors, if we keep faith with the hopes of those who came before us, then with God's grace we will see an even greater America in the twenty-first century.

So as we take the bumpy ride into the future, we might seek comfort in these words from the Epistle of James: "Consider it pure joy, my brothers and sisters, whenever you face trials of many kinds, because you know that the testing of your faith produces perseverance. Let perseverance finish its work so that you may be mature and complete, not lacking anything." James concludes with a note of hope: "If any of you lacks wisdom, you should ask God, who gives generously to all without finding fault, and it will be given to you."

Yes, wisdom will be given to us. And from there we must add our own perseverance. Because as a great president once said, "Here on earth, God's work must truly be our own."

CHAPTER THREE

Minnesota to Israel to Winona

ONE day when I was twelve, as I was playing in the basement of our home in Cedar Falls, Mom came down and said we were moving to Minnesota. Dad had gotten a good new job in Minneapolis.

From a logical point of view, this was good news for the Amble family—it meant more responsibility, more money. My father was, after all, smart and talented; the first in his family to attend and graduate from college, he had worked his way through school, and now, having earned his engineering degree, he was ready to move ahead. A white-collar job at Honeywell, a big multinational company. A bigger piece of the American Dream.

But all that logic was lost on me and my adolescent mind. My thoughts raced: *We aren't really leaving, are we? I don't want to leave Iowa. I love living in Iowa. Iowa is home—everything I know. It's family, friends, church. A happy place. A wonderful place. I never want to be anywhere else. And when I die, I want to be buried in the Garden of Memories Cemetery, alongside my grandparents. We can't go to some faraway land with no relatives nearby.*

Of course, Minneapolis is just a little more than two hundred miles from Waterloo—but to a twelve-year-old mind that seemed an unfathomable distance.

I started crying. Then I gave what I thought was a good argument: "But I've never even been to Des Moines! Our state capital!" Yet my reasoning fell flat and we moved.

That was 1968. For the nation as a whole, it was a grim year of war, assassinations, and riots. America was being torn apart. And my world too would soon be torn apart.

Minnesota, of course, is a wonderful place to live. Yet after this drastic change for the family, it took a little time for the Gopher State to feel like home. For one thing, it was colder. Now, over the years, I have come to love the outdoor winter sports of Minnesota, including cross-country skiing, ice-skating, and, of course, hockey. It just took some getting used to, that's all.

We moved into a four-bedroom, split-level house on an acre of land nestled in the pleasant Minneapolis suburb of Brooklyn Park. In terms of material possessions, we had a far better life. Our VW Beetle, for example, was soon joined by another car, a Ford LTD. I thought we were the richest people in the world.

At first the other kids in sixth grade teased me for being different. They thought I said "thank you" and "please" too often. They were good kids, but they asked, "Why are you so polite?" Well, maybe I was always polite, although I like to think that good manners are something that most parents teach their kids. Being polite at all times was one habit that our mother insisted we never break. And certainly a nation of polite people is preferable to a coarsened culture.

I was a good student—I got mostly *A*s. How did I do it? I worked hard and read a lot—it remains my favorite pastime. I like to say that I learn with my wrist. That is, I write everything down, and as I write things down, the words and ideas become imprinted in my mind.

We settled in, and we even bought a brand-new exotic machine called a snowmobile. It was gold and black and gorgeous. Our dad pulled our toboggan behind the machine as we went racing through the snowy woods and over the frozen lakes; we kids thought we had really moved up into an exciting new world of technological luxuries. So while I still missed Waterloo, I began building up a store of fond memories from my new life in Minnesota.

But then, in 1970, everything in our happy little home changed. Our parents made a decision to end their marriage of nineteen years. We knew no one in our family who had divorced. Security was gone. Stability was gone. And our dad was gone. I will always honor both my father and my mother, but the fact remained that our family was irretrievably broken.

Dad moved out, and we didn't see him again for six years. It's one of the oldest stories ever told, and it's been played and replayed many times, but it still hurts. Dad moved to California, and just five days after the divorce from Mom was finalized, he married another woman. Now I had two new stepbrothers, but six years would pass before I got to meet them.

And so I resolved that I wanted, more than anything else in life, to have, someday, an intact and happy family. I told myself that I would marry a man who would be committed to me and to our family—and we'd have lots of kids! And we would stay together, happily ever after. And so in my teenage mind, I resolved to turn something bad into something good. Four decades later, that determination—which I now share with my husband and children—still burns inside me.

When Dad left, the economic impact on the rest of us was immediate. Overnight, we literally fell below the poverty level. For nearly two decades, Mom had been a full-time homemaker, taking care of us kids; now, all of a sudden, she had to go out and find a job. Sadly, she had few marketable skills. She hadn't stayed long enough at Luther College to get her BA, because when she married, she had followed Dad out to Colorado when he was in the Air Force. She had only a one-year teaching certificate, and that wasn't worth anything in the Minnesota job market.

But she was willing to work, and work hard. We qualified for welfare, but Mom wouldn't think of it. She did not consider herself a political conservative; she just didn't see us as poor enough to take government help. She knew she could get a job. And so even if we were barely getting by, she was sure she wasn't going to rely on the government to provide for us.

So Mom got a sales job at a department store, then found better work as a bank teller—for $4,800 a year. She did her absolute best for us, but it was still an uphill struggle. Soon, it was obvious that we couldn't afford to stay in our home in Brooklyn Park, and we had to move out. In the small apartment we were moving into, in the farther-out city of Anoka, there wasn't much room, and because we desperately needed money, Mom held a garage sale. I remember gazing at many of our nicest belongings—my mother's wedding gifts, all the china—just sitting there on a card table in front of the house we were leaving. People would pass by, looking for bargains, and then snap up something for fifteen cents, or maybe a quarter or a dollar. I remember thinking to myself, *That's our whole life going away.*

All these years later, I am a relentless bargain hunter at yard sales, but even so, when I see something that was obviously someone's treasured heirloom, I feel a twinge in my heart.

My parents' divorce in 1970 was a mile marker in our lives; nothing was the same after that. Our relationships with our extended family changed, and our support structures were altered. Millions of families go through this trauma with disappointed, disillusioned spouses and children who are deprived of the daily support and presence of both parents. Some divorced parents, to be sure, manage their duty to their children with a sense of sacrifice and service—and some don't. Either way, it's nearly impossible for the kids to come away from the experience without a sense of loss. But Mom had the blood of all those sturdy forebears running through her; she came from strong stock. And thanks to her, and the child-support checks from our dad, we all survived—and ultimately thrived.

As the oldest child still living at home, I helped care for my two younger brothers, Gary and Paul. So to inspire them to do their share of the chores—or maybe sometimes more than their share—I developed a point system, scoring various activities, such as doing the dishes or picking the weeds in our itty-bitty garden. Earning points, I assured my little brothers, was a good thing. And what did they get for piling up points? Well, that was a tricky question—because in truth, I didn't have anything to offer them, except . . . more points! And, of course, compliments, smiles, and hugs. They thrived on sisterly praise. You don't always have to have material things in life.

My mother's mother, Laura—the petite widow who had carried huge trays of bacon around the Rath meatpacking plant in Waterloo till late in her life—would come to visit, bringing canned food and hams in the trunk of her car. I can remember seeing her beige Ford Fairlane, bearing those black-on-white Iowa license plates, and thinking of happier times back in Waterloo. My grandmother had been widowed with seven children before her fiftieth birthday. She was poor before her husband's death, and after, of course, it was even harder on Mom and her six siblings. Grandmother was resilient, that's for sure. She was one of the hardest working people I have ever met, she saved her pennies, and yet at the same time, she was generous and kind. Pure love. She was always a lady, but she was always strong. Indeed, she was both ladylike and strong at the same time: When she was eighty-three, she changed the snow tires on her car in her garage while wearing one of her favorite Shelton Stroller dresses. She was ever a lady!

Meanwhile, I was working. I started babysitting; the going rate back then was fifty cents an hour. I took every babysitting job I could get, because by ninth grade, I was growing conscious of my appearance. In those days, girls had to wear dresses to public school, and if I wanted pretty dresses, I had to buy them, because Mom couldn't afford them for me; she couldn't afford lunch money. I remember during my parents' divorce I asked Mom for ten cents for some activity at school. Her face was pained; she didn't have it in her purse. So she looked through her dresser drawer and eventually found a dime, which she gave to me. After that experience, seeing the look of pain and loss on her face, I vowed to never ask her for money—or much of anything else—again. If she had had it, I knew, she would have given it to me, but clearly our lives were reduced to about as low as we could go.

I quickly realized that expenses were piling up faster than my earning power, so I taught myself how to sew. I went to summer sidewalk sales at the local fabric store, picked up a pattern and small swatches of marked-down fabric, and then figured out how to vary the pattern so that I could make two dresses for the coming school year. But I wanted to do better. I had always been a hardworking student, but after the divorce my mother had told me, "Your education is one thing that can never be taken away from you." Those words inspired me to work harder than ever. As they say, adversity can either break you or make you—and I was determined to make it.

After all, I was now in high school, and I could see a path to my future life and career. In fact, I was fortunate enough to be at Anoka High. Go, Tornadoes! Anoka is the alma mater of Garrison Keillor, of *Prairie Home Companion* fame. His politics are very different from mine, but I love his gentle, knowing humor. Keillor understands Minnesota, from Lutherans to lutefisk, and his ability to squeeze laughs out of serious-minded mid-westerners makes him a legend. The way he writes, it's as though he was present at our grandmother's Sunday table. Clearly, looking at his skill, he received a good education at Anoka—I know I did.

Anoka High offered a wealth of academic, vocational, and extracurricular activities. I joined everything. I was in seemingly every club and

every group, and I had at least a small part in every play. I knew I might not
be the star, but I could always learn something and contribute something.

But I soon settled on a big goal: the cheerleading squad. I have never
been athletic or well coordinated, and yet I knew I wanted to be a cheerleader more than anything. So I practiced, practiced and practiced. I was
a disaster at first, and I rehearsed my cheerleading routines in our living
room with the shades down in order to avoid humiliation in case anyone
saw me, even though our apartment was on the second floor! My brothers
poked fun at me as I crashed around on the carpet, but I kept at it until I
mastered the Anoka Tornadoes fight song:

> Fight, fight, Anoka, fight;
> Go, go, Tornadoes!
> Win, win, maroon and white
> We're with you tonight, Tornadoes!
> Fight, fight to victory,
> Team, team, it's your game.
> Score, score, score and then
> Score some more
> Tornado men!

Astonishingly I made the cheerleading squad! I even made the varsity
cheerleading squad. And to top it all, I was football cheerleader. A girl who
tripped, who couldn't run, who couldn't play normal sports without embarrassing herself—I had made the squad.

Fortunately, I could lead the Anoka cheers without really being able to
see beyond the girl next to me—or the girl standing on my shoulders to
make the Anoka *A*. I had always had poor eyesight. I couldn't read anything without my glasses; indeed, I can barely see my hand in front of my
face—I need my glasses. For cheerleading, I could take my glasses off, but
the rest of the time I was a hopeless four-eyes. And as I got older, my glasses
had to be thicker and clunkier. Not good.

So what to do? I knew that I needed to see, but just like every other
teenage girl, I wanted to look my best. The answer? Get contact lenses. But
such vanity was not in our budget, and because we as a family couldn't
borrow or print money—as the U.S. government could always do—I had
to be both thrifty and strategic.

So I worked even harder to save up money. Happily, I loved babysitting; I loved being around children, watching the way they learn and grow up. So babysitting was a wonderful way for me both to make money and to prepare for a family of my own. I had a little jar on my dresser for keeping the coins and dollar bills that I had earned. Once a week, I sent my earnings to the bank with my mother, where she made a deposit. It was exciting to watch my bank balance increase, week after week, month after month, year after year. After three years, I had saved up three hundred dollars, and now I could pay for my contact lenses.

So I made an appointment to see the eye doctor, and he measured me for contact lenses. I was so excited! Another step on the path to adulthood.

But back in those days, in the early seventies, contact lenses were hard, not soft, as they are now. People don't know what that's like anymore, but back in the days of hard lenses, putting in a lens felt like putting a sandbur into your eye. And so for two weeks, it was just sheer pain, until my corneas built up calluses. I remember weeping and weeping for those two weeks, because it was so painful to have the lenses in my eyes. But I had worked for three years to get them, and I wasn't going to give up.

One afternoon I went out bike riding with the new contacts, even as my eyes were still watering from the pain. But one of the lenses suddenly flew out of my eye, landing on the gravel shoulder alongside West River Road. I got off my bike and searched for it as cars whizzed by just a few feet away. I had this feeling of horror: I had worked for three years, and now the lens was gone, and I was out that three hundred dollars.

Unable to find the lens, I rode home in tears and told Mom the bad news. Always determined and always the optimist, Mom said that we would go out together and find the missing lens. So we went back out to the highway, and together we got down on our hands and knees on the gravelly side of the road and looked for that lost lens. It probably seemed ridiculous, but that's what families are for—to solve every crisis that arises, no matter how ridiculous. Then, miraculously, the sun glinted on the lens—and we saw it! That little piece of plastic represented three years of work and savings to me. I was thrilled to know my labors weren't for nothing. So we took it home and washed it off, and I put it back into my eye. I was utterly grateful to Mom, and utterly happy at the same time—so I ignored the pain.

With the help of my new look, I felt more confident in high school. I wasn't really a beauty-pageant girl; there were scads of girls far more attractive than I was. But I was chosen twice as a princess for the homecoming court, and, yes, I even won the title of Miss Congeniality I borrowed friends' prom dresses to wear to the court; we couldn't possibly swing buying a fancy gown. But there was one problem: the tradition at Anoka was for a girl's father to walk the queen, and all the princesses, across the football field at halftime in their ballgowns. I borrowed a gown, but I didn't have my dad. What to do? We had no adult male relatives in Minnesota, so I looked to a man who laid down the law at Anoka, our principal, Art Dussel. I made an appointment with the school secretary to speak with him. I was very nervous and felt a little ashamed to ask him if he would escort me across the football field. My emotions overcame me and though I didn't mean to, I started to cry when I asked him to do this. I'd never spoken of my parents' divorce, and it was harder than I had even anticipated to talk about it. Mr. Dussel couldn't have been more gracious or kind. He immediately agreed, and seemed honored by the request.

At the Friday-night homecoming game, sure enough, Mr. Dussel met me at the fifty-yard line in his suit and tie. He had a little gift-wrapped box in his hand that he gave me which contained a small pearl pendant necklace. Gifts were rare to nonexistent in our family, and I couldn't believe that he and Mrs. Dussel would be so generous. I've never forgotten his kindness or how he "stood in the gap" for me when I needed a dad's presence at that important event in my life.

I went on a few dates in high school, maybe to the movies or to a school event, but not many. In addition to the fact that I was always studying, working, or rehearsing, I wasn't fun in the way that so many high-school boys defined "fun." I didn't drink, didn't smoke, didn't do drugs—and didn't fool around. Despite serving as prom chair, I didn't get asked to the junior prom. I felt bad when I didn't get asked my junior year, but I was really embarrassed and sad that I wasn't asked my senior year. I was working as a grocery cashier at Country Club Market and was scheduled to work prom night. Because girls couldn't ask boys, and because I had no idea how to flirt, I found myself literally minding the store rather than primping for the prom.

Meanwhile, my home life was changing yet again. In 1973, when I was seventeen, my mother remarried. She had met a man named Raymond J. LaFave, a divorced father with five kids of his own, at a Parents Without Parents meeting and dance. My mother hadn't had much success at these meetings and decided this would be her last try. Ray was, and is, a wonderful man. He worked hard all his life and is a true salt of the earth. And he has always been good to Mom. Finally, our economic situation had stabilized. My stepdad was a proud Army veteran of World War Two, with a great smile and a great sense of humor. He had been a single father to his five kids, and clearly he was crazy about our mom. So in May 1973, I became a bridesmaid at my mother's wedding. In October of my senior year, I got to see my mom and stepdad purchase their own home, a three-bedroom rambler. Thanks to everyone's pitching in, from Grandma Laura to the youngest sibling, all through those tough years, we had made it. During the lean years, my mom had told us, "Don't worry, it won't always be this way. Things will get better." It was tough, but we all learned a work ethic, we learned to save, we learned that if we wanted something, we'd have to work for it, and we learned the value of a dollar. We also learned that material possessions could sprout wings and fly away overnight; we also learned to look at material possessions as temporary, rather than permanent. It was my first lesson that I didn't want material things to own me or define me.

But even so, the new LaFave-Amble "blended family" was mostly older, out-of-the-house kids. By my senior year, I had piled up enough credits that I only needed to spend half a day in school for my first semester and could work the rest of the time, and then I graduated.

But by that time, I was almost out of the house anyway. I got my driver's license and bought my first car, a three-hundred-dollar Rambler with a manual transmission with "three on the tree." Ray taught me how to drive the stick shift while my mother drove me crazy with her backseat-driving "suggestions." Ray had me drive back home and told my mother to get out of the car. Once she was gone, Ray directed me to the high school parking lot and in no time I learned the feel of a manual transmission and was on my way. So I could now drive to work as a restaurant hostess. Then I got a job picking up and dropping off special-needs children at events around Anoka. Once I organized a trip for the kids to go to a Vikings football game. They loved it.

I graduated from Anoka High in 1974 and with less than nine hundred dollars in the bank, I had limited options for college. I had no money for a four-year university, but I signed up to attend Anoka-Ramsey Community College to pick up some academic credits at eight dollars a credit hour, because I was determined, no matter what, that I would go to college and then figure out how to earn a living. My mom meant well, but she didn't encourage me to attend college. She thought I should try to get a job as a secretary, as she had. It would offer stability, she told me. My dad hadn't been in my life to offer direction, but I knew that there was no way I was going to miss getting an education. So I filled out forms, made calls, and assumed that my only option was community college. I paid rent to my mother and Ray to live at home while I was at community college, because I wanted to pay my bills as I was going to school. It was a bit of a lonely time for me; most of my friends had moved away, and I, too, wanted to be at a four-year school and find new friends and adventure. But with little money and even less guidance, I looked for an adventure the summer after my first year of community college.

During the first nineteen years of my life, I had never been outside the Midwest, except for just across the northern Minnesota border to Rainy Lake in Canada. So when the doors began to open and I finally got the chance to travel, I jumped at it. My uncle Donnie, my mother's brother, was an adventurer; he had lit out for Alaska as a young man with his wife Sylvia and their young family in the forties and stayed there, working as a big-game hunting guide and dabbling in other businesses. So I spent the summer of 1975 working for him at his fishing lodge in the Aleutian Islands, where he often hosted geologists looking for oil finds. I not only cleaned fish but also did the laundry and cooked—I even tarred roofs.

Those were exciting times in Alaska, as the oil boom was just beginning. Down in the "lower forty-eight," as Alaskans referred to the continental United States, the talk was all about "the energy crisis"—the inevitability of gas lines, the need to turn our thermostats down, the need generally to live with less. According to the self-appointed experts, the seventies had become the "the era of limits." But I surely didn't see any limits in Alaska. Everybody up there in the "last frontier," as they called it, knew that Alaska was blessed with an abundance of oil, natural gas, and other precious raw materials to share with the world. It was just a question of accessing them responsibly, that's all. It made no sense to anyone, especially Alaskans, why federal-government restrictions were blocking the extraction of all this wealth, as well as preventing the creation of good jobs that paid good wages.

Having seen up close in Alaska the enormous God-given potential of our nation, I grew permanently skeptical of claims about shortages and demands for rationing. And in my young mind, I could see that America faced a stark choice. On the one hand, explorers and wildcatters were finding and producing wealth for the benefit of all; on the other hand, politicians and bureaucrats were trying to limit output, in accordance with a politically correct dogma that further entrenched the power of a distant and arrogant elite, many of whom had never been to Alaska.

So I learned a lot in Alaska. And yet as I thought about my own future, including college, I knew I wanted to be closer to home. Once again, God's hand intervened in my life. I met a geologist there who had formerly taught at Winona State University in Winona, Minnesota; he took a kindly interest in me. I told him I didn't want to go back to community college but didn't have the money for a costly school. He recommended Winona, not far from the Twin Cities. He explained that it was inexpensive, was situated in a wonderful little town, and offered great academics. He sold me on it. So I sent away for the school catalog; my letter went out on the airplane that came to and from our small Aleutian camp once a week. A couple of weeks later, the plane dropped its regular mailbag, and in the pouch was a catalog from Winona State. I read it, filled out an application, sent a check for the application fee, and was soon accepted. That was the beginning of my new life—first as a student and then, later, as a wife, mother, and career woman.

I borrowed my cousin's college guidebook and sent requests for catalogues for fifty colleges across the country. We had no TV, radio, or telephone; only a shortwave radio we used for emergencies. With long sun-filled days and evenings—we had three days when the sun never truly set—I had nothing to do after work except read college catalogues. So I scoured them all, even as I was teased each week by my uncle and cousins, because I was the one getting all the mail and packages. One day while cleaning the cabins, I read the Winona State catalogue. The school had it all: every department, a beautiful romantic campus; it was the oldest college west of the Mississippi. And it was eight dollars a credit hour! I could do this! When we were little, our dad had told us never to go into debt. That's the way everyone we knew lived. No one had much money, but everyone saved a little, they gave their money to church, and spent less than they had. Democrats, Republicans, apolitical, we all lived that way. "Bankruptcy" was a dirty word. Taking money from the government was something we wouldn't consider doing. Besides, there was no need. Our parents were careful and were not foolish with their money. I knew that finishing college was my goal and that there would be a better life thereafter, so I made it my mission to pay as I went and to not graduate with debt. I wouldn't even put a quarter in the pop machine on campus, much less spend money on a spring break trip. I worked. I went to school, because I had that greater goal.

But I should pause here and step back a couple of years to describe the single most important relationship I will ever have—my relationship with God through Jesus Christ.

If you had asked me growing up if I was a believing Christian, I would have said, "Of course!"

I loved the Lutheran Church. I had been baptized as a Lutheran, went to church every Sunday, attended vacation Bible school every summer, and prayed a traditional Lutheran prayer at night before I went to bed. And I was proud that I came from a long line of Lutherans; I remember, as a kid, driving through Iowa with my parents and stopping at a Lutheran church near a little place called Jericho, where many of my ancestors had once lived and were buried. There we were able to look at the old church records and see all sorts of family names—including that of Halvor Munson, my great-great-grandfather. I was proud that my ancestors had been actively involved in their church, but as far as I was concerned, that was mainly a matter of history. For me as a girl, being a Christian was a simple duty, doing what was expected, it was what we did on our way through life. I didn't know that I could have a personal relationship with Jesus. There was something missing in my life—a God-shaped hole—even if I didn't yet realize it.

As I mentioned, in high school I participated in lots of activities. One activity was a prayer group that met before school. I went to the meetings, and I enjoyed studying the Bible, just as I enjoyed listening to sermons on Sunday. I believed in God; I behaved myself. I didn't go out drinking, never did drugs, never fooled around with boys. None of that had ever held any attraction for me, because I had seen that it led to personal downfall.

But my friends knew what I didn't know—that I was not saved, that I had not made my own personal commitment to Jesus. When my friends would make this point to me, I would smile politely and, in my mind, wave them off. I was fine, I said; after all, I was a Lutheran. And I didn't need to worry about going to heaven. Of course I was going—I was a Lutheran. So my friends prayed for me, and waited, and hoped.

Let me pause again here to say that I am sure that the Gospel was preached at our church and that folks in the pews all around me heard it just fine. At that church, they heard God's word, and they were saved, just as He promises salvation to all who believe in Him, anywhere in the world. It's just that I, as a teenager in Minnesota, had missed the true import of His message. Maybe I thought it was automatic; that I wouldn't have to do anything except sit in church and nod. Well, in any case, that was all about to change.

On Halloween night 1972, my friends and I heard that our local church was holding a Halloween party, and so we decided to check it out. We soon discovered that there was no party, but the church doors were open, so we went inside. I was with three of my friends, and we all, at the same time, felt the same need.

We were all good kids, but none of us had a close relationship with God. At that stunning moment, we knew that we needed more. I had seen enough pain in my life. I had seen how darkness had afflicted my own family. Now I knew I wanted all that behind me.

So on that Halloween, something was nudging the four of us away from the goblins and the spiderwebs, away from the candy and soda pop—and toward the church sanctuary. We felt pulled. Later I learned that it had been the Holy Spirit that had lovingly led all four of us to our Savior, to our knees in prayer.

My Bible study had taught me that I needed to confess my sins and put my trust and faith in God's redemptive power through his son, Jesus Christ. I had read about that. Now I truly knew what it meant.

I remember saying, "I believe that Jesus is the son of God, I believe that He is true, I believe that I am a sinner, and that Heaven is where I want to go, to be with Him for eternity." All four of us poured out our hearts to Him, proclaiming that we needed Him to come into our hearts. Not just on Sundays but always. Each and every moment.

And that's how it happened. I went home that night, and in my bedroom I prayed again at the foot of my bed to the Lord. And this time, really for the first time, I sensed His peace and His presence. I took the wisdom of Thessalonians to heart: "Pray without ceasing." And ever since, I have been assured, as written in Hebrews 13:5, that He would never leave me nor forsake me. I had radically abandoned myself to Christ, and that's when my life truly began. I was born again. I was a new creation, thanks to Him.

You know the famous line from the hymn, "Was blind, but now can see"? That's exactly the way I felt. The next morning, November 1, 1972, I woke up with a new vision—not because of my contact lenses but because Jesus was lighting my path. I had a new heart; I was a new person. The difference was like the moment in *The Wizard of Oz* when everything shifts from black-and-white to Technicolor.

Now I felt real confidence. Profound confidence. Finally I felt armored and equipped, ready to confront the world and its many challenges. I knew that I belonged to God and that He loved me, and so I no longer had to depend on the approval of others. My cheerful childhood outlook had been damaged by the move away from Iowa, then more damaged my parents' divorce. And while I had kept plugging away through my early teen years, learning and working, I had felt a gnawing insecurity—an insecurity that is common, I realize, among children of broken homes and blended families. Maybe that's why I had joined every club, thrown myself into every activity.

Now, looking back on my life before Christ, I realized that I had been searching for something and not finding it. I had sought approval from teachers and classmates, and while they were almost always nice, they could never fill the real void in my life. What I needed was a close personal relationship with the Lord Jesus. It was upon the rock of that revelation that I would build my life, and if I kept faith with Him and His Word, even the gates of hell would not prevail against me. I was one with Christ, and I knew I would be one with Him forever.

From that day on, all the ordinary fun of high school—even cheerleading—seemed far less important. It wasn't about me anymore. Now it was about Him. I had to listen, through prayer and Bible study, for His plan for my life, and how I could use my talents and my abilities to glorify Him. That next summer I joined my dear friend Barb Norbie—my sister in Christ, as well as my sister in life—as a counselor at a Lutheran Bible study camp in Bay Lake, Minnesota, way up north. We all did the usual camp things—swimming, boating, arts and crafts—but every morning and every evening we learned about the Lord.

I had always been hardworking and success oriented, but now I felt an inner motivation. I was going to work even harder and aim even higher. But

I would not labor for the sake of material possessions; I would labor to follow His precepts and was profoundly gratified for God's grace and mercy in my life. Tests and challenges, to be sure, come to everyone, but they are never more than we can handle, with His help. By trusting in God and His Covenant Word, we can find the strength to overcome. The world may buffet us, but the Word bolsters us.

So now, more than ever, I looked forward to being happily married someday, surrounded by a lovingly united family. That was my commitment to the Lord: In addition to following the Lord, I wanted to be a good wife, a good mother, a good citizen, and a good American. And with God's help, I would do everything I could to leave the world a better place.

Yet as I grew older, I came to see forces at work that were making America a worse place, not a better place. It was hard for me to comprehend that certain forces in society were seeking to undermine the family, to undermine the traditional structures of our society, and, indeed, to undermine all the moral and political achievements of our Judeo-Christian heritage. It was an onslaught against the goodness of the American tradition. And the worst of all was the devaluation of human life. Life, I realized, was losing its value.

I had always loved children, and yet well into my teens, I was naive about abortion. I guess I had a hard time even imagining that a mother would not want her baby. I was sixteen at the time of the Supreme Court's *Roe v. Wade* decision, and I will admit that I didn't quite understand what it was all about. But then a Catholic friend explained it to me, the full disastrous dimensions of what the Supreme Court had just done to our culture and to our nation. I was shocked by what she said, and I immediately realized that I was completely committed to a pro-life position. Why would our government legalize taking the life of an unborn baby? Why should an abortion-minded young woman not be told of the negative emotional and physical repercussions she would face as the result of an abortion? How could anyone kill a little baby? How could such a crime be allowed? I have enormous sympathy for unwed mothers, to be sure, and for those who live with doubt and fear of the future; it is the duty of the rest of us, of course, to help them. Which Marcus and I chose to do. We reached out to offer counsel and friendship to women in unplanned pregnancies. We drove them to an adoption agency nearby. I went through child-birthing class with an unwed mom and held one woman's hand as she gave birth to her daughter—that was nearly thirty years ago. It takes courage for an unwed mom to see her pregnancy through to birth, and I thank the fathers who stand by the mothers of their children and do all they can to support the mother and the children that together they brought into this world. But at the same time, we have to stand up for the unborn. And with God's help, we can do both; we can keep faith with the mother *and* with the child, seeing it not only to term but to a good life beyond.

And yet in our efforts to protect the family and to preserve what Pope John Paul II called the "culture of life," I began to see that our government was often on the wrong side. Government officials were praising, even subsidizing, the worst kinds of behavior—not just abortion but also idleness, dependency, and delinquency. The pundits of the era, speaking down to us from their high perches in their ivory towers, called it "justice" and "liberation." But here on the ground, in real-world America, where I was living, the rest of us could see that the government was fostering injustice and anarchy. Indeed, in the seventies the bad trends were moving steadily up and the good trends were moving down; abortion, crime, divorce, drug abuse, and venereal disease were on the rise, while test scores, the purchasing power of the dollar, and traditional family values were drastically falling. And of course, the nation's morale and standard of living were stagnating, even declining. That's when I came to see that if the average household was suffering, then the country was suffering. Good moral behavior, I realized, is not just the path to a virtuous civil society; it is the prerequisite for economic growth. A healthy society, a healthy economy.

In other words, America needed once more a firm foundation. It needed a framework for good living; it needed sturdy walls against wickedness. I had felt safe as a girl in Waterloo in the sixties; why did I not feel as safe as a teen in the Twin Cities in the seventies? And yet Minnesota was safer than most parts of America. The problem, then, was national, not local. Something had hardened the heart of America. Our defenses against evil had weakened. Some Americans applauded that weakening, to be sure, and many did their best to ignore it. Yet a few of us wanted to do something about it.

So I came to appreciate and venerate Nehemiah of the Old Testament, the Jewish leader who rebuilt the walls of Jerusalem and restored the city to goodness. In today's terms, that task would mean restoring the moral foundation and framework of America, so that we could once again have a country in which children grew up safe and well educated, in which husbands and wives loved each other and stayed true to their vows, where they fought to make the marriage work despite less than ideal circumstances, and in which work and faith were honored, not scorned.

Such is the great work before us today. In the words of the prophet Isaiah: "And they that shall be of thee shall build the old waste places: thou shalt raise up the foundations of many generations; and thou shalt be called, the repairer of the breach, the restorer of paths to dwell in."

As for my own role, I esteemed and identified with the men of Issachar, one of the Twelve Tribes. As we are told in 1 Chronicles, they were "men that had understanding of the times, to know what Israel ought to do." And I like to think that the women of Issachar too knew what to do. Now, thousands of years later, it is my generation's turn to do our part to rebuild the foundation, to reestablish the framework, to help repair the walls. After all, in the time of the Twelve Tribes and in the present time, we worship the same eternal and unchangeable God.

My struggle to change those destructive government policies would ultimately bring me into politics. But first I had to get through school, to see what else life held in store for me.

In 1974, during my senior year in high school, as I was beginning my walk with Jesus, I wanted to see where He walked as a man in His brief life on earth nineteen centuries ago. I also wanted to see all the other places of the Bible, the storied places where godly men and godly women had done His work here on earth.

The more I studied and the more I learned about the Bible, the more I wanted to go to Israel.

I was involved in a Christian ministry, Young Life, when the group decided to arrange a trip to Israel. This was to be no junket; we would be students in the Holy Land—and yet we would also be working on the land. And that's a good thing; as Proverbs tells us, the souls of the diligent will be made rich.

But first I had to raise money to get there. The trip was nine hundred dollars. The mother of a good friend of mine, known for her excellent skills as a baker, went to work and sold her creations at a bake sale and donated the proceeds for my trip. Another anonymous businessman donated money, and I came up with the rest.

Our departure was slated for the day after I graduated from high school.

It was to be a moving and memorable experience. I remember the sweaty intensity of Ben Gurion Airport when I landed; I remember the heat, the customs officers right there on the Tarmac, the soldiers with their guns. Indeed, the whole country seemed poor, dry, and dusty; I saw chickens roaming, and there was noise and action everywhere. It was a stark contrast to the placid tranquillity of Minnesota. But of course, the Israelis had bigger things to worry about than making a good impression on visitors.

Just the year before, in 1973, during Yom Kippur—the sacred Jewish day of atonement—Israel had been sneak attacked by Arab armies; for a few days, it seemed as if the Jewish state might be lost. But then the Israeli Defense Forces rallied, and, aided by the United States, they turned the tide of battle. Zion was safe once again. That was a lesson to me: Whether the country is Israel or America, a strong defense and national security must come first. If a nation doesn't have military strength, it could lose everything.

We Christian lovers of Israel were going to work at Kibbutz Be'eri, in the Negev desert in the south of Israel. Our youth housing—a bare Quonset hut—was really just a barracks. It was dubbed "the ghetto." Bugs and lizards crawled and slithered everywhere. Our hosts would wake us up at 4:00 A.M., put us on a flatbed truck pulled by an old diesel tractor, then drive us out to the cotton fields. Armed soldiers provided an escort; before we began working, they scouted the fields for land mines. I will never forget their stoic good nature, even their ironic black humor. For us Americans, this was an eye-opening adventure; for them, safeguarding Israel against terrorism was a weary necessity for the whole of their lives. Our work involved mostly pulling weeds from the fields, but occasionally I was allowed to operate the rig; it was my first experience driving with a clutch.

We would work till noon, then ride back to the communal kitchen; then we'd go to sleep. In the afternoons and evenings, we'd study the Bible, maybe learn a few words of Hebrew from some of the girls in the kibbutz, including my new friends, Ziva and Hagar. In a mix of languages, we would swap stories, tell little jokes, and do girly things, such as braiding one another's hair.

It was hard work—sunburn, blisters, sore joints—but it was a wonderful experience. After that, we traveled to Jerusalem, where we stayed for a week in a quaint little hotel in the Old City, just inside the Jaffa Gate.

I felt closer not only to Jesus but also to all the great figures of the *Tan-*

ach and the Gospel. And I was able to do my small part to help Israel build itself up. The area had been sorely underdeveloped when the Jewish settlers defiantly declared Israel's independence in 1948. And after surviving a terrible war and winning a miraculous victory against invading Arab armies, the gallant Israelis had made the desert bloom. I thank God for America's thirty-third president, Harry S Truman, who backed Israel immediately after she declared her sovereignty, extending diplomatic recognition to the newly independent Jewish state, helping it to gain needed legitimacy. More than sixty years later, Israel today is still gravely threatened, and yet it is by now not only an agricultural powerhouse but also an economic tiger, a citadel of high-tech development. Its advanced technologies provide both prosperity and security—a lesson too for America.

So while the Israel of the ancient world gave us the living foundation of the Christian faith, the Israel of today is a valued and valuable ally to the United States. And for me, many decades later, it is a privilege to show my support in Congress for a strong and sovereign Israel.

Several years ago, I was happily reminded of my time in Israel. One of the girls whom I had befriended, Ziva Yellin, had saved a little card with a heart on it that I had written to her at the time. It was later published in the Israeli newspaper *Haaretz*: "This is especially for Ziva who has such a pretty smile. You and Hagar can speak English so well. I feel stupid next to both of you. Thank you so much for your friendship, I will remember and think about you always. Your friend, Michele from Minneapolis, Minnesota, United States." Now *that* brought back memories for me!

But I am getting ahead of myself.

In 1975 I arrived at Winona State University, about a hundred miles southeast of Minneapolis. The campus was all new to me; I had heard only the geology professor I met in Alaska describe it and had seen just a few photos in the catalog. My mother and stepdad helped me move into my new dorm room, putting sheets on the bed and clothes in the closet, and then she had to head back home.

So now it was just me. I was out of the nest.

Yet I had no time for homesickness or self-pity. Not only did I have school, but I also had to get a job. So while I enjoyed my classes, growing increasingly interested in law and political science, I have to make a further point: Frankly, my most profound memory of the 1975–76 school year was not academic.

CHAPTER FOUR

Marcus

IN my second semester at Winona, I got a job as a lunchroom and playground supervisor at nearby Lincoln Elementary School. It seemed like a great job; it was just a short walk to campus, and I loved working with children. But I had no idea how great it would really be.

On my first day on the job, in late March 1976, I saw a tall, handsome man at the same school—but he seemed too young to be a teacher. It turned out that he was a fellow Winona student and that we shared the same job assignment: to watch over the kids so that the teachers could take a break. The young man walked up to me with an expression of kindness and the sweetest smile and extended his hand: "I'm Marcus Bachmann." That was Marcus. Always nice, always straightforward.

"I'm Michele Amble," I replied.

That was it. That's when and how I first met my husband. I had blue jeans on, maybe a gray sweater, and my hair was long—down below my waist in those days. He had on a down jacket, sweater and slacks. We chatted only briefly, because the kids were always running around and our job was to watch them, not each other. But as our shift ended in the early afternoon, we found ourselves walking back to the Winona campus together, along the little path that connected the elementary school and the college.

And as we walked back to campus that day—the day we had first met—the kids in the playground started humming a familiar tune: the famous bridal chorus from composer Richard Wagner. You know, "dum-dum-de-dum"; it's the tune that everybody plays at weddings as the bride comes down the aisle. And I must say, even now, it all seems strange. Marcus and I knew the kids were just teasing, yet we were both embarrassed, which, of course, is what the kids intended! But later we were reminded that sometimes, out of the mouths of babes comes great wisdom.

In other words, those kids, in their own juvenile way, knew that something magical was happening long before Marcus or I did. Yet one thing we both knew immediately was that we could be friends. We could chat easily, we had similar interests—notably, children and how to raise them—and we both shared a living faith. He was more fun loving than I was; to this day, he is more outgoing and jovial at parties. So we would often meet on campus simply to banter back and forth; I guess, looking back, our times together were semidates, but I don't think either of us thought of them as such. In our minds, neither of us was there yet.

Marcus had an interesting background. His parents were born in Switzerland, not coming to the United States until after World War II. His father, Paul, hailed from a long line of farmers while his mother, Elma, grew up in a business family that at one point during the war had assisted in the resettling of Jewish refugees in neutral Switzerland, helping to offer them safe haven from a genocidal madman. During the war, my future father-in-law had served in the Swiss army, guarding Switzerland's border with Nazi Germany; he often heard the Wehrmacht soldiers taunting the Swiss soldiers: "We will come and get you next." Of course, the Nazis never attacked Switzerland, mostly because the Swiss were strong in their determination to defend themselves. Strong defense. That's what we always need in the face of evil.

Paul and Elma married in 1950. They journeyed to America shortly thereafter, sailing on the *Queen Mary*. While still living in Switzerland, they bought a dairy farm in Independence, Wisconsin, not far from the Minnesota border, that they had seen in an advertisement. Farms were much bigger in America, compared with the twenty to forty acres that were common for a farm in Switzerland. At home, Marcus's family spoke in the mixed languages of Switzerland—German, French, Italian. Marcus and his two older brothers, Peter and Reinhard, went off to school; the boys helped their parents learn English, although that Wisconsin household was always a jumble of languages and accents.

Paul Bachmann's real passion was work, and he instilled that passion in his three sons. Marcus, born on April 10, 1956, four days after me—he likes to joke that he married an older woman—would wake up, start milking the cows at 5:30 A.M., take a few minutes for breakfast, go to school, come home, change clothes, and then get back to milking the cows. At 9:00 P.M., he finally had time for homework, albeit knowing that he would have to be up again early the next morning to start all over again with the cows.

Marcus wasn't a big complainer; he was fun-loving and sweet tempered and good natured—when he wanted to be! Yet at the same time, he felt a spiritual hunger in his life. One evening in 1972, he came in from the barn and saw Billy Graham preaching on TV. As Marcus later told me, "It was as if Billy was speaking directly to me. I asked Christ to come into my life that night, and He has been with me ever since." Little did Marcus know, of course, that in that same year, also at the age of sixteen, a hundred or so miles to the west, I was coming to my own salvation experience.

Marcus chose to attend Winona State because it was inexpensive and close to home. He knew he wanted to work with young people, bringing his Christian perspective to the challenges of adolescent development. But because Winona didn't offer a psychology major, he settled on the next-closest topic, sociology.

And of course, Marcus continued to work. In addition to his job alongside me at Lincoln Elementary, he put in hours as a tour guide for the Winona State admissions office. And every weekend, he drove the thirty-two miles back home to help with the cows and the farm. That was our college life. Because we were each responsible for our college bills, we held various jobs. But working was good for both of us. Our parents had strong work ethics, and we had worked when we were younger, so it was perfectly normal for us to work multiple jobs and attend class.

Through it all, Marcus kept not only his sense of purpose but also his good humor. He has always been the hardest-working man I have ever met, as well as the nicest.

And so, of course, while we were "just friends" for a year and a half, it was only a matter of time before I fell in love with him.

Near the beginning of 1977, I knew, quietly, that he was the man for me. I think it was a little bit later that Marcus came to see me as a future life partner as well. Having lived and worked—mostly worked—on the farm all his life, he had never really had the chance to go anywhere; he once told me that his original plan had been to see the world while in his early twenties, then get married when he was twenty-seven or so. But as they say, men make their plans and God laughs.

But the bond between us was strong and growing stronger. Always a perfect gentleman, Marcus told me over ice cream, "I have enjoyed our friendship together."

Then he paused, regarding me thoughtfully. My mind raced as I absorbed his words. I knew something more was coming—I just didn't know for sure what. Marcus, having studied people for so long, has always been better at reading me than I've been at reading him. Trying to stay cool, I said to myself, *Michele, he is about to tell you that he wants to stay "just friends," or else that he wants to get more serious.* But which was it? I knew what I wanted, and I thought maybe I knew what he wanted—yet I wasn't quite sure. So what was the answer? As we all know, in pressure situations, a million thoughts can race though our heads in the time between two words, in the time between two heartbeats. And my heart was beating fast.

Then he continued, "Would you . . . be interested in a . . . more romantic relationship?" He looked right into my eyes. Not accusing, just wondering—hoping.

Once again, my mind was off to the races. *Think hard, Michele. This could be big. Really big.* My fingers tensed; my teeth clenched just a little. Not out of fear—I had felt completely safe around Marcus from the moment I met him—but rather out of nervousness. Or maybe I just wanted to feel something so I'd know I wasn't dreaming. In other words, there were lots of thoughts and emotions inside, even as I struggled to keep my composure. For a moment, I couldn't say a thing. No sound would come out.

And then that peace that passes understanding descended on me; calm came over me, and it was settled. Now I could speak. And I did. Like water from a spring brook, simple but sincere words poured out of me: "I would be open to that." Shakespeare could rest easy; I was no threat to the Bard in wordsmithing. And yet my response to Marcus was heartfelt, because my heart was entirely his.

Marcus later told me that he had been nervous too, that he had practiced his words for days before. That's how Marcus does things; he thinks things through, then acts with both care and precision. He's like a Swiss watch. And making a Swiss watch takes a lot of know-how, but once it's made, it always ticks true. Inspired by his example, I have tried to be the same way—that is, careful and precise. Although I'll admit, not always—I think again of that one April Fools' Day, decades in the future, when I suddenly found myself plunged into politics. That's why, when I say something wrong, I'm hard on myself, because I'm trying to communicate information accurately. I've learned the hard way at the national level that any erroneous statement will very quickly be magnified. So, as someone who talks for a living, I've learned to check, double-check, and triple-check my sources. And yet still I make a mistake or two!

Meanwhile, Marcus and I, up to that point, hadn't even held hands. But now everything was different; the arcs of our lives were converging. Not long afterward, we rode together on a church-group hayride; it was a Minnesota winter, and we were both bundled up—and Marcus reached out his hand, clasping mine. I didn't do a thing. Contact! From that moment on, I didn't remember a thing about the evening other than that he was holding my hand. That sounds innocent, considering some of today's dating standards, but it was our true story. We both knew that this was what we wanted—to be clasped together for life, under the watchful eye of a loving God.

And believe it or not, it was politics—Democratic politics—that accelerated our romance. In 1976 the Democratic presidential nominee was Jimmy Carter, who had introduced himself to the nation as a commonsensical Democrat, as well as a born-again Christian and a good family man. All that sounded promising to Marcus and me, and when Carter picked Minnesota native son Walter Mondale as his vice-presidential running mate, the two men seemed like a perfect national ticket. And speaking of Mondale, Mom pointed out to me, "He's Norwegian, you know."

In college, Marcus and I had become familiar with the work of Dr. Francis Schaeffer, author of a seminal book of Christian apologetics, *How Should We Then Live?* The book also served as the basis of a widely watched ten-part movie. In his work, Dr. Schaeffer points out that God is not just the God of theology, not just the God of the Bible, but also the creator God, creator of everything. He is the father of biology, sociology, political science, all human inquiry and creative endeavor. Dr. Schaeffer transformed our way of thinking; now we understood more fully that God's plan included all aspects of our existence, even our careers. Dr. Schaeffer further declared that life itself is the watershed issue of our time and that how we view the sanctity of human life informs all other issues. Each life is absolutely precious, we realized, from conception to natural death.

So Marcus and I decided we didn't want to be pro-life in name only. We wanted to live our lives and our careers being fully and actively pro-life.

So we began counseling single mothers, praying with them and helping them in any way we could. We volunteered to drive these expectant moms to crisis-pregnancy centers, where they could be offered a safe and saving alternative to abortion. I'll add too that I never condemn any woman who has had an abortion or who has participated in one, because I know that God is always there, offering grace and mercy in such tragic situations. Yet I felt called now to do everything I could for these women in difficult situations and their babies.

At that time, I was still a Democrat. The Democratic Party, while it was then edging toward an abortion-on-demand stance, still allowed room in its ranks for pro-life leaders. Carter himself proved to be a clever waffler on the abortion issue, suggesting that he was pro-life to the pro-lifers and prochoice to the prochoicers—and yet the media, always Carter friendly, never nailed him on his hypocrisy. So in our naïveté, we failed to realize that Carter was playing a duplicitous double game. And the Republican Party, meanwhile, still seemed at that time to be dominated by defenders of the proabortion stance. But today, thanks to the tireless efforts of conservative leaders such as Phyllis Schlafly, Father Frank Pavone, the late Henry Hyde, and, of course, Ronald Reagan, the Republican Party has rediscovered its moral origins as a champion of human liberty and human life. Today, we have witnessed, in the party platforms, which one of the two parties stands up for life and which one doesn't.

Yet back in the seventies, the parties had not yet sorted themselves out on the vital issue of abortion. So in 1976, many pro-life and socially conservative Americans could be found conscientiously voting for the Carter-Mondale ticket, thinking they were voting pro-life. And Marcus and I did more than that; we helped on his campaign, handing out fliers and making phone calls.

And of course, the Carter-Mondale ticket won the general election that November. A few weeks later, Marcus and I both received an invitation to attend the presidential inauguration in the coming January—at our own expense, of course. Marcus found me on campus one day and said he'd figured out how we could travel to D.C. and back for just a hundred dollars. Neither of us had ever been to Washington, and I wanted to go, to be a part of history. But still, mindful of the cost, I hesitated. A hundred dollars? To this working-her-way-through-college student, that was real money.

But Marcus was persuasive. So eventually, eight politically involved Minnesotans clambered into an RV, having packed in plenty of food, and took off from Winona to Washington. It was like a scene from *Planes, Trains, and Automobiles,* in which a group of strangers from the provinces heads off to see the bright lights of the big city. We didn't have money for hotels along the way, so we took turns driving, making it straight through to Washington in twenty-four hours. This was no raunchy road trip; one of the passengers was a nun, and the rest of us were starry-eyed idealists. We sang sing-alongs, talked about current events, and dreamed about how America would be a better place thanks to the Carter-Mondale administration.

Disappointment, of course, was to come in the future, but Washington, D.C., as a city did not disappoint; it far exceeded my expectations. I remember coming over a hill and seeing the horizon, and there was the capitol—and, honest to God, tears were streaming down my face. I had read all about Congress, the White House, and the Supreme Court, but actually seeing those places—there was nothing like it. We were admiring, up close, the three branches of government, the landmarks where our Constitution came to life each day. Or at least that was the hope.

And we got to see the Carter-Mondale inauguration, albeit from a great distance.

And the parties! We went to the Minnesota ball, where we got to meet two of Walter Mondale's children, Eleanor and Ted. That was a thrill, but what left an even bigger impression was the cornucopian richness of the parties. We went from party to party to party; free food abounded everywhere in the public buildings of the Capitol complex. To the dainty eater, tasty hors d'oeuvres and cute little finger foods beckoned; to the hearty eater, big stacks of deli meats, hunks of cheese, and those delectable little pigs in blankets were shouting, "Come and get it!" Because I brought a grand total of eleven dollars with me for food, transportation, and spending money, I was myself both types of eager eater. The heaping silver platters of huge brownies were like something I had never seen before. As I said, we came from a simple background; we'd never seen so much food at so many venues and at no charge. Giving away exorbitant goodies and we didn't have to pay for them—that was our introduction to Washington's ways!

But I remember thinking to myself, *Washington has surely gotten big—*

and yet the rest of the country seemed actually to be shrinking. That is, Washington is a rich city, a permanent boomtown, while Minnesota and the rest of America had been suffering, all through the seventies, from slowing growth and rising prices; "stagflation" they called it, a wordplay on "stagnation" plus "inflation." I remembered reading in history books that back in the nineteenth century American presidents had managed to do their jobs with the help of just a few aides. So, I wondered, what had happened since, as White House staffs had ballooned into hundreds, and then into thousands? I came to see what critics meant when they jibed about "palace guards" and "imperial presidencies."

On the way back home to Minnesota, I continued to wrestle with what I had seen in Washington. It was a paradox: The public "servants" seemed to have more money than the taxpayer "masters." And yet during that same time, as I had seen in the summer of '75, some areas of the nation—Alaska, for instance—were rich, holding great natural resources. Or, I should say, *potentially* rich, because most of Alaska's wealth was locked in the ground by federal bureaucrats, functionaries obeying the "zero growth" edicts of elitist environmentalists. Yet Washington, D.C., was obviously excessively rich, grown fat on federal tax revenues. Washington thrived, after all, on its Internal Revenue Service money spigot; in those days the IRS could take as much as 70 percent of someone's annual income. I myself was light-years from a high income, but such a confiscatory tax rate didn't seem right to me, even if few in positions of power seemed to object.

Then we were back home. And back to work. Marcus too was working hard, both on campus and back on the farm. In retrospect, it might have seemed like a long courtship from the time we first met, in early 1976, till the time we were married, in late 1978. But let me tell you, the time flew by, because we were both busy working and finishing our studies. During all of 1977, we were going steady, as you might say, but we didn't have nearly as much time together as we would have liked.

In the fall of that year, Marcus invited me to come meet his family in Wisconsin. We drove in an old Ford Pinto that he had borrowed from his brother; it featured a gaping hole in the back floor. Riding with Marcus through the rolling hills of Wisconsin, I thought to myself, *How beautiful this country scenery is!* Marcus was pointing out the trees that were bare and brown; the Wisconsin countryside, he said, was prettier in the winter, when all was velvety white, or else in the spring and summer, when everything was leafy green. But it was beautiful right now, I insisted. The stark trees looked like the romantic ruins of an old cathedral. And Marcus agreed. So here were two lessons for me: First, every season of nature has its own kind of beauty, and second, with the help of someone you love, you can see the world anew. Everything can be made fresh.

Arriving in Independence, Wisconsin, I instantly bonded with Marcus's parents. His father and I talked about cows and milk; his mother and I talked about baking bread. It was all so natural, so comfortable, so obvious.

Next it was Marcus's turn to meet my family. He drove up to Anoka to meet Mom and Ray. It was a Saturday, and Mom had said to come by anytime, so we did. When Marcus and I arrived, we found Mom and Ray scraping their wallpaper in the hallway. Marcus was eager to help, so that's what we did. Such gallantry might seem more practical than romantic, but let me tell you, it was both—practical *and* romantic. By pitching in so readily on a chore, Marcus made a good impression on my folks. Men, here's a lesson for you: Flowers and candy are wonderful for a girl, but if you really want to convince her that you're Mr. Right, it helps to be a handyman!

A few weeks later, unbeknownst to me, Marcus asked Mom and Ray for permission to propose to me. She told him he had to promise always to take good care of me, and Marcus promised earnestly to do just that. And so Mom and Ray nodded, and that was that. Marcus also called my dad, met with him, and asked for, and received, permission to marry his daughter.

But in the meantime, it was work, work, work. Neither of us had yet graduated from college; we were both still paying our way through school doing a variety of jobs. I was an intern at the state legislature, but my most satisfying job was as a nanny for a wonderful family. There I saw a positive vision of family life. For his part, Marcus's job was at a day-care center in downtown Minneapolis, a place called Soul's Harbor, where he taught employment skills to those who were down and out. But all that time turned out to be time well spent, because he enjoyed listening to people; he has always said that everyone's story has value. And then, of course, Marcus would do his best to help and minister, sharing not only his savvy about getting a job but also his ever more mature Christian worldview.

Marcus proposed to me on February 15, 1978. You may be thinking: Why not February 14? Well, Marcus wanted to be different. For all his

Swiss precision, he can be quirky sometimes. And so he proposed at 12:01 A.M. on the fifteenth, because, as he told me, he wanted our engagement to be unique! But as a hopeless romantic, I told myself it was still the fourteenth in Mountain or Pacific time.

We set the date for September, so that we could both graduate from Winona and then have plenty of time to prepare a grand wedding. So that May I graduated with a BA in political science with a minor in English, while Marcus earned his BA in sociology.

The wedding was on Sunday, September 10, 1978. A beautiful Wisconsin late-summer day! Marcus, always a good workman, had built a lovely stone altar on his parents' family farm, on top of the "horses' hill," surrounding it with wildflowers. The scene was breathtaking, as was the temperature—ninety degrees and full sun! I wore a simple, long, white dress that I had bought off the return rack; it was ninety dollars. I also wore a floppy white hat—those were big back then. Marcus's mother had her silk wedding veil stored in the attic; never sentimental, she planned to rip it up into sections to tie her tomato plants. "Elma!" I said, "you can't do that. Let me sew the holes in the fabric and I'll use it as my veil." And that's what I did. I spent five dollars on a pair of shoes at Payless, and if I do say so myself, the bride looked great!

For his part, Marcus wore a dark blue velour suit—hey, this was the seventies! I'll admit, incidentally, that I never liked the suit; I later gave it to Goodwill during a garage-cleaning frenzy without telling him. Two pastors, Dick Alf and Bill Hagedorn, presided over the ceremony; we pledged our troth using the beautiful words of traditional wedding vows, declaring before God and these witnesses that we would remain lifelong companions. And because this was a working dairy farm, the Holstein cows joined in—they made plenty of noise. I thought of the Bible verse "Ask now the beasts, and they shall teach thee." I knew that God was with us on that blessed day, as He is with us every day, as His hand guides every living thing.

Because we had some four hundred people joining us, we had to borrow chairs and benches from a local church. Marcus's best man was his brother Peter, while my maid of honor was my college roommate and close friend Dana Primrose. My lifelong pal Barb Norbie had moved out to California by then, and sadly, she couldn't afford to come to the wedding. After the ceremony, we drove to our reception in Winona, where we offered M&Ms as party favors and served root beer and homemade chicken, mashed potatoes, and vegetables for our wedding feast—good food, prepared by local farm women, but nothing fancy. And the price was something like $1.25 per plate. My, how times have changed!

We spent our wedding night at the Schumacher Inn, a lovely old bed-and-breakfast in New Prague, Minnesota, which back then featured four-star Czech and German dishes.

For our honeymoon we flew to California, the first time that either of us had ever set foot in the Golden State. We flew to San Francisco, and from SFO we flew to Monterey, where we spent two weeks in the Carmel area. For two nights we stayed at the Gosby House Inn, a beautiful old Victorian perched on Lighthouse Avenue, overlooking the ocean in Pacific Grove. Those nights were a wedding present from my best friend Barb. Then Marcus and I stayed with Barb at the home she was renting with two other women. Barb gave us her bedroom; she slept on the couch. Then we drove down the coast, zipping along the curves of the scenic Pacific Coast Highway to the Hollywood Bowl, where we caught Steve Martin and John Belushi.

I must pause again to say how close I feel to Barb. After we came back from Israel, we promised each other not only that we would stay friends but that we would see each other at least once a year. She has lived out in California since the midseventies, but we have never missed a year. Over the decades, we have talked and prayed together about everything—from boyfriends and husbands to babies to politics. Both of us are ardently pro-life; Marcus and I focused on foster children while Barb became executive director of a pro-life center. She is godmother to one of our children, and she is Auntie Barb to all five. And I am godmother to her twins. For nearly forty years now, we have been with each other in times of joy and times of tragedy. But perhaps most of all, our friendship is built on the foundation of our faith.

Marcus and I still didn't have much money, of course, and so two weeks later, when we came back to Minnesota, we returned some of the duplicate wedding gifts, because we needed cash. For the next year, the new Mr. and Mrs. Bachmann stayed out on the family farm. Marcus worked the cows—what else?—while I got a job at a judge's office in Buffalo County, Wisconsin, just across the Mississippi River from Minnesota. I answered phones and did typing for Judge Schlosstein, and along the way, in little side moments, I learned a lot of practical things about the law, courthouse life, and our legal system. The judge would always take time to explain to me the finer points of law. I knew that this was how lawyers had once been mentored and trained; that is, aspiring lawyers worked for an experienced lawyer and thus were schooled by him. It worked for Lincoln! In fact, that system still would be good today, it seems to me, because too many law schools have become overfunded hothouses for avant-garde legal theorizing, as opposed to teaching the details and practicalities of the law itself.

Meanwhile, Marcus and I were trying to hold down our spending and build up our savings. I had zero debt when I graduated from college; Marcus owed fifteen hundred dollars. Our first paychecks went to pay off his student loan debt, and by Christmas, we were 100 percent debt free—and we liked it that way. Frugality and taking good care of the things we had—that's all in my blood. I can remember, when I was a child, my mom and dad bringing home a brand-new dining-room table and chairs made of hard-rock maple. I was ten, and it was the first time my parents had had a stick of new furniture. He said it had cost a lot of money, nine hundred dollars, so we weren't allowed to touch it—or even get near it! Dad made his point about the value of fine things, but in our own family, we mostly preferred secondhand furniture that the kids too could enjoy. And besides, there's a lot of good that you can do with polish and paint!

In that scrimping spirit, Marcus and I bought our first car, a used Datsun. Actually, it was more of a *wrecked* Datsun. It had been totaled and then restored—mostly. It ran, but it never quite ran right. We called it "the bomb."

The first year of our marriage, 1978–79, was a happy time for us newlyweds. We lived in an old red farmhouse belonging to the Bachmanns, out there with the cows in the middle of the Midwest. In lieu of rent to Marcus's parents, we fixed the place up and gave his labor to the farm, working the crops and the cows. I sewed new curtains, and Marcus fixed up the rooms. But the main thing was that the two of us were together. Marcus, always analytical, kept saying that our most important task as a couple was to knit together as one. And that's what we did. We have been knitted together ever since, for thirty-three years.

Meanwhile, the larger world was steadily, scarily unraveling.

CHAPTER FIVE

Jimmy Carter and Me

WHILE Marcus and I were gelling our relationship as a couple together, back in the late seventies, the Carter administration was coming unglued. Marcus and I had both voted for Jimmy Carter, but it didn't take long for us to become disillusioned. I remember being appalled by Carter's energy policy; he was going on TV, telling us to turn the thermostat down and wear sweaters, and he also wanted the government to build giant "synfuel" plants. These proposals struck me as either an unnecessary sacrifice or an unnecessary boondoggle. After all, I had seen for myself the natural abundance of Alaska—although little did I know, as yet, about the untapped energy supplies abounding also in the lower forty-eight, both underground and offshore.

Meanwhile, as day follows night, Carter's bad policies were leading to bad results. In the late seventies, America was suffering from a severe gasoline shortage, all the worse because it was government created. Like so many other Americans, I remember sitting in my Rambler in a gas line for more than an hour, only to see the station owner come out and put up a "no gas" sign right in front me—he had run out. I was literally running on fumes by that time and wondered if I could even make it home after an hour of idling in line. The bureaucrats simply weren't allowing him enough gas. I thought to myself, *This is ridiculous. Off in fat and happy Washington, bureaucrats are toying with our lives and livelihoods—and then when they get it wrong, when they misallocate energy supplies, they're still no less fat and happy.* Working for the government means never having to say you are sorry.

And at the same time, during the Carter years, inflation was surging.

The White House tried to blame inflation on everyone else, but the truth was, the Democratic administration was running big deficits while telling the Federal Reserve to print money without value behind it to make up those deficits. Do we see a recurring pattern here? That is, too much government spending, so government pays for its binge by firing up the printing presses. That means a reduction in the value and the soundness of the dollar; in other words, theft by government. So now, during these years, prices and interest rates were rising, and Washington seemed helpless, even complicit, in the foul-up. For his part, Carter kept trying to blame us, the American people, for his self-made problems. He didn't give any evidence that he understood either his contribution to hurting the nation or how he could turn the country around.

The pieces were now coming together for me: It was a case of ivory tower big government thinking versus the real people who, as Jimmy Stewart said in *It's a Wonderful Life,* the classic film, "do most of the working and paying and living and dying in this community." So I wondered: Were we, the people, going to live with overspending, government-created inflation, high interest rates that only allowed home purchases by contract for deed, and gas rationing? Were we going to oppose this hapless embrace of big government? In 1978 I remember cheering as the voters in California enacted the property tax–cutting Proposition 13 by a nearly two-to-one margin. Prop 13, it turned out, was the opening salvo of a nationwide tax revolt.

And that tax revolt could not come soon enough for me. One summer, when I was still in college, I had an eye-opening experience proving that the federal government was capable of operating by both deception and force. Examining my modest paycheck from working a summer job as a reporter for a small local newspaper, I could see how much the government was withholding from my check. I was shocked. The income-tax bite was bad enough, but what was this about FICA taxes? I was, and am, all in favor of everyone having a safe and solid retirement, but I started to wonder if the current system was the best way to achieve that goal. As I dug around on the issue of Social Security, I learned about the illusion that each of us had his or her own Social Security account; we had no such thing. Uncle Sam had no account labeled, for instance, "Michele Amble." Instead, all the money went into a big general fund, allowing the politicians to do whatever they wanted with it. And what have they done? They have raided the fund and left behind IOUs that the labors of generations of Americans, as yet unborn, will be required to repay. In other words, more governmental theft. In fact, according to the U.S. Supreme Court's 1960 decision in *Flemming v. Nestor*, we American citizens out in the provinces had no legal right to the Social Security benefits that were supposedly "ours," even though we had paid all those FICA taxes. I was really fried, I must say.

I thought to myself: *I'm young, and I have my whole life ahead of me, and they're taking this big chunk out of my check. I'd rather take the money myself and put it in a savings account and watch it grow.* So I wrote a letter to the Social Security Administration saying I didn't want to pay those Social Security taxes. I'll take care of my own retirement, I added; just let me keep my hard-earned money, and I'll let you off the hook, thank you very much. The next thing I knew, I got an intimidating phone call from Washington, D.C. The caller on the other end of the line said this was coming from the White House! The man said, "We've received your letter, and we want you to know that you have to pay your Social Security. It's a crime not to; you will go to jail if you don't pay us the money." I was shocked, but I argued anyway. But the man from the government was not there to help me or even to listen to me; he was there to put me in my place. After a few more moments of not listening, he curtly ended the call. Staring at the dead phone receiver in my hand, I thought to myself, *Wow, so this is how it is. We have no choices over our retirement and how we fund it. There has to be a better way,* I thought to myself, *for the government to interact with the citizenry.* A little courtesy, a little respect, and a lot more candor— that's what we needed then and what we need now. I wanted to invest that money from every paycheck, not turn it over to the government. I would willingly save and invest that money by setting it aside. Instead, I later found out, the government wasn't investing my retirement money for my best interest; it wasn't even investing it at all. The government was taking my money and spending it on current recipients, providing no guarantee of return on investment.

If Carter's energy and economic policies were bad, his foreign policy was worse. In the late seventies, the shah of Iran—a friend not only to the United States but also to Israel—was in trouble, challenged from within by Islamic forces led by the Ayatollah Khomeini. You remember Khomeini: He was the man who called America "the great Satan." So we saw a decisive fork in the road: Iran would be led either by the pro-American shah or by the anti-American Khomeini. The Carter administration seemingly couldn't decide what to do about it; the president talked about "human rights," not seeming to notice that the Ayatollah had no intention of respecting anyone's human rights. Soon the shah was falling, Khomeini was rising, and still the Carter administration was dithering.

During those years, 1978–79, Marcus and I had Marcus's little nine-inch black-and-white TV from college that we set on the kitchen counter. Before I went to work in the morning, I always turned on the news, and I remember seeing that the shah had been forced to flee his country. Meanwhile, Carter kept just sitting on his hands. I couldn't believe it. Then I watched as the Iranian people chanted and shouted, eagerly welcoming Khomeini as he entered Tehran. I thought to myself, he is the scariest-looking person I have ever seen. I felt that I was looking at the face of evil.

I also thought that if past generations had been forced to confront the evil of Nazi Germany, then maybe this generation would be forced to confront the evil of Islamic fundamentalism, which led to radical jihadism in Iran. And that was before the new Iranian regime seized the American embassy in Tehran, holding our diplomats hostage for an agonizing 444 days. The hostage takeover—again, Carter seemed helpless—was a hinge moment for me and, more to the point, for all of America.

Looking back, we can see the results of Jimmy Carter's failure to confront the Ayatollah before he could take and consolidate power. Since then, the Middle East and the world have suffered a dramatic surge in Islamic radicalism and terrorism. And so now we have to live with the lethal jihad ideology that produced the 1983 Beirut barracks bombing, the endless terrorism against Israel, the epic tragedy of 9/11, the prolonged wars in Afghanistan and Iraq, and the continuing terrorist threats around the world.

And here on the home front, airline travel is forever changed by the dehumanizing aspects of the Transportation Security Administration. The Israelis have the best airport security procedures I've ever seen. Why not pattern our security procedures after what works? The American people aren't guilty of terrorism, and we shouldn't all be treated as suspects when we travel on an airplane—I myself seem to get screened quite often. Let's have a little judgment so that ordinary Americans can move around the country unmolested. The way that the Israelis screen airline passengers includes screening everyone, of course, but they screen with a skilled professionalism that enables their screeners to quickly zero in on potentially dangerous individuals; there's a reason that El Al, the Israeli airline, hasn't suffered a hijacking since 1969 and that no airplane, ever, that departed from Ben Gurion Airport has been hijacked.

It's been said that liberals want a strong government and a weak country. Speaking for myself, I want a small government and a big defense. Even an unashamed apologist for free markets like me has to agree that national defense is the single most important function of government. And the father of free-market economics agrees: "The first duty of the sovereign," Adam Smith wrote more than two centuries ago in *The Wealth of Nations*, is "protecting the society from the violence and invasion of other independent societies." And that protection requires military force. Moreover, if we are going to have military force—and we must—we should have the best. During the seventies, I remember reading news reports about our military personnel being so underpaid that they were depending on food stamps to make ends meet. At that time, Uncle Sam was suffering from a "hollow military"—that is, not enough resources to protect America. And I must add, those concerns about a hollow military are reemerging ominously today.

In addition, a strong military requires a technological edge. In order to sustain the margin of safety needed to support a policy of "peace through strength," the Pentagon needs top-notch scientists and engineers. Back in the seventies, the Soviets were busy building new weapons, and many Americans wondered if the United States was keeping up, to say nothing of staying ahead. During the Carter years, General Daniel O. Graham, retired from the U.S. Army, went on to lead a campaign to get Americans interested in the idea of missile defense. We should occupy the "high frontier" of space, Graham argued, so that we could launch satellites and deploy other devices to destroy attacking Soviet missiles. Graham's idea was so obviously sensible to me. It was foolish to depend on the nuclear doctrine of mutual assured destruction (aptly called MAD). Instead, we should figure out how to shoot down enemy missiles fired by the USSR or other potential enemies. Such a defensive capacity could save not only many millions of American lives but also many millions of Russian lives. It made good sense: You should be able to defend yourself. But to most adherents of the establishment's pseudotheology of arms control, missile defense was completely anathema. We shouldn't defend ourselves against the

Russians, they declared; what we should do instead is negotiate with the Russians, because we can trust the likes of Kremlin leader Leonid Brezhnev. It made me wince to listen to the sophistries of State Department officials as they touched down in America long enough to write another anti–missile defense op-ed in the *New York Times*—before they jetted off to another round of expense-accounted "arms reductions talks" at a deluxe hotel in Zurich or Vienna. And speaking of Vienna, I was shocked that Carter would share a kiss with Brezhnev at the signing of an arms-control treaty. Or maybe by then I wasn't shocked.

So America's foreign-policy establishment united around the idea that General Graham's defense vision shouldn't even be considered. Sensing that their arms-control-talks lifestyle—the diplomatic equivalent of *la dolce vita*—was on the line, these diplomatic lifers could never admit that missile defense might actually be possible. And they were joined by leftist scientists who also insisted that missile defense could never work. Yet I knew that such deliberate fatalism about technological potential was ridiculous, because if antiaircraft weaponry could be made to work—as it had worked successfully as far back as the Second World War—so too could antimissile weaponry be made to work during the cold war. It was a matter of a can-do America making the effort and exertion, that's all. So here was the question: Did we want to defend the American homeland against a missile strike or not? Most conservatives said yes; most liberals said no. I was convinced that missile defense could and should be built.

Let's look at today's Israel for a moment: The Israelis are firm believers in missile defense. Confronted by thousands of missiles and Qassam rockets launched against them from beyond their borders, they are moving as fast as they can to deploy what they have poetically dubbed Iron Dome, so that they can protect their people from rocket assault. Indeed, the Kibbutz Be'eri, where I spent an inspiring summer nearly four decades ago, has come under repeated rocket attack from Palestinian terrorists firing from the nearby Gaza Strip. It's always been clear to me: The Jewish State of Israel has the right to exist, the right to self-defense, and the clear need to build up its defenses. And if they do so, they will be helping themselves and ourselves to perfect the technology to confront new potential threats from countries such as Iran. And we will benefit, too, as we confront potential threats from around the world.

But perhaps the concern that hit me the hardest back then was the urgent need to protect the family and family values. During the 1976 campaign, Carter had promised to hold a White House conference on the family. I believe he might have meant well when he made that campaign pledge; perhaps he thought that a conference on the family would generate policies that would, in fact, help the family, such as school reform or tax relief. But if so, he was naive. He couldn't control the liberals and the bureaucrats in his own administration. So instead of examining pro-family policies, the Carter administration got bogged down in avant-garde discussions of new kinds of family, seeking to appease liberal-left constituencies that had little or no interest in preserving traditional values and norms.

And so the idea of a White House conference on the *family* morphed into a conference on *families*—that is, a politicized gathering that expressed agnosticism and bewilderment as to what a family should be. In 1980, after years of wrangling, the Carter administration's White House Conference on Families was finally held and, needless to say, was a festival of liberal relativism. For his part, Carter just went along with what the activists said.

Out in the Midwest, watching all this foolishness on TV, I said to Marcus: "The president can't define what a family is? Any three-year-old knows what a family is! So why are we spending millions of taxpayer dollars on such foolishness?" As I studied the whole sorry saga more carefully, I learned an important lesson: Inside the government, personnel is policy. Carter himself might have had some good Georgia values, especially on social issues, but he couldn't, or wouldn't, ride herd over the radicals who had burrowed into his own executive branch.

So yes, I was disappointed and disillusioned by Jimmy Carter. And yes, we could see that in regard to the three major components of modern American conservatism—economics, foreign policy, and social issues—Carter was wrong on all three.

But I still thought of myself as a Democrat. I don't make big changes suddenly.

Then one day while I was still in college, I was taking the train from Minneapolis to Winona, and I had with me a copy of *Burr*, Gore Vidal's 1973 novel about the Founding Fathers. In the novel, Aaron Burr—the man who killed Alexander Hamilton in an 1804 duel—was portrayed basically as the hero. This portrayal seemed strange to me, because the historical truth is that after killing Hamilton, Burr fled the United States—then consisting of just seventeen states—and headed for the Louisiana Territory, where he attempted to raise an illegal army for the purpose of conquering Mexico. These misadventures, of course, were gravely serious, violating the Neutrality Act of 1794; Burr was subsequently tried for treason. And although he was acquitted, he spent the rest of his life in disgrace. This man was a villain, not a hero.

Moreover, America's legendary Founding Fathers, according to Vidal, were all seriously flawed. George Washington was a hopeless bumbler, and Thomas Jefferson was nothing but a hypocrite. In fact, none of the founders were much good. So I could only conclude that the author of *Burr* was, well, snotty. At best, the book was jaded, and at worst, it lacked truthfulness. The book horrified me. *What it says isn't true,* I told myself, and I put it down. Then, looking out the train window, I saw instead the green fields and trees of the midwestern landscape, dotted with pleasant houses and welcoming little towns. *Here, truly,* I thought, *is our wonderful nation—the nation that the founders fought for two centuries ago.* These immortals had no idea that there would ever be a state called Minnesota, or that people with names such as Amble and Bachmann would be coming to the United States to find a better life. Nevertheless, the founders had been willing to put everything—their lives, liberty, and sacred honor—on the line for us, for all of us. Indeed, the nation had prospered, just as they had envisioned. And this was the thanks they got?

The idea that Vidal—at the time a major figure in American literature, as well as a regular guest on TV talk shows—would write such a book was disgusting to me. And the fact that critics would love that book was even more disgusting. Indeed, I realized, a snide dismissiveness toward American history and American institutions had become the essence and thinking of the chattering-class gatekeepers of the culture. Then I pondered: *So who has the greatest influence today in the Democratic Party? Who is now setting the party's attitudes and policies?* The answer was obvious: *It's the same liberals who have given us policies of scarcity on energy regulation, government spending, and high taxes. It's the same liberals who have given us a weak-kneed policy toward Iran—and also, of course, the Soviet Union. It's the same liberals who have given us abortion, racial quotas, school busing, and that ridiculous waste of time and money White House Conference on Families. And now, as the last straw, it's these liberals who are smearing our own history, and doing a hit job on the founders.*

These trendy-left people spoke as though they had no understanding of, or connection to—and only contempt for—my own working-class folks back in Waterloo. Nor did they evidence any connection to or affinity for the working-class folks who were once the backbone of the Democratic Party as a whole. You know, the kind of Democrats, like my mother's mother, who loved Franklin D. Roosevelt because they believed he had put people back to work, or the kind of Democrats who supported Harry Truman because he gave 'em hell and stood up to Stalin, even as he stood up for Israel. These old-line Democrats, I concluded, had no real place in the new-left Democratic Party. Everything had flipped. And so at that moment, I became a Republican and never looked back. I was through. I realized I wasn't in line with the new antifamily, antistrong national defense, antifiscal sanity Democratic Party. I was now a Republican.

As Ronald Reagan always liked to say, he didn't leave the Democratic Party—the Democratic Party left him. Now I too knew the feeling.

Indeed, during the late seventies, Marcus and I grew increasingly attracted to Reagan and his conservative philosophy. We loved it when he said that Americans wanted a conservatism of bright colors, not pale pastels—we sure did. That is, we wanted someone who would unabashedly take the fight directly to the economic declinists, the foreign-policy defeatists, and the antifamily relativists who seemed at the time to dominate both parties. Indeed, Republicans of the "me too" persuasion—that is, Republicans supporting everything the Democrats wanted to do, although maybe for a little less money—held no appeal to us. We wanted a GOP that would fight to make real change. So we liked Reagan, and also a newcomer, a charismatic congressman named Jack Kemp, who had been highlighting new and better approaches to economics, such as marginal-rate tax cuts.

All the things I remember hearing from my Republican grandmother, Anna, began now to make sense to me. I started reading more: The weekly magazines, *Time*, *Newsweek*, and *US News & World Report*. And yes, the *Wall Street Journal*—I was truly becoming my grandmother's granddaughter. And another publication, *National Review*, became a must-read; I needed to know more about the intellectual, ethical, and theological origins of the conservative movement. Indeed, I learned a few new words from *National Review*'s fearless—and fearlessly polysyllabic—founding editor in chief, William F. Buckley.

I had been a reader my entire life, but mostly I read biographies and especially mysteries. I loved solving puzzles, but now that I was in my twenties, I saw that I had new mysteries to solve—the mysteries of history and economics. I never finished *Burr—and never, of course, read another Gore Vidal novel.* Instead, I began consuming books on American history that told the real story—that George Washington, for instance, was not only a military hero but also a good and honorable man. I felt convinced, with patriotic certitude, that the founders were great men, and great women, who bequeathed to us a great country.

I also read a lot of economics. Keynesian economics made absolutely no sense to me; I rejected the notion that you could "spend yourself rich." Just the opposite was true, as far as I was concerned; if you spent too much, you spent yourself poor. Keynesianism proved bankrupt in the seventies, when both Republicans and Democrats tried it, and it has been proved even more bankrupt in the last few years, when Barack Obama tried to revive it. The truth is that basic economic realities never change in any era. The economy is not propelled by Keynesian fine-tuners calculating and recalculating their arcane equations about "multipliers" and "money velocity"; the economy is propelled instead by actual, real-world doers. It is animated by "human action," in the phrase of the Austrian economist Ludwig von Mises, who titled his famous 1949 book *Human Action: A Treatise on Economics.*

Indeed, it's pure folly to think that someone in a marble palace somewhere can dictate the economic activity of people far away, all of them pursuing their own individual wants and needs. Instead, von Mises argued, the force that creates economic activity and growth is, simply, people getting up in the morning and making something—that is, free enterprise. The ideas of von Mises were thrilling to me; he put a rigorous intellectual framework around the commonsense observations that we all make. It is, indeed, hard work—a very basic "human action"—that creates wealth and prosperity. So yes, absolutely, the work of von Mises—as I told Steve Moore of the *Wall Street Journal*—makes for great beach reading.

Applying von Mises's wisdom, we Americans can all remember a basic truth: No bureaucrat ever put the idea of the lightbulb into the head of Thomas Edison. As Edison said, his inventions were 1 percent inspiration and 99 percent perspiration. Similarly, no economic planner ever put the idea of the assembly line into the head of Henry Ford; it was Ford himself, using his talents, plus his education, plus his sheer hard work. God gave Edison and Ford and all the other business heroes their first sacred spark of life; then those go-getters did the rest.

And just as important as free enterprise is the free market, the place where producers meet consumers. The empowered and informed consumer is the crown jewel not only of the free market but also of freedom itself. That was the message of Milton Friedman in his classic work *Capitalism and Freedom*. In the free market, I get to decide "Coke" or "Pepsi," and the market then responds to me. In fact, we *all* get to decide on one or the other—or decide on none of the above—and always, the market responds. And if we decide we want something completely different, the marketers will again come running, offering any other beverage we might desire. Capitalism: It's a beautiful thing. Indeed, as I think about all these great economists, I am reminded again: Freedom is inspiring, and liberty is beautiful.

Another eye-opening book for me during those years was William Simon's 1978 best seller, *A Time for Truth*. After a successful career on Wall Street, Simon, in the 1970s, worked for the federal government, first as "energy czar" under President Richard Nixon, then as Treasury secretary under Nixon and President Gerald Ford. As energy czar, Simon was tasked with making sense of all the idiotic price-control regulations that the government was using to straitjacket the energy market. All that red tape had been a failure, of course: It had decreased energy production, caused those unending gas lines that I had sat in with my Rambler idling, and ultimately raised prices, allowing the OPEC nations to maintain a stranglehold on the American consumer, holding us up for even more billions. Simon, having been inside the belly of the federal regulatory beast, emerged from those depths warning Americans that they were headed toward ruin—that is, if current trends of taxing, spending, and regulating were allowed to continue. And he was right: We had reached a grim point of reckoning. Yet thanks to Ronald Reagan, those negative trends were finally reversed in the eighties. The late Bill Simon's status as an economic truth teller is thus enshrined forever, even as we realize now that we must take up his fight once again.

Warning against runaway statism, the Gipper liked to quip, "A government big enough to give you everything you want is big enough to take it all away." And that truism reminds me yet again that the ultimate point of free enterprise and free markets can be summed up in just one word: freedom. The bigger the government, the smaller the freedom. And if the government controls the economy, it also controls the media and the right to free speech. As they say, the only way to be guaranteed a free press is to own one—private ownership is a vital check against state power.

Moreover, when governments grow big enough, they develop an oppressive sameness, relying on common characteristics of regimentation and control. As the great libertarian economist Friedrich Hayek explained in his 1944 book *The Road to Serfdom*, the communists and fascists of the era might have hated each other, but in the end, the reds and the browns were similar. That is, totalitarians are all united in their belief that personal autonomy is the enemy. In a later work, *The Constitution of Liberty*, Hayek further laid out his argument for simultaneously structuring a system of freedom and limiting the power of the state.

The emphasis on personal freedom and free will took me back to my own biblical thinking. As we are told in Second Corinthians 3:17, "Where the Spirit of the Lord is, there is liberty." Liberty is a gift of God. We must not misuse it, and we must always treasure it. We are each made in His image, and when He made us, he wrote a series of truths on our hearts. That's what natural law tells us—that we each have a soul, that God loves each of us in our uniqueness, and that each of us is born with inherent dignity. The Bible tells us that each one of us, no matter what our surface imperfections, is in fact made in the perfect image of God. This essential equality of all souls, graced by the Almighty, is the ultimate redoubt of our individual freedom.

I also started following thinkers and activists who helped articulate my Christian conservative worldview. But first I had to see through the faddish fog of "feminism," the radical school of thought propounded by such well-known figures as Betty Friedan and Gloria Steinem. I'm all for strong women as role models; I knew many of them growing up, starting with my mother and both of my grandmothers. Yet in the seventies, women were solemnly instructed by the liberal media to believe that family, tradition, and even faith were merely the disguised manifestations of an oppressive "patriarchy." We were further told that "women" wanted to be liberated—as if "women" were a bloc, and as if liberals knew what was good for all of us, all across the country.

I rejected that kind of feminism. First and foremost, I rejected it because of the issue of abortion. Pro-life is a bedrock principle for me. Even hard-core feminists should understand that girls are the biggest losers in abortion, because it's unborn females who are most frequently selected for elimination. But I was repulsed also by the generalized worldview of liberal-left feminism, which tended to say things like, "A woman needs a man like a fish needs a bicycle." It's a free country, of course, and everyone is entitled to his or her opinion, but I wanted no part of an ideology that praised wives being apart from husbands or children being apart from fathers. That was the sort of thinking that had gone into the regrettable conference on "families" back in the Carter years.

So instead I found myself reading the works of Phyllis Schlafly and Beverly LaHaye. I read a copy of the *Phyllis Schlafly Report*, and soon I was a regular reader. I remember reading about Beverly and her organization, the Concerned Women of America, as a young bride. I opened my mailbox one day and found some of Bev's cassette tapes; I listened to the first tape as I was driving across Wisconsin. I was immediately a fan. Beverly's words were inspiring. And I realized that while I might be in the minority, I was hardly alone. And soon, with the 1980 election, I saw that the values and beliefs I held were actually in the majority. As they say, never despise small beginnings. Conservative women started small, but thanks to leaders such as Phyllis and Beverly, we have now become a real force.

One of my goals was to learn from these wonderful women and to connect with them—and then to take up their great causes. Later I would be blessed enough to spend time with both Phyllis and Beverly and to count them as friends.

Marcus and I talked about all of these ideas. The difference was that he was focused on his career, and I was developing my own. He would be the listener and the counselor; I would be the speaker and the activist. But we both agreed: We were going to do more than talk the talk. We also wanted to walk the walk. We were going to say to liberals: "Not with my country, you don't."

So Marcus and I became solid, active Republicans. We could see that it wasn't just a problem of Jimmy Carter; it was the liberalism of the Democratic Party—with, unfortunately, assists from some in the Republican Party—that had enlarged the government, weakened our standing in the world, and decreased responsible liberty at home. We needed energized conservatism, and nobody epitomized it better than Ronald Reagan.

We enthusiastically voted for Reagan in 1980. We were so proud of him, and also of Nancy for being such an inspiring first lady. Our new president not only cut taxes but also eased up on regulation, thereby unleashing a new generation of entrepreneurs and job creators. He forthrightly declared the Soviet Union to be an "evil empire," then used the idea of missile defense—which he called the Strategic Defense Initiative—to strike fear and doubt into the hearts of the Soviets, accelerating the collapse of their regime. And he appointed mostly pro-life judges to the federal court system. As for the Supreme Court, he appointed some brilliant individuals, such as Antonin Scalia, appointed and confirmed in 1986; lamentably, the equally talented Robert Bork was shamefully disrespected in his confirmation hearing and was ultimately rejected by the Senate in 1987. We the people are poorer for that reprehensible action.

It was in the perilous fires of the Carter administration that my ideology was forged. In the seventies, Carter taught me what I was against, and then in the eighties, Reagan taught me what I was for.

In the meantime, in our own lives, Marcus and I were determined to put "feet to our faith." That is, not just to believe it but to live it. We enjoyed listening to and supporting the fortieth president, so charming and engaging. And yet we realized that he couldn't do everything. The nation had spent decades digging itself into a deep trough of misguided policies; it would take more than eight years to climb out. So Marcus and I knew we had plenty of work to do in our own neighborhood, our own state, our own time. So while Reagan was saving the world from communism, Marcus and I had to do what we could to save Minnesota from liberalism.

But where to start? We started with what we knew to be true, of course—our faith in God. I had always loved reading the Old Testament, especially the story of how Moses carried the Ten Commandments down from Mount Sinai. I also believed that the immutable truths of the Ten Commandments served properly as the conscience of our Judeo-Christian civilization. The commandments, I knew, provided immutable and universal truths. So I came to see further the need for objectivity, not subjectivity, in the law; that is, the law must be based on solid moral foundations, not on slippery situational relativism. And that process of understanding deepened my interest in the law, because the American concepts of law and justice indeed found their roots in the Decalogue. No wonder the frieze depicting Moses holding his two tablets graces the center of the pediment on the east facade of the Supreme Court building in Washington.

Some secular activists claim, of course, that the founders have been misinterpreted, and so what we really need now is relentless secularization—for instance, pulling down crosses and crèches on public property. And these ACLU-type activists will gleefully trample public opinion if they can find one judge who agrees with their antireligious bias. Was that truly the founders' view? What did they have in mind when they authored our founding documents? Many well-qualified scholars have offered undeniable historical proofs attesting to the Judeo-Christian roots of American law. We might note, for example, that the Declaration of Independence makes America's devoted relationship to God fully clear and manifest. The first sentence of the Declaration asserts:

> When in the Course of human events, it becomes necessary for one people to dissolve the political bands which have connected them with another, and to assume among the powers of the earth, the separate and equal station to which the Laws of Nature and of Nature's *God* [emphasis added] entitle them . . .

So there's God, right there, in the first fifty words of the Declaration. And He appears again in the very next paragraph:

> We hold these truths to be self-evident, that all men are created equal, that they are endowed by their *Creator* [emphasis added] with certain unalienable Rights . . .

It's worth noting that the Declaration is brief—little more than 1,300 words. But then again, there's the ringing conclusion:

> And for the support of this Declaration, with a firm reliance on the protection of *divine Providence* [emphasis added], we mutually pledge to each other our Lives, our Fortunes, and our sacred Honor.

So in their own immortal words, there you have their thinking. From the beginning, American leaders have put their trust in God. In God We Trust—our national motto. Our whole history as a nation has been shaped and guided by our faith in God. We have always used public money to employ chaplains, for example, and to write out oaths and other public statements that acknowledge our enduring devotion to God.

Mindful of that deep connection between our Judeo-Christian heritage and the formation of American law, my determination to go to law school grew even stronger. I could now see a career for myself as an advocate for these immutable truths. Scripture tells us to walk in a manner worthy of the Lord, and by God's grace, that's what I wanted to do. I felt called to attend a Bible-based Christian law school. So I chose one of the few available, the O.W. Coburn School of Law—named after the father of Oklahoma's great U.S. senator, Tom Coburn—at Oral Roberts University in Tulsa, Oklahoma.

Marcus and I traveled there in the fall of 1979. I loved Tulsa, I loved ORU, and most of all I loved law school. I worked hard. I respected my teachers and my fellow students, and I learned to think and talk on my feet. And I did many presentations, developing a skill that would come in handy in the years to come.

But there was a problem—a big problem. Marcus didn't feel he had a place in Tulsa. He had made plenty of contacts for jobs back in Minnesota and Wisconsin, but Oklahoma was new territory for him. He got a job as a director of a senior citizens center and loved the folks he was working with. He has always had a love and affinity for seniors. As a second-generation immigrant, Marcus did not have grandparents in the United States. Elma made it a habit when she went on her weekly shopping trip to town on Fridays to take young Marcus along and regularly visit both shut-ins and nursing-home residents. That habit carried over to some of our dates in college. Because we had no money, we would occasionally go to visit some of Marcus's favorite senior citizens at nursing homes in Winona, at Sarnia, and the Watkins Home. These were very unusual dates, but I got to see what a loving, sensitive, and caring man Marcus is, and afterward, rather than being depressed, we found great joy in recalling the stories and jokes of these seniors. To this day, we still do. It was wonderful work that Marcus was doing with the elderly, and it well fit his personality, but it was not what Marcus was truly meant to do. He wanted more direct contact with helping young people who needed mentoring. He wanted the chance to look into their eyes to come alongside and help them get back on a positive path. While I was in school that year, Marcus traveled to San Antonio—we had no car to spare, so he took the bus—for a Youth for Christ convention. That's when he realized that he was most truly called to help young people, to offer them better hope than the dumbed-down and often corrupted culture we were seeing all around us.

Marcus is never a complainer, but when he returned from San Antonio, I could tell that something was troubling him. We just looked at each other, not saying a word. And I thought of the verse from Isaiah: "In quietness and trust is your strength." So we both prayed, sharing our feelings and our concerns with God and with each other. For now we faced a dilemma: I loved being in Tulsa, but Marcus didn't.

But then I came to see that it wasn't a dilemma at all—I knew what I had to do. Marcus was my husband, the leader of our home and family. Between my law school and my marriage, it wasn't even a contest. I now realized, deep in my heart, that however much I would hate to leave ORU, I would hate even more causing hurt to Marcus. And then God reminded me of the famous words of Paul to the Corinthians: "Love bears all things, believes all things, hopes all things, endures all things."

So at the end of my first year in law school, in the spring of 1980, we packed up in Tulsa and moved back to Minnesota. I won't say I didn't shed a few tears, but I knew it was for the best.

Now, back on his home turf, Marcus was thriving. Helped along by mentors Peter and Susan Roehl, he established a youth ministry as part of the Youth for Christ organization, teaming up with ten local churches that couldn't afford to set up a youth outreach program on their own. This work is what Marcus was meant to do. He could help create a wholesome environment for kids while carefully advancing his goal of helping kids find faith in God. And cleverly, he held meetings at exactly 7:17 P.M. on Tuesday nights. "Why 7:17 P.M.?" I asked. "Because kids will remember it," he answered. And he was right. As always.

I could now see that Marcus was on an upward career path, the path that God intended him to walk. But unfortunately, now I wasn't sure about mine. I wanted to finish law school. To that end, I had worked hard to get into college, just as hard to get into law school, and yet now I felt I was stopped short of my goal. On the other hand, far more important, I was in the arms of a loving husband, and, of course, in the arms of a loving God. So as I cheered Marcus on in his new career success and asked the Lord for strength, I myself felt that I was waiting, waiting for whatever might come next. I was calmed with love, hope, and faith. And sure enough, new challenges—and greater joys—awaited both of us.

CHAPTER SIX

Life and Taxes

I wasn't all that happy to be away from law school, but then something big happened that changed everything. We knew we wanted to have a baby, but I also wanted to be prepared. So I spent six months changing our nutrition habits. We adopted a 100 percent health-food eating regimen so my body would be ready for my baby. And sure enough, six months later, I was pregnant! When I told Marcus, we hugged and then we prayed, recalling the 127th Psalm, which tells us that children are a gift from the Lord. Now my priorities were different; I talked with Mom about what to expect during pregnancy, and, of course, I read books that helped put me at ease. I knew that God was shaping the baby in my womb, but I wanted to do everything I possibly could to help. My overwhelming goal was to be a good expectant mother and then a good mother.

Lucas Barrett Paul Bachmann was born in Winona on April 30, 1982. Delivery took all of an hour after we got to the hospital. It was 12:30 a.m. The birth of a first child is so exciting! I wanted to call everyone, all our friends and family, to share the good news, but Marcus was exhausted and wanted to go to sleep. The irony: I had just had a baby, but he was tired. My mother said she would drive right down to stay for a week. Marcus also called my father, who by now was living in northern Illinois. Lucas was dad's second grandchild, but first grandson; soon, Lucas was the proud owner of a Chicago Cubs jacket. Marcus and I reconfirmed a decision we had made when we got married—that one of us would always be there for the children. And so we would get by on one paycheck, if need be. Our children would be our first priority as a couple; money would come second.

Marcus continued his work in the youth ministry and I assisted him.

When he came home, he helped care for our very colicky baby boy. We didn't have much money, but we always had fun as a young couple. We realized that walking was free; we could stroll along the banks of the Mississippi River and watch the Father of Waters, as the Native Americans called it, go flowing by, headed all the way down to the Gulf of Mexico. We could look at the blue sky and occasionally see the eagles that made their nests in the hilly woods all around us.

About the only luxury I had back then was a 1983 visit to California to see my lifelong friend Barbara Norbie, who was now Mrs. Meyer, having married a wonderful man, David Meyer. Barbara and David had by then moved to the northern part of California, to a little town called Willits, where David taught school. There they had been blessed with twins, Christy and Daniel, born just six weeks after Lucas. So all three of these kids have more or less grown up together, even two thousand miles apart. Indeed, Marcus and I are godparents to Christy and Daniel, just as Barbara is godmother to one of our children. On that trip west—Marcus stayed at home to work—Barbara's husband David volunteered to take care of the toddler trio, and so Barbara and I sneaked off to a little inn for a couple of nights devoted to girl talk, prayer, and heart-to-heart discussions about the challenges we faced as new mothers of seemingly perpetual screamers. This was during the early Reagan era, when things had been getting better after the "malaise" years of Jimmy Carter; yet both of us still felt called to do our part in renewing the nation, especially in the supremely important issue of life. In later years, Barbara would enjoy a fine career as the director of a Christian clinic, where the goal was always to provide compassionate, life-affirming health care to patients, including, of course, the unborn baby.

In the meantime, Marcus was making a new decision for us. He was enjoying his work at the youth ministry, but as he prayed about it, he sensed that it was time for me to finish law school, that my career calling was to be a lawyer. And that meant finishing law school in Tulsa. It was a poignant reversal: Four years earlier, I hadn't wanted to hurt him by staying in Tulsa, and now, because he didn't want to hurt me, we were once again going to Tulsa. I love my husband, truly and deeply, for a million reasons, but that reason is way up toward the top. He is a good man and a prayerful man, and when prayerful consideration told him what he should do, he did not hesitate to put his own interests second. In fact, we both knew we would have grad school in our future—Marcus was eager to gain at least a master's degree in Christian counseling—and so we agreed that we would somehow "tag team" our way through the next few years. That is, I would finish law school, and then he would pursue his own graduate degree.

So in the fall of 1984, four years after leaving Tulsa, the Bachmanns, now "plus one," returned to T-Town, as residents sometimes call it.

This time, Marcus found jobs more suited to his talents. He worked as the vice president of admissions for Oral Roberts University, which meant he could continue his work with young people. Also, interestingly, he once again became connected with the elderly; he became director of a senior center in the nearby town of Jenks. He organized the usual activities and events: coffee and doughnuts in the morning, ice-cream socials in the afternoon, art and exercise classes, plus the occasional speaker. In addition, Marcus arranged excursions; he and the seniors visited local churches and a nearby synagogue. Marcus loved every minute of it—these oldsters were the grandparents he had never really had; Marcus had seen his grandparents only rarely. And these seniors, too, were more than happy to share their life experience with a young man eager to learn more about how best to deal with social and psychological concerns.

Meanwhile, I attended my law school classes, then left immediately for home to care for Lucas. Then after work, Marcus stayed with Lucas so I could return to study at the law school library at night. We lived a Spartan life—all work, studying, and caring for our son. I earned my JD in 1986. Although matters of life and family would always be central to me, I grew increasingly interested in economic issues, including the nation's tax code. My reading in economics had told me that a too-complicated tax system and too-high tax rates were particularly damaging to the economy. But if I wanted to make a real change in the tax code, I knew I had to come armed with more than just my own personal opinions. I needed to know the facts of each particular case. I also needed to understand how the tax code was shaping—and misshaping—the American economy. That summer I took and passed the bar exam back home in Minnesota.

In the meantime, as the other half of the Bachmann tag team, I knew it was my turn to follow along after Marcus so that he could continue his own schooling. Marcus was equally committed to education with a biblical worldview, and so he chose what is now Regent University in Virginia

Beach, Virginia, founded by the evangelist Pat Robertson. Marcus entered the school's Christian counseling program, seeking a master's degree. At the same time, he worked full time counseling people over the telephone for the Christian Broadcasting Network.

Yet during the summer of 1986, friends pointed out that given that we would be living in the Tidewater area of Virginia, it was silly not to think about my studying tax law at nearby William & Mary; the university boasted one of the best tax-law programs in the nation. I already had my JD, but now I wanted to earn a *legum magister*, or LLM, a master's degree, in tax law. I knew I had received a great education at Oral Roberts, but I was looking forward to specializing in understanding the tax system because I wanted to lower taxes!

Now the pressure was really on both of us. Marcus and I shared in the homeschooling of Lucas, while I commuted, sometimes by car pool, to my new school in Williamsburg, more than an hour's drive away. And Marcus was going to school too, of course, as well as working. We were two full-time graduate students; Marcus also worked full time as we homeschooled Lucas. Our universities were an hour apart, and we could afford only one car. I often caught rides with other students, or Marcus figured out an alternate plan. I had back-to-back classes sometimes, evenings and mornings, and through the kindness of a married couple at the law school, I could sleep on their couch in a small graduate-dorm apartment. I was by now in my early thirties, and yet I was still sleeping on a couch!

And oh, by the way, during that time, we welcomed our second child into the world—Harrison Sterling Bachmann. Perhaps realizing that we were busy and didn't have time for a lengthy labor, Harrison took only seven minutes to be born. I kid you not. It is called a precipitous birth, and it happened suddenly one morning. In other words, our little boy was in the world before we were barely awake. It is the best way to have a baby! That was on February 2, 1987.

By this time, Marcus was so overworked and tired that he fell asleep in the dentist's chair; it wasn't from novocaine but from sheer exhaustion. As for me, there were days when I wondered if I would ever have time even to put conditioner in my hair. In a typical week, Marcus and I were able to find time for each other only on Friday nights and on Sundays. But I'm proud to say that Lucas and baby Harrison always saw at least one of us. We were tag-team parents; one of us was always there to care for the boys, but we couldn't both be there simultaneously. So while it was sad to miss some together times, Marcus and I always had plenty of stories to share about the boys and what they were up to. Still it was tough sometimes, but as I liked to remind myself, I had the built-in advantage of being married to a marriage counselor!

Moreover, Marcus and I both knew we were doing something important. Not just in raising those two boys, but also in the work we were preparing to do. Tax law is tough, even for those who love it. We were very tired pups that year, but we knew our sacrifice would be worth it. I worked hard because I always wanted to be prepared for class; I went to class and paid attention because I wanted to absorb this fascinating material to the best of my ability. With hard work and God's help, I made it through.

I earned my LLM degree from William & Mary, Marshall-Wythe School of Law, in 1988. And Marcus too received his master's in Christian counseling from what is now Regent University.

We moved back to Minnesota in the summer of 1988, just as the Reagan presidency was coming to its glorious close. Ronald Reagan had done what he had promised. For one thing, he had dramatically cut taxes, reducing the top income-tax rate from 70 percent to 28 percent. He had also pared back regulation, notably energy price controls, bringing big government at least somewhat to heel and giving the economy room to grow.

More than that, Reagan had restored the basic confidence of Americans not only in their economy but also in their country as a whole. Reagan had put the bitter hangover of Vietnam behind us; I still remember watching the ceremony, back in 1984, when our president presided over the laying to rest of the Unknown Soldier from the Vietnam War. And when Reagan presented the Unknown with the Congressional Medal of Honor, tears were streaming down my face. Later that year, our president traveled to Normandy for the fortieth-anniversary commemoration of D-day, reminding Americans of the heroism of U.S. forces, particularly the Army Rangers: "These are the boys of Pointe du Hoc. These are the men who took the cliffs. These are the champions who helped free a continent. These are the heroes who helped end a war." Not since the Gettysburg Address had a U.S. president paid better homage to our fighting men.

In fact, I wonder if we would have seen the revival of interest in World War II—Tom Brokaw's book *The Greatest Generation*, Steven Spielberg's *Saving Private Ryan*—were it not for the Reagan presidency.

But of course, Reagan was much more than a rhetorician. He was real in his deeds—he walked the walk. Don't take my word for it; ask the post-Soviet Russians. Reagan stood tall against the Soviet Union, which he rightly labeled, in a 1983 speech to the National Association of Evangelicals, the "evil empire." In that same speech he went even further, boldly predicting the demise of the USSR and its dictatorial system: "I believe that communism is another sad, bizarre chapter in human history whose last pages even now are being written." That was a remarkably prescient statement, at a time when the foreign-policy elites were saying that communism would last forever, maybe even ultimately prevail.

Yet Reagan never left anything to chance. To put pressure on the Soviets, he launched the Strategic Defense Initiative, working toward neutralizing the Russian nuclear threat. In addition, he coordinated with British prime minister Margaret Thatcher and two courageous sons of Poland, Pope John Paul II and Lech Wałesa, to block Soviet expansion and to support anticommunist dissidents. Reagan and company broke communism's grip, first on Eastern Europe, then on Russia itself. And so international events were unfolding just as Reagan had said they would. In 1987 he traveled to Berlin, standing in the shadow of the Berlin wall. He told the Soviet leadership what it had to do: "Mr. Gorbachev, tear down this wall!" Two years later, in 1989, the Berlin wall came down, and in 1991 the Soviet Union itself ceased to exist.

So it was in that resonant 1983 speech, years before the collapse of Soviet communism, that Reagan had foretold the future; he had predicted communism's "last pages." How did Reagan know what would happen? What inspired him in this prophecy? Well, the man answered those questions in the very next sentence of that speech: "The source of our strength in the quest for human freedom is not material, but spiritual. And because it knows no limitation, it must terrify and ultimately triumph over those who would enslave their fellow man." Right there, Reagan's words provided an instructive window into the vital concept of God-given natural law—that is, the realization that God has imprinted certain truths on the hearts of all mankind, including knowledge of our inherent right to life and to dignity. And if totalitarian oppressors stomped on those rights with which we were born, that's when the people rise up. And so we can see the powerful fusion of the natural-law tradition and the American Revolution. The founders held natural-law truths to be self-evident, and when they saw that the British were trampling their liberties, they took up arms. They knew that Providence was on their side in the fight for freedom.

And in that same 1983 speech, Reagan didn't just cite a spiritual source of strength; he cited chapter and verse from the Bible, quoting from Isaiah 40: "He giveth power to the faint; and to them that have no might He increaseth strength." Continuing, the president added: "But they that wait upon the Lord shall renew their strength; they shall mount up with wings as eagles; they shall run, and not be weary." Amen to that.

I love those verses of Isaiah, because while Reagan invoked biblical words to help inspire worldwide opposition to communism, those same hopeful words—"He giveth power to the faint"—also prove useful in helping to heal wounded hearts here at home. And let me tell you, as a married mom out there in the provinces, when I heard the president of the United States saying, "They shall mount up with wings as eagles," well, my heart soared. God spoke to me in those words, and here on earth, so did Ronald Reagan. Now I knew I had to do something. I thought of the commitment that God made to each of us in Hebrews 13:21, offering to make us fully perfect instruments of His plan. I wanted God to lead me to do what I could, each effort of which "is well pleasing in His sight."

Meanwhile, as the eighties edged into the nineties, many bulwarks of the American home front were seriously crumbling. Even while Reagan was busy saving the U.S. economy and saving the world, pernicious social forces were causing severe damage to the soul of the nation. Epidemics of crime and drug abuse, of dependency and family dissolution, continued to worsen during this period. A brave new governor in Wisconsin, Republican Tommy Thompson, began a push in the right direction, enacting landmark welfare reform, showing once again that individual states—those "laboratories of democracy," as Supreme Court justice Louis Brandeis once described them—could do a better job of managing social programs than could the federal government. Yet in most of the country, the faltering liberalism of the bureaucratic welfare state remained firmly in place, inflicting its relentless damage on all Americans. It was as if a sad stream of social pathology continued to rise up from the depths, drowning innocent lives and threatening to engulf the nation.

Of course, we remember that the basic human condition itself brings problems. That is, humanity has always known imperfection and iniquity. And it's true that any of us can stumble and fall, and we can't always blame the government for our troubles—nor can we always look to the government for help. As Samuel Johnson wrote, "How small, of all that human hearts endure, / That part which laws or kings can cause or cure." That is, the problems that are caused by laws or governments—as well as the problems that laws or governments can cure—are perhaps fewer than we think; many problems occur simply within the oft-flawed human heart. So in order for us to find help, and to help others, we must look to ourselves, to our friends and family—and, of course, to God.

And that's yet another reason why I admire Marcus. In his counseling work, he focuses on individuals, or on small groups of people, and then makes an enormous difference in their lives. With God's guidance, Marcus lights one candle in the darkness. And then another, and another.

So as always, Marcus found work—lots of work. He served as an individual counselor and group therapist at an inner-city church in the Twin Cities. It was obvious to all by now that Marcus had developed formidable skills as a counselor. A counselor from a Christian perspective.

In our troubled world, many varieties of therapy and self-help compete for attention. So why did Marcus choose Christian counseling? What makes it different? Marcus was obviously fully aware of other approaches, but he believed that faith in Jesus Christ is the strongest approach of all. It's that simple. With the power of Christ, he knew he could make a positive difference in people's lives. God works. He delivers. In applying Christian concepts, Marcus could offer clients direction, correction, and hope.

A key concept in Christian counseling is *integration*. That is, the Christian counselor seeks to combine, or integrate, biblical truths with the best of psychology and neurology, thereby imparting new life and new hope. The Bible, of course, is the greatest counselor of all. As Paul tells us in 2 Timothy, "All Scripture is given by inspiration of God, and is profitable for doctrine, for reproof, for correction, for instruction in righteousness: that the man of God may be perfect, thoroughly furnished unto all good works."

We all look to something for guidance in our lives. Should we look at our own hearts for guidance? Often, our shifting whims are what lead us into trouble in the first place. Some say we should look to philosophers. But which ones? Why not look to our Judeo-Christian heritage, to a God who made us and created the heavens and the earth? Surely, if He made us, He should understand the owner's manual!

Moreover, because God is the author of all good things, including science and medicine, it makes sense to use all good things to help others. And that's integration: We start with the Bible and a biblical worldview and then integrate more tools—all the insights we have gained over the centuries—into an effective plan for aiding and counseling. Just as the goal of all Christians is to become one with Christ, so the goal of those who are troubled is to seek oneness with Christ—they just might need more help.

So what would Marcus do in a typical counseling session? How would he put his Bible-based training to work? He would gather a small group of seekers into a circle of seven or eight—seekers of relief from, say, anger or alcohol. Then he would begin the discussion by asking questions: "What's a good response to anger?" or "How do you handle a spouse who is drinking?" And then, for the next half hour or so, Marcus would listen as each individual brought up his or her personal issues.

Marcus knew he had to proceed in his counseling with patience and subtlety. As Paul said to the Corinthians, the goal is not to shame but to instruct, to counsel. These seekers had come to Marcus because they wanted to change their lives—and that wish to change, of course, was truly critical. After all, the Bible tells us that a change of heart must precede any true and lasting change of conduct.

So Marcus might not immediately confront or condemn unacceptable behavior. Instead, he would remind his group that while everyone, at times, feels weakness and temptation, everyone can nevertheless feel strength through Jesus Christ. Indeed, the goal for all Christians is to emulate Christ. If we think of Him and rely on Him, we will gain in strength.

Marcus's innate empathy, his academic training, and his informed sense of Christian ethics told him never to accommodate or validate negative behavior. Instead, with the grace of God, he was there to *change* such behavior. We all have an enormous capacity for renewal in our own lives, but our capacities are microscopic compared with God's. To those he was counseling, Marcus would cite Scripture to bring hope. For example, the 146th Psalm tells us: "The Lord gives sight to the blind, the Lord lifts up those who are bowed down, the Lord loves the righteous, the Lord watches over the foreigner and sustains the fatherless and the widow, but He frustrates the ways of the wicked." That marvelous psalm, in a nutshell, points to some of the major problems that people have always faced, both in King David's time and in our own. In that verse, we see God's concern for those who are suffering from disease or depression, for those who have lost a father or a husband, for those who find themselves as strangers in a strange land. To all of them God offers his love and comfort. Amen!

As Marcus once pointed out to me, the 146th Psalm is also part of Jewish liturgy, included in the prefatory portion of morning prayer. The observant recite the *Pesukei D'zimra*, verses of song or praise. And so we can see that the whole of the Judeo-Christian tradition affects all facets of day-to-day life, imbuing them with sanctity and godliness. And that's what Marcus was doing each and every day, serving God in his dutiful and quiet manner. He was helping care-laden people get over the many hurdles they faced in their daily lives. He was encouraging folks to conduct themselves with sanctity and godliness. That's Christian counseling.

Marcus was doing good work, but it was not well-paying work. We lived in a tough area of St. Paul, an area where the boys couldn't play outside, and also an area where our car, our stroller, and anything else not nailed down was stolen. A nearby biker bar guaranteed plenty of rowdiness and noise; more than once, late at night, drunks would pound on the door wanting to come inside the building or just make trouble. Marcus would have to go down and tell them to go away. If those same drunks had pounded on the door and asked for help, Marcus would have been happy to talk to them—although he would have preferred daytime hours! Meanwhile, we both realized we needed more room, and a backyard, to raise our family.

For my part, during those years I took a job with the IRS, a division of the Treasury Department, working out of the St. Paul district office. I know it might seem strange for me to find such work, as I am now often called an "antitax activist." My ultimate goal was to change the tax code and help people in their fight to keep more of what they earned. So I chose to learn how to change the system from the inside out, to take a reconnaissance mission inside "enemy" lines. Rule #1: Know the enemy. But the truth is, I am not against taxes *per se*. I agree with the great Supreme Court justice Oliver Wendell Holmes, who said that taxes are the price we pay for civilization. And so, for example, I believe that everyone should pay at least some tax, at least a symbolic amount. In so doing, we are all reminded that if we are going to preserve our republic—a word coming from the Latin *res publica*, or public thing—we all must be good citizens. That is, we all have a duty to make our union ever more perfect, and so we all need a reminder that the government has no money of its own. It has our money, held in trust. So taxes are necessary. But as the Bachmann corollary to Justice Holmes, if taxes are the price we pay for civilization, then the taxes themselves should be civilized—not confiscatory.

As a Treasury Department employee, I worked on hundreds of civil and criminal cases. Typically, I would represent the government against delinquent taxpayers. Most of the time, my work involved negotiation rather than litigation. I would say, "You owe the government this much," and the negotiations would then begin; only a few cases ended up in court. And I will admit I enjoyed negotiation; although I revere the absolute nature of the law, I also savor the matching of wits and wills in a legal setting. I've never been a poker player, but I can see the appeal of playing for real stakes in a pressure situation. And the negotiations I engaged in were usually intense—people weren't happy to see me, and quite a few had criminal issues as well—and yet the intensity of the negotiations was sometimes exhilarating. I also found instances where I believed that the government had erred, where an injustice had occurred. And I wasn't afraid, either, to make that argument to my managers.

Yet at the same time, I could see how devastating the U.S. tax code could be, not only to individuals but also to the economy as a whole. The Internal Revenue Code today consists of some 3.8 million words; even the IRS has told me that it doesn't know the exact number of words! Yes, Reagan had cut tax rates during his presidency, but subsequent presidents had lamentably agreed to raise those tax rates again, and so the U.S. tax code was once more ratcheting up to both higher rates *and* greater complexity.

Those millions of words in the tax code—many of them opaque, many even contradictory—contain enough traps and snares to catch just about any taxpayer. So I realized that if IRS auditors wanted to nail someone, they usually could do so. And the people who were targeted usually chose to settle, because they knew they couldn't win—or couldn't afford to win—against the IRS.

In other words, the infernal complexity of the tax code almost always favors the IRS. People often end up paying more than they should just to get relief finally from the tax man. Why was it, I would observe, that the government nearly always won and the people nearly always lost? Yet to us on the side of enforcing the law, the complexity ended up being a demoralizing burden as well. Once I called the IRS office in Washington for help on a particularly puzzling fourteen words in the tax code. It took nineteen calls—no kidding—even though I myself was a Treasury Department employee, before I found the expert who could give me a proper answer. That was my "lightbulb" moment. After the call, I set the phone in the cradle, turned around in my chair, and looked out the window. I thought: *If the government can afford to hire one employee just to interpret 14 words out of 3.8 million, then how do ordinary Americans have a chance against such a well-fortified bureaucracy?*

I thought further: *This is a terrible system—and yet it's the system on which the whole federal edifice rests. No wonder we have so much trouble.* My colleagues at the St. Paul IRS office were thorough, consummate professionals, well meaning, and considerate. I didn't find them taking joy in deliberately trying to undermine the taxpayers. They worked hard to do their jobs well, but they, too, were trapped in the same nefarious system. And meanwhile, back in Washington, all the bureaucrats continued to make good careers by writing—and all the lobbyists continued to get rich by rewriting—those monstrous million words of the tax code.

So at that moment, I resolved to do everything I could to bring about a simpler and better tax system. And I still hold to that firm resolve today: We should deep-six the code and move to a simpler system and to lower rates. A tax code is required, of course, to raise the revenue that the government needs, but it should not be a job killer to the American economy. We need to nurture the golden goose of free enterprise, not kill it with 3.8 million pinpricks.

In Congress and on the campaign trail, I often find myself speaking to victims of the IRS and the tax code. I tell them: "I know what you're going through. I've seen it from the inside. And as bad as the tax code looks from the outside, it looks even worse from the inside!"

CHAPTER SEVEN

Our Twenty-nine Children

IN any case, the home front was changing too.

In 1988, while I was just beginning work as a federal tax litigation attorney, I became pregnant with our third baby. Although unexpected, Marcus and I were so happy. Our two sons, Lucas and Harrison, were then five and two. Lucas had already developed his own little personality as a demanding, willful "leader of the pack," while Harrison, alas, was in his "terrible twos," although we could imagine that he would grow up to be an actor or a dancer—he was a happy baby. What great little boys they were! I could have had five boys—boys are so much fun. They were good brothers to each other; they would take turns playing spacemen, and then cowboys, and then cowboys again—or maybe they would be back in time with the dinosaurs. I had three brothers, no sisters. And Marcus had two brothers, no sisters. We already had two boys, so I presumed that there were no girl genes between us; so no girls in the cards, it seemed.

But it was not to be. Three months later, I lost the baby in my womb—a miscarriage. It seemed as if my waist had stopped expanding; something was off. Marcus took me to the doctor for an examination. An ultrasound was ordered, and we anxiously awaited our first look at our new baby. Something, I could see, was wrong. I asked the technician why the baby was lying down at the bottom of the screen, as if it were sleeping. The technician got up and left the room and called in a midwife. The midwife looked at the screen, paused for a moment, and then told us: Our baby wasn't sleeping, our baby was no longer living. We were completely unprepared for this news; it was devastating.

The midwife advised me to go home and that over the next few days, the baby would naturally expel. And then, even as she was speaking, my water broke as I was lying on the table, and the baby instantaneously delivered. The midwife put the baby on a paper towel and held it in her palm. Marcus was overcome with emotion; he couldn't bear to see the baby and left the room. I needed to see our baby, who was now gray and lifeless, the umbilical cord had disintegrated. But nonetheless, that tiny baby was perfect, maybe four inches long. I memorized every feature of that baby, although I didn't touch the baby, nor did I know its sex.

I had to have an emergency dilation and curettage, because my body wouldn't stop bleeding. Afterward, the momentousness of what had happened struck us. We had lost our child—this miscarriage was as real to us as if we had lost Lucas or Harrison. Marcus and I wept in each other's arms. Friends called, but I couldn't muster the ability to speak with them. I didn't speak to anyone else for three days. I was profoundly affected by this loss of life. My little sons would crawl into bed with me, and I would just hold them tight—tighter than ever. *Life is so precious,* I thought to myself. And as so often has happened during our marriage, Marcus picked up the load of family duties. Both of our hearts were broken, but he knew that our lives had to go on.

Although Marcus and I hadn't considered ourselves to be overly career minded and certainly not overly materialistic, we made a new and life-changing decision. We resolved to receive however many children God chose to give us. Moreover, the loss brought us even closer together as a couple, in a depth of feeling that we hadn't experienced before. Afterward, women at church and at work shared their stories of miscarriage with me. I hadn't heard much about miscarriage before, and now it seemed that so many women had also gone through the same tragic experience. Our respect for human life, for the primacy of children and the family took deeper root.

And of course, Marcus and I prayed. We knew that death comes to all of us here on earth, and yet through our faith in Christ Jesus, we also knew that God will come again for us, taking us to Himself, so that where He is, we may be also. And so too our baby. Amen.

We told God that our hearts were broken but that we were absolutely committed to life, and so we would gratefully receive into our lives as many more children as He wished. And even if it was only for a short time, well, we would be grateful for those precious moments.

The ambulance had taken me to St. Mary's, a Catholic hospital. In the midst of the frenetic activity at the hospital, we hadn't thought about the burial arrangements. Once home, Marcus called the hospital. We waited and prayed, hoping to be able to bury our baby. And because the Catholic Church is so profoundly pro-life, the hospital had buried our little baby in a proper grave. The hospital hadn't even asked us—it was just the right thing to do. We cannot thank the hospital enough for burying our baby. Later, we drove out to the burial site, and there, in a little patch of sacred earth, nestled in the grass, we saw the small marker. Lot 24, row 18—a place that would be etched forever on our hearts. We dropped to our knees and wept again. We thanked the hospital for doing right by our baby, and we prayed again to God, thanking Him for allowing our baby's body to find a holy resting place, even as He carried its soul up to be with Him. Someday, with abiding hope, we look forward to reuniting with that baby, whom we count as our third child, now in heaven. Meanwhile, here on earth, we dedicated our children and our family to God.

More than two decades later, tears come to my eyes as I think back to that day. Yet I have often thought that sometimes events are so sad that just at the moment when you think they can't get any sadder, a new event opens up and reveals a new kind of wonderment.

Soon, thankfully, I was pregnant again. Marcus and I prayed constantly, beseeching God to bring that baby to term. And yes, Elisa Laura Bachmann—her middle name after my mother's mother—was born on April 14, 1990. Our first daughter! Marcus had only brothers growing up, as did I. Finally, we had a baby girl to grace our lives. She was pretty in pink—and, if I may be permitted a boast, pretty in every other color.

One day Marcus and I were sitting together in the kitchen, watching her. That's all we were doing—watching her every wiggle and gesture. In that moment, I thought of Whittaker Chambers's famous discussion of his baby girl's ear in his soul-searing book, *Witness*. Chambers had once been a communist—a spy for the Soviet Union, in fact—but then he saw the light. He took his story to the FBI and so became not only a witness against other Soviet spies in the 1940s but also, in a larger sense, a witness against godless communism. Chambers's moment of epiphany came to him as he watched his baby:

> My daughter was in her high chair. I was watching her eat. She was the most miraculous thing that had ever happened in my life.

I liked to watch her even when she smeared porridge on her face or dropped it meditatively on the floor. My eye came to rest on the delicate convolutions of her ear—those intricate, perfect ears.

The thought passed through my mind: "No, those ears were not created by any chance coming together of atoms in nature (the Communist view). They could have been created only by immense design."

Chambers then thought to himself, "Design presupposes God." And so, he wrote, "at that moment, the finger of God was first laid upon my forehead." Marcus and I were already firm believers, of course, as we gazed on Elisa's little ear, but we revere Chambers and his memory. We revere the author of *Witness* as more than a witness to faith; he was a champion of faith. No wonder President Reagan awarded him, posthumously, the Presidential Medal of Freedom.

Meanwhile, in our lives—it was now 1992—we were ready to take our three children out of the city and into the suburbs. We had enjoyed our time in St. Paul, but we needed more room, and the kids needed a safe place to play.

So Marcus, having completed much of his PhD course work, found a new job as a Christian counselor in the suburbs, and we moved to the town of Stillwater, about ten miles east of St. Paul; we have been here ever since. Our little town sits on the banks of the St. Croix River, which serves as the boundary line between Minnesota and Wisconsin. It's not far away from Anoka, where my mother and her husband Ray reside, and it's not far from Marcus's family farm. When you have aging parents, it's always nice to be close.

Stillwater is a place rich in tradition. Along with much of the western Great Lakes region, it was settled originally by the Dakota and Ojibwa, or Chippewa, tribes; they thrived on the abundant local fish and game, as well as wild rice and other indigenous plants. In 1855 poet Henry Wadsworth Longfellow wrote his famous "Song of Hiawatha," based on legends of the Ojibwa, describing "happiness and plenty / In the land of the Ojibways, / In the pleasant land and peaceful."

Stillwater is often called the birthplace of Minnesota. It was here in 1848, right on the corner of Main and Myrtle, that folks from the area convened and set in motion the legal process leading to the formation of the

Minnesota Territory and then, in 1857, to the joining of the great State of Minnesota with the larger federal Union.

In the nineteenth century, Stillwater's economy was driven by forestry. Timber harvested upstream flowed down the St. Croix, each log having been stamped by its owner. In the river at Stillwater, a boom, or barrier, was stretched across the water to catch the logs, which were then tallied and tracked as they went on to the sawmill. It was a marvelously intricate system in which people who had never even met one another managed to work together, following a complex process that turned trees into valuable building materials. This process might be called an example of the "spontaneous order" that the economist Friedrich Hayek was later to describe so ably. That is, it's the process of thousands of people cooperating with one another for the benefit of all—and no bureaucrat in some faraway place could have made this system work so effectively. Yes, these loggers might also be competing with one another, but as long as common-sense laws were put in place, and as long as contracts were honored and enforced, then cooperation and competition could occur profitably at the same time. To this day, the St. Croix Boom Site is a notable tourist attraction, reminding visitors of the mighty lumberjacks and their legendary deeds.

In addition to hard workers, Stillwater has had its inventors. Back in 1921, Charles Strite received a patent for the pop-up toaster—the greatest thing since sliced bread, we like to joke! Five years later, Strite opened a factory in Minneapolis. Today Stillwater remains a town full of hardworking folks; the locals, along with visitors, enjoy boating on the river, strolling through the many stores clustered in the downtown, and visiting the local vineyards—and there's even a brewery cave tour!

In other words, Stillwater, population eighteen thousand, has its own proud history, as well as its own homegrown entrepreneurial and civic energy. Indeed, we Stillwaterites continue to be responsible, civic-minded citizens, fully capable of making all the big decisions about ourselves, our families, and our community. We raise our kids responsibly, we make our own local decisions, and we run our lives in an accountable, transparent manner. So here's a question: Why do the state capital, St. Paul, and the national capital, Washington, insist on telling us what to do? How did it happen that individual autonomy and local control were arrogated to state and federal bureaucrats? Here's an even more important question: How can we take our power back, away from the bureaucrats who took it away from us in the first place?

All those questions—and a few answers—were becoming apparent to me during those awakening years. But first, Marcus and I had kids to raise. More kids than we had ever dreamed of.

When we moved to Stillwater in the spring of 1992, we had three kids, and a fourth soon joined us; Caroline Cathleen Bachmann was born on June 15, 1992. These four kids seemed to fill up our four-bedroom house, and yet we asked God for more—and we got more.

Sophia Anna Bachmann—her middle name honoring my father's mother, the *Wall Street Journal*-reading Republican—was born on May 31, 1994. So there we were, at a total of five kids. We would have been happy with more, of course, but after that pregnancy, I realized I couldn't have any more biological children.

During my early thirties, I found that I was developing severe headaches. They were diagnosed as migraines. The word "migraine," I learned, is derived from the Greek word for "skull," which is *kranion*, or "cranium," plus the Greek word for "half," which is *hemi*. So the term "hemi-cranium" was sanded and silted down to "migraine." But let me tell you, a migraine hurts your whole cranium. Yet with the right medication, these headaches are entirely controllable; I thought to myself, *Thank God that medical science has developed such effective treatments.* As a child, I had read about how scientists such as Louis Pasteur and Jonas Salk had used their brilliance to identify and alleviate the causes of disease. Thanks to their genius, the blind could now see and the lame could walk. And so God's plan for us unfolds here on earth.

I later learned that some thirty million Americans suffer from migraines, about three-fourths of them women—and that migraine incidence in women spikes after the change of life. At the time, I thought to myself, *Welcome to the club, Michele.* And while I am reluctant to cite sexism as a political issue, sexism certainly can exist. Many years later, when migraines briefly became a campaign issue for me, it appeared that political foes were maybe playing the gender card. After all, at one time or another, all of us, both men and women, suffer pain and get sick.

Meanwhile, back in Stillwater, I threw myself into raising all these kids. During the years 1992 to 2000, I didn't work outside our home, although I certainly was busy. At the Bachmann household, it was "kids r us." I was always cooking, cleaning, sewing, painting, wallpapering, and generally mothering. I thought of the nursery rhyme, "There was an old woman who lived in a shoe / She had so many children, she didn't know what to do." Of course, I hadn't seen anything yet.

Marcus had a good job, but with seven of us, money was always tight. And I will admit, my natural frugality—handed down to me from thrifty ancestors and reinforced by lean years while I was growing up—came into play. I knew all that I had done to make ends meet, to stretch dimes into dollars, and I knew all that Marcus had done as well. And we wanted to share those values with our kids. I was very tight at the grocery store, buying generics, skimping on meat, and making nearly all of our menus from scratch. For instance, we bought dehydrated milk powder at the store, then added water at home. The kids *hated* it, so Marcus and I finally gave in. But to this day, we are always on the lookout for discount coupons from any source; even on the campaign trail, Marcus picks through newspaper inserts looking for bargains. Most of my clothes, even today, are from consignment stores. As for our children, we wanted them to be good shoppers, and we also wanted them to think in terms of paying cash, not using a line of credit.

Lucas likes to tell the story of the time we went to the Goodwill store to buy him a pair of winter boots. Usually, Goodwill is a great place for bargains—but not on that day, or at least not for boots. I took one look at the price tag and said, "This is just too overpriced!" Okay, maybe I said it a little too loudly. Okay, maybe I said it loudly enough so that everybody else in the store heard me. My apologies to the other shoppers, who might not have needed to hear my audible price-point analysis, but I am glad that Lucas remembers. "Come on, kids," I said, "Goodwill is too expensive for Mom!" The kids said, "Wow." Listen to your mother—always good advice!

In Minneapolis, there was a great store called Discount 70. The rule is, everything is 70 percent off. And that's a good start. But on the day after Christmas, all Christmas items are 90 percent off. Now *that's* more like it! So every December 26, we would trek over to Discount 70 and load up on gifts for the year ahead, plus Christmas cards, plus wrapping paper, plus everything else we needed. It was always a great teachable shopping moment for the kids.

And I probably shouldn't tell this story, but one time Marcus saw that a car dealer was offering roast beef sandwiches to visitors coming into the showroom. Not just hot dogs, but real roast beef. So Marcus went in, kicked a few tires, and ate a few sandwiches. Anything to stretch the paycheck!

Those were fun years. Lucas, who became a teenager in the nineties, probably has the quickest wit of anyone in the family, as well as the best vocabulary. He attended both Bethel University in St. Paul and the University of Minnesota in Minneapolis; he is now a medical doctor.

Harrison, five years younger than his brother and thus closer in age to the three girls, proved to be a wonderful big brother. A jock himself, he would always encourage his sisters to be athletic. In the manner of his father, Harrison has always been a social animal; he made a lot of friends in high school and made even more at Wheaton College in Illinois. Since graduating, he has nearly completed his master's in teaching and worked for two years as a special education teacher for SomaliAmerican and Ethiopian refugee kids in St. Paul.

Elisa, the oldest of the girls, took enormous responsibility in raising her little sisters—and in helping all of us. She packed the knapsacks for the littler ones on their way to school, scheduled their dentist appointments, and made sure their permission slips were always ready. As the middle child, she has been the hub of the family—the go-to girl for all her siblings. She got the job done for us at home and then later went off to a Christian college in Florida.

Caroline is the most bubbly, the most animated, the most athletic—and the tallest of the girls. She makes friends easily; in high school she always took part in sports and ran cross-country. She was, and is, an avid reader and also takes a diligent approach to shopping; she and her little sister know their way around all the bargain outlets in the area—although, primarily, they are "Maxxinistas." As in T.J.Maxx. Caroline is now in college.

Sophia is the youngest—and let's talk about her name; she is perhaps the child that Marcus and I had the most trouble naming. Come to think of it, we have always had trouble naming our kids. Lucas went unnamed for six weeks, because as nervous first-time parents, we wanted to get his name right. Our first choice was Christian David, and of course our parents and friends all weighed in with comments and criticisms. Ultimately, it was embarrassing to have an unnamed baby, so we made a decision,

Lucas Barrett Paul, and told our family and friends that they would have to live with it. After that, we wised up and resolved that future baby names would be *our* decision, not a family group project! Still, sometimes we were grateful for help. Harrison's middle name, Sterling, came from the nurse at the hospital, who was just trying to nudge us to get something down on paper, in order to complete his birth certificate. But as soon as she said it, we loved it.

And of course, all the kids have nicknames. Lucas has been called "Deedee" since Elisa was little. She couldn't pronounce "Lucas," and so she called him "Deedee," and the name stuck. So now, at home, he is known as "Doctor Deedee." And at one time—I can't remember why—Caroline assigned her siblings nicknames based on breakfast foods. So for years, the kids called us and each other names such as "Sausage," for Marcus, or "Orange Juice" for Lucas, or "Honeypie" for Harrison. In that same fun spirit, Elisa became "Eggs," Caroline was "Pancake," and Sophia was "Waffle." The nicknames have all evolved now, but we still have them. I am the main user of nicknames, and Marcus relies on me to decode who is who. He only knows them by their given names. "Is Sophia now 'Toffee'?" he'll ask.

Indeed, food seems to be a major theme around the Bachmann household. We play "turkey bingo" after Thanksgiving dinner is complete, keeping all the usual rules of bingo, except that instead of the winner saying, "Bingo!" he or she yells, "Gobble gobble!" And the winning prize includes treats Marcus knows each child wants, including beef jerky or Swiss chocolate. Depending on who wins the other's prize, the loser might say, "Hey, that's my prize—not fair!" Then there'll be some chasing around the house, the losers chasing after the winner. Now we all know what will happen and the kids figure out who will chase whom around the dining-room table. Perhaps you had to be there, but for us it is hilarious and highly anticipated. And Boomer the beagle, whom we rescued from the pound, seems to love turkey bingo too. No wonder he's gotten a bit hefty. Marcus makes sure that his treats are the rule, not the exception. Note to self: Boomer needs to be in the garage when too much food is being passed around.

Marcus always joked, "Life is short. Eat dessert first!" Of course, whenever I ate dessert, I thought of those two great Minnesota girls, Mary Richards and Rhoda Morgenstern, as Rhoda confronted weight issues on the great *Mary Tyler Moore Show*. Once, as Rhoda held a piece of candy in her hand, she said, "I don't know why I'm putting this in my mouth. I should just apply it directly to my hips." Rhoda's predicament rings true to women everywhere. My own food weakness runs more toward cookies, and so I have to count every calorie—even if I sometimes count them retroactively!

Regarding Sophia and her name. I had always liked the name Sylvia or Solveig. And then Sigrid, which seemed like a nice way to remember my Norwegian ancestors. But Marcus pointed out that she'd inevitably be known as Siggy. But who knows, maybe Sophia could have handled that name with aplomb, as she has always been the most theatrical of our kids. Yet I might note that her career on the boards had its moments. One day, when she was onstage at a school play, she fainted. She was at the Christian school—it was a Bible play, and she was an Old Testament prophet—and then she swooned, right in front of the audience of mostly parents. I was in the front row, about twelve feet away from her, and jumped so fast that I caught her before she hit the floor. Marcus was there, too; he and I got her to the hospital. She fainted a second time at school; I was then serving in the Minnesota state senate, and I came running back from work. As a result, I missed a vote—which made the newspapers. This year, Sophia is off to college. Although technically a high school senior, she will do college work this year. She has always been unusually mature; the kids call her a forty-five-year-old woman.

Meanwhile, because there are so many of us in the family, and because we are always trying to save money, we celebrate birthdays on the cheap. Yet for holidays such as Easter, Memorial Day, Veterans Day, and Christmas, we never scrimp or hold back. At Christmas we have a gigantic tree in the living room—a live tree, crowned by an angel. Christmas is a special family time, of course, and yet I missed it once, with great reluctance. That was Christmas 2007, when I went to visit the troops in Iraq. Family means everything to me, and yet that Christmas with the troops seemed even more important. On the flight back, our military transport plane stopped for an extra-long layover in Ireland, and I went out and bought sweaters for the kids as presents.

We got through those years with the help of a mortgage, but we incurred no other debt. Except for that home loan, Marcus and I have never been in debt. We always knew that fat years could turn into lean years, and we always wanted to be ready.

How did we do it? Well, I think there are some lessons here, especially for the greatest debtor of all, our own Uncle Sam. In the seventies, we often heard a slogan: "The personal is political." That meant that everything one did in one's personal life needed to be judged according to left-leaning politically correct standards. I disagree vehemently: I am against all attempts to pressure people into meeting arbitrary political standards. Here in America, we should be free to live our lives—bounded, of course, by basic ethics and by the law—without being hectored by a nanny state or even the nanny media.

But I will give liberals credit for this much: Sometimes the personal is indeed political. If the American people, in their personal lives, need to be thrifty and prudent or else risk bankruptcy and ruin, Uncle Sam too should be thrifty and prudent. If people shop at garage sales and second-hand stores, if they go online to eBay and other bargain-hunting sites, if they wait till the day after Christmas to buy presents—then surely the federal government too should pick up some pointers on how to lower its spending. The basic rules of common sense apply equally in Washington, D.C., and in Stillwater. The difference, unfortunately, is that the people in Washington don't seem to think these rules apply to them. And as long as the American people let Washington get away with such arrogant thinking—taxing, borrowing, money printing, avoiding the tough choices that the rest of us constantly have to make—then, of course, Washington will never stop its profligacy.

During the nineties, whenever I had a free moment, I could be found reading everything from political philosophy to *Investor's Business Daily*. At the same time, I would listen to the music of Bach—and I should note that I was a fan even before I met Mr. Bachmann! I enjoy Bach and Handel because I find it soothing to think that mortal men could compose such immortal melodies. And the rest of us, too, can enjoy this music across the centuries.

So there I was, sitting in the backyard and studying current events, feeling increasing concern—and growing stronger in my determination to do something positive. In particular, I followed the news about Bill Clinton's presidency with greater and greater alarm. And not just the scandals and the impeachment trial but also the even more ominous news about an evil new figure on the world stage, Osama bin Laden. In 1998, when I heard about Al Qaeda's terrorist attacks on two U.S. embassies in East Africa, I remember thinking, *This is going to get a lot worse before it gets better.*

And during that same decade, the nineties, I realized once again that the government was often hurting us, not helping us. The politicians and the bureaucrats in both St. Paul and Washington were using our tax money to make our problems worse. I asked myself: *What is wrong with this picture? What terrible things are they doing with our taxes?* Marcus and I had homeschooled our kids for many years, then sent them to Christian schools, and yet we kept hearing from other parents that some public schools were not only inflicting harmful values on kids but also watering down the curricula. And so I became an education activist, fighting against the government-imposed Profile of Learning, an effort that took me to that fateful Republican district convention in Mahtomedi on April 1, 2000.

As I grew busier, the child-rearing responsibilities were increasingly shared with Marcus. We have always been a good team, as husband/wife and parents. Marcus and I each did what had to be done, so each carried out nontraditional roles. Our focus was taking care of the kids and getting the job done, not on who should own each task. Back during our wedding sermon, we had been told that it is often said that in marriages, it should be 50–50. But that was wrong, our pastor said. We need to each be prepared to give everything. We took that to heart, and each of us has striven to give 100 percent to the family. I think that's the key to why our family works, because we each do whatever is needed to get the job done. If I was in St. Paul or later in Washington, D.C., or out on the campaign trail, Marcus took care of the kids and our business. He always did everything he could— but now he did even more. And with his own brand of enthusiasm.

It was Marcus, a real steady-eddie, who held the fort. Every night, no matter where I was, he would have dinner ready at home. On school nights, our kids were not allowed to watch TV, although we made an exception for *American Idol*. He kept the TV and the computer in the family room, next to the kitchen, making a point of always being nearby to keep an eye on things. If any of the young adults wanted to talk, he would be there for them. He knew that sometimes they wanted to chitchat, just to get out of going to bed, but that was a fair trade. Marcus knew that if a teenager started talking, he or she would eventually open up, and an observant parent would quickly figure out if anything was wrong. As they say, quality time occurs within quantity time. And Marcus spent quantity time with our kids when I had to be in Washington. We also observed that as much as our children needed us when they were little, it seemed that they needed us more as they neared adulthood, because they needed our minds and attention. They needed to know we were dialed in to them, paying close watch, providing guardrails for their decisions. We were blessed. They were raised with restrictions, yet they became very happy, confident, young adults.

During holidays, he would make sure that the kids helped with the Christmas decorations, inside and outside; he would make sure that they sent their Christmas cards, that they remembered their duties as a Secret Santa to someone else. The proper observance of holidays, of course, is the great joy of family traditions. In addition, such observances are comforting and reassuring to children.

Marcus and I agreed that the world imposes adult situations too early and quickly on kids. We thought, "We can't let them lose their childhood." So the movies that we let them watch were always on the wholesome side anything without bad language or adult situations was okay. We also enjoyed *My Big Fat Greek Wedding*, and *That Thing You Do*. And, of course, the Narnia movies. Every Christmas, we would watch *It's a Wonderful Life*. Now, when Marcus walks in through the garage door after driving home from work, I often say, "Welcome home, Mr. Bailey!" We also have made it a point to see, almost every year, *A Christmas Carol* at the Guthrie Theater in Minneapolis. That's a show, and a story, that just keeps getting better and better. We loved the positive moral and ethical vision of Charles Dickens and the high quality at the Guthrie.

Or course, kids being kids, and families being families, there's always an unpredictable impishness. For example, the baby of the family, Sophia, didn't understand how goldfish could breathe in water, and she'd want to pull them out of the water and into the air so they could "breathe." So someone had to come and grab the fish as they flopped around and put them back in the bowl. But once Lucas put some pieces of chicken in the microwave, cooked them up, and then showed them to her, saying this was what happened to the goldfish once they were out of the water. "Not a fish! Deedee, not a fish!" Sophia wailed, till Lucas explained to her that it was just a joke.

Indeed, Marcus himself was not immune to the imp impulse. As we celebrated our twenty-fifth wedding anniversary, he looked at me and deadpanned, "You know, we might have a chance. This thing might actually work out."

As the kids grew older, it was time for them to take on responsibilities of their own. Marcus decreed that every summer, the kids had to either get a job or do volunteer work somewhere. And so they all were busy. All across Stillwater, young Bachmanns were mowing lawns, busing tables, hostessing at restaurants, volunteering at hospitals and Bible camp—you name it. But always busy—it was expected.

No matter what happens to me or to Marcus, he and I agree: Those kids will always be the proudest accomplishment and legacy of our lives.

In the meantime, Marcus's career was advancing. In 1995 he earned his PhD and thereafter we launched Bachmann & Associates, a Christian counseling service. I was cofounder of the company and have been involved in the business side of its operations. As I like to say, I have signed both sides of a paycheck, the front and the back. That is, I have endorsed paychecks made out to me, and at Bachmann & Associates I have signed paychecks going to others. Our company has been a success; we have created some fifty jobs. Yet even as I was learning about job creation, I was being reminded, yet again, of the challenges that small businesses confront. Taxes, regulation, bureaucrats: I've dealt with 'em all. So whenever I speak to a gathering of the National Federation of Independent Business, I can truthfully say, "My husband and I have walked in your moccasins. In fact, we still are walking in them—or trying to."

But in our business we will never apologize for being pro-life and pro-marriage, and we want everyone to know that we approach all our work from a Christian perspective. We are respectful and honoring of every person entering our clinic. We make no secret of the fact that we endorse biblical values and integrate biblical principles into our counseling.

For years, even before we were married and all through our marriage, we had been actively speaking to and contributing aid to unwed mothers as we helped them find the strength to carry on with their pregnancy.

These expectant mothers, most of them, were teenagers; as newlyweds, we reached out, on an informal, one-to-one basis to help and encourage young women to choose life. We never judged, only helped as best we could. And we prayed and prayed and prayed. We beseeched God to help these mothers to keep their babies, not only till birth but after that, if possible. But if that wasn't going to be possible—and it often wasn't—then we would help as best we could to find a new home for that child and a new start for the mother. We drove them to pro-life adoption agencies, and I even helped one woman through her childbirth experience—again, strictly as a volunteer, trying to support this courageous mother's decision, after being abandoned by the baby's father, to stick to it and choose life.

I must say, Marcus's therapeutic work opened my eyes to the myriad troubles that people were confronting in the modern world. These troubles included syndromes that I had never heard of as a child, such as anorexia and bulimia. Marcus did everything he could in his counseling, but he and I still wanted to do more. We thought about it and prayed about it, and we knew we had the energy and capacity to open our hearts and home to people who had need. It was risky. We had little kids to think of, but we still wanted to be part of the solution for people who were hurting and who needed help.

During the nineties, we learned of friends at church who were accepting foster children into their homes. Marcus and I agreed at the same instant—that's what we want to do as well. We began by providing short-term care for girls with eating disorders who were patients in a program at the University of Minnesota. These girls moved into our house—the house didn't get any bigger, but our hearts were broken for these girls and their families, and we wanted to help. As Psalm 68:6 tells us: "God setteth the solitary in families." Well, that's exactly what He did in our home.

Marcus and I knew that this was the last stop for some of these girls before they finished high school. We weren't trying to save the world; we were just trying to give consistent care and love to some kids in need of a new start. That is, to show them a home where the dad comes home from work each day and kisses the mom. This is what it looks like when husband and wife cherish each other; this is what it sounds like in a family that doesn't pretend to be perfect by any stretch of the imagination, but which was open to helping to heal the hurt in a few kids' lives.

For their part, our biological kids were good sports through the whole experience. Yes, we had to bunch them up in bunk beds to make room for the new kids, and yes, we had to form long lines to use the bathroom. But our kids shared in our passion for helping others, so everything was fine. It's sometimes said that homeschooled kids grow up being naive about the world; I don't think that's true, and I know for sure that our kids grew up knowing about the many challenges of adolescence. In fact, Marcus and I are confident that such knowledge has armored them.

The girls moved in with us and became part of our family. Most stayed with us for about two years; the shortest stay was a few weeks, the longest three and a half years. They had the same chores as the rest of the kids. And so we all learned to grow and adjust. I hope that many more families too, as they are able, will find it in their hearts to accept foster kids. If they do, they will find it a deeply rewarding experience. But that's not to say it's easy. We had all the sorts of difficulties that one might expect from teenagers, but that goes with the territory of parenting any teen.

We had as many as four girls at once, so that's four plus our five biological kids, making a total of nine. Quite a crew! Marcus had been working with people all his life—he was a natural! We eventually had to move a wall to make a bigger kitchen to accommodate our burgeoning census.

Some of the foster kids asked if they could go to Christian schools, but state law required them to go to public school. I am proud to say that all of our foster kids graduated from high school.

And yet at the same time, I came to be concerned about some of the curriculum they brought home. One day, when one of our girls came home and showed me her eleventh-grade math "homework," which was just coloring in a poster, that was my decisive moment on the path to school-reform efforts. If anyone needed a leg up in life, I realized, it was these girls, as well as other at-risk young people. And increasingly, I was worried that academics seemed to be displaced by curricula that imposed politically correct attitudes, values, and beliefs. That's not an education; that's an agenda. And a loss for the kids' future.

Of course, people ask many more questions about our foster kids. We love them and their families, always. Those girls were each a unique blessing and a gift to us, and we know that their parents also loved those girls, even amid family challenges. But those kids have been through enough. They have a right to privacy. They have all had challenging lives, and surely they don't need be pushed into the spotlight. No doubt curious reporters will pursue them, but Marcus and I wish they wouldn't. Just as we encourage foster care, we also pray that all of our foster children will be able to get on with their lives without embarrassment or harassment.

So those are our twenty-nine kids. The five biological children who are here with us, the sixth who is in heaven, and the twenty-three foster kids. We love every one of them and are proud of each of them.

Today, our foster children are grown and launched into the world, and our biological children, too, are out of the house. Now, for the first time in twenty-nine years of parenting, our parenting responsibilities are no longer daily. Dare I say, "Bring on the grandkids"?

CHAPTER EIGHT

Stillwater Activism

IT was the declining quality of education—ominously visible in Minnesota by the nineties, and in America as a whole—that proved the decisive factor in getting me into politics. There would be no stillness in my life in Stillwater.

As a kid back in Waterloo, I had always enjoyed taking the Iowa Tests of Basic Skills. Every year, we would sharpen our number 2 pencils and hear the familiar instructions, always the same: Fill the oval, don't mark outside the lines. I was proud that the famous tests, offered nationwide, were produced by the University of Iowa, located in, of all places, Iowa City. It was Iowa all the way! I instinctively believed that tests were a good idea, because some things should be measured. After all, if you want to improve something, you have to be able to measure its progress—to see whether or not it has really improved. Also, as a kid, I was always proud that Iowa placed first in the nation. So I would pull out my trusty pencil and happily start scratching away on the tests.

But if tests are a good thing, there's still a danger in centralized testing. And in my lifetime, the benefits of testing have often been lost, especially when the testing—and the judging and the controlling—are administered by a distant bureaucracy. We should all seek to measure and improve ourselves, but at the same time, we should rightly fear the power of one-size-fits-all "improvers." When Marcus and I were raising our children, we wanted to know exactly how well they were doing. But we didn't need the federal government to test our children; we would test them ourselves.

Happily, my husband and I were to various degrees able to home-school our five biological kids—the boys for longer periods of time, and the girls until they were proficient in reading. And then we sent them to Christian schools. Marcus and I believed that if we taught the kids to read, they would be able to succeed in school, and they have. But at the same time, we could see that other parents might not be so fortunate. Indeed, it was both a shame and a waste that while governments at all levels were spending increasing amounts of money on the public schools, the federal government's regulatory burden, piled on top of the schools, increased much faster than federal aid. These "unfunded mandates," as they are called, proved to be an enormous weight on local schools. We knew plenty of motivated teachers and administrators, and yet the educational bureaucracy was grinding them down into defeatism and fatalism.

During this same time, in the early nineties, a new idea, charter schools, came onto the scene. Charter schools are a sort of public-private educational hybrid in which the charter school—run, perhaps, by a motivated group of experts, activists, and parents—could contract with the government to run a school independently of the traditional public school system. I have always believed that parents should be able to choose the school that their child attends, just as we are empowered to choose most other things in our lives. Charters were therefore a creative and constructive step in the right direction—toward full autonomy for responsible parents and local communities.

One idealistic education activist in Stillwater was a man named Dennis Meyer. A former junior high school teacher, Denny had a vision of improving education by returning to the traditional verities of reading, writing, and 'rithmetic. So in the fall of 1993, Marcus and I joined with Denny and other motivated neighbors to open the New Heights Charter School; immediately, some two hundred students signed up. Denny was the CEO, while I served on the board of directors. Our goal was simple: We wanted to provide the best possible education for children in the area, based on sound and proven principles. We wanted rigor. We wanted our kids to gain knowledge, facts, and information. We also wanted a special emphasis on help for kids with troubled backgrounds—and that was a lot of kids, even out in the leafy suburbs. Most of all, we wanted to impart the classical building blocks of knowledge for each student, not the latest fads and attitudes to emerge from an ivory-tower school of education.

Unfortunately, within months, we were confronting dissidents and protesters who accused us of trying to advance Christian values in the school. Yes, we were Christians, but we never sought to impose Christianity on our students. However, some liberal activists seemed to think that the word "rigorous" was somehow code for "religious." They even accused us of objecting to showing the movie *Aladdin*, because we allegedly feared the depiction of a magical genie. Well, of course, that was bogus. We weren't afraid of Robin Williams and his character; our objection to showing *Aladdin* was that kids don't need to go to school to see fantasy movies. They can see them at the movie theater or at home. Students should go to school to learn the best that has been thought and said. If you wonder why kids get less than they should in education and why they graduate with minimal skills, it's because too many "experts" think that comedy cartoons are a legitimate part of a curriculum.

The Minnesota charter school law mandated that 51 percent of the school board be composed of licensed Minnesota teachers, so parental input was always going to be outnumbered by the professional staff. Unfortunately, rather quickly it became apparent that the original mission of the school's founders wasn't shared by the board. If the board couldn't agree on the school's direction, how could we go forward? Parents put time and effort into the school because they wanted high-quality academics for their children. When they sensed that the mission of the school had changed, to focus primarily on at-risk kids with lower levels of academic achievement, they took their children and left. Ultimately, Marcus and I saw we wouldn't succeed in restoring the school's original focus, and so I and other board members stepped down. The school survived, and many excellent and dedicated staff remain. The focus was, indeed, on "at risk," and today, I am proud to say that the school fulfills a positive purpose in reaching out to kids who otherwise could have fallen through the cracks of the system.

The New Heights experience taught me a lot. I learned about school governance, and also about the ins and outs of dealing with state and local authorities. And I certainly learned that the fight for education reform would not be won easily. Yet at the same time I could see hope. I could see, among the majority of folks in Stillwater, and among a majority of Minnesotans, a great hunger for better education. The relentless dumbing down of the schools since the sixties had inspired an unexpected boomerang. By the nineties, parents had wised up; they wanted better schooling for their kids because they wanted them to succeed. And that inspired me. *I might not always succeed,* I told myself, *but I will always keep trying.*

In 1980, Ronald Reagan campaigned for the presidency on a platform that included abolishing the U.S. Department of Education. Only recently created by President Jimmy Carter as a political favor to the teachers' unions, the department had failed to deliver either better test scores or more rigorous curricula dedicated to academic excellence. That sounded like a good idea to me, because I have never believed in federal control of the schools. The vast majority of parents can figure out for themselves how to educate their children and how to provide them with good values. And if some parents can't do so, well, there's most likely someone nearby who can step in. That's what I mean by local control and by the wisdom of letting the fifty states—all those separate laboratories of democracy—chart their own courses on education. The challenge of good schooling, I firmly believe, is best addressed as close to the student as possible.

Yet during the eighties, a new idea took hold: that the federal government should take the lead in education, not just as a matter of national policy, but as a matter of *international* policy. That is, the U.S. government should work with the United Nations to remake American society, as part of global "solidarity." This story seems astonishing, I know—it astonished me when I first learned about it. But this larger context for education reform is so important that I am providing details and documents in an appendix at the back of the book even as I focus here on the American part of the story.

As a result of new-style educational thinking, Americans were saddled with Goals 2000, enacted by Congress in 1994 and signed into law by President Bill Clinton. That piece of legislation sets forth a lofty set of goals for the nation, starting with the blanket statement "By the year 2000, all children in America will start school ready to learn." Well, obviously, everyone is in favor of such a goal. But how do we go about accomplishing it? And did anyone honestly think that a federal program would produce that? That seems like a nice notion, but in the real world, such goals can be achieved only in the old-fashioned way—by working for them. Can the federal government do it? Can Uncle Sam, in view of his abysmal track record on social policy, be relied upon? Can we trust Bill Clinton—or any president—with our children?

So as we poke around in Goals 2000's fine print, we see, for example, that an official federal goal is to make sure that "every parent in the United States will be a child's first teacher and devote time each day to helping such parent's preschool child learn." Okay, that sounds fine, in the aspirational sense, but here comes the kicker: "and parents will have access to the training and support parents need." And what "training and support" is that? Who will provide it? Well, it means that if a parent can't handle his or her parental duties, a benevolent-seeming bureaucrat will step in to "help." You know the old line, "We're from the government, and we're here to help you." Indeed, as Goals 2000 makes plain, if children and parents for any reason don't measure up to federal requirements, there's a "partnership" or "team" of agencies that will happily move in and take charge. Yes, that's our federal government—always efficient, always effective, always at your service!

Here's another goal: "By the year 2000, United States students will be first in the world in mathematics and science achievement."

Oh my, who can be against that? Who can be against winning the international brain race? But wait, there's a small detail left out: actually doing it. How will this victory happen? And will these same people who brought failure now bring success? I recall my foster daughter, the one whose eleventh-grade math homework consisted of coloring in a poster: Was her colorful homework helping to fulfill Goals 2000? The truth is, the United States hasn't been anywhere close to first place in math for a long, long time. These days, countries such as Finland and South Korea are always at the top; they are the new Iowa, you might say. Typically, the United States ranks down in the teens and twenties in international rankings of math and science; a recent study the World Economic Forum ranked the United States forty-eighth in the quality of math and science instruction.

But wait—there's more! Goals 2000 still had more to offer: Washington now decreed that a greater percentage of students would graduate from high school, that more students would be proficient in foreign languages, that the dire achievement gaps between population groups would disappear, that all students would be knowledgeable about diversity—and, of course, that the lion would lie down with the lamb. I made that last one up, but the fully delusional quality of these goals is captured in goal (7)(A): "Every school in the United States will be free of drugs, violence, and the unauthorized presence of firearms and alcohol and will offer a disciplined environment conducive to learning."

Needless to say, I am 100 percent in favor of our having safe schools, free of drugs and violence, offering "a disciplined environment." But it's preposterous to claim that a federal government that can't even be bothered to defend the U.S.-Mexican border against human traffickers and narcoterrorists is qualified to lecture the rest of us on how to keep our schools safe.

Indeed, the Goals 2000 pledges were so ambitious—and so ludicrous in their pseudodetailed optimism—that they are worth recalling in full (they are appended in the back of the book). Yes, they make for turgid reading, full of stilted bureaucratese, but trust me: Every word therein was crafted by "experts," working their part of a grand central plan in which a new kind of bureaucratic-corporatist ideology—of schools as state-supervised education factories, doling out dumbed-down instruction to meet the plan—replaces our traditional love of children and the child's innate and joyful striving for excellence.

It's worth remembering, again, that these fantasy goals became the law of the land in 1994. And if now, seventeen years later, they read like some cosmic practical joke, well, please be advised that you paid for it—through the nose, with your own hard-earned money. Your tax dollars at work. The federal government has indeed spent hundreds of billions of dollars trying to do all these things. Moreover, while the goals statement consists of only about 1,300 words, each item comes with its own wagon train of fine print and regulation. And it's within all that red tape that the bureaucrats find their power—and even more of your money.

So if the gap between the stated goal and the reality is so vast—wider than a mile, to quote the songwriter Johnny Mercer—as to make the whole goals process comical in its costly incompetence, well, now you know why I got so fired up in Stillwater.

Because even as the central bureaucrats in Washington were grinding away, peripheral bureaucrats in each state capital were similarly grinding. In Minnesota, the state department of education bureaucrats in St. Paul were all too eager to join in on the effort, creating their own mini version of Goals 2000. So in 1998 the state launched a new education plan called Profile of Learning, as mentioned in chapter 1. And as always happens when the government unveils a new program, eager spin doctors rushed to herald the "historic breakthrough"—while relying on the silent assumption that nobody would actually read the fine print. Or remember how the previously heralded "historic breakthrough" had worked out.

In reality, of course, when the bureaucrats do their thing, educational verities erode, reduced to their lowest common denominator. Moreover, the many localities out in the provinces are disempowered—not by accident but by design. The bureaucrats' hope is that the public will give up and a passive fatalism will set in, so that the rule makers rule, overseeing a long slide into politically correct mediocrity.

As my friend Allen Quist, a former Minnesota state legislator and Republican gubernatorial candidate, said at the time, the Profile was a power grab. Yet it was not just a power grab of our schools, but a power grab of our whole way of life as free Americans. Students were now to be seen for their value to the economy, for their usefulness to a future employer. No parent sees his or her child only in such utilitarian terms, but central planners do—and that was the problem. Embedded in the Profile was a vision of top-down control in which children become mere cogs in a vast bureaucratic machine.

For my part, as an ordinary citizen, I came to understand that if a leader isn't actively paying attention to the procedural workings of government—that is, if he or she isn't drilling down into the day-to-day shuffling of papers—then a reckoning will come, and he or she will discover that cunning underlings, operating on little cat feet—or, I should say, bureaucrat feet—have altered the political landscape to their own liking. Corner offices for all!

In other words, it was the Minnesota bureaucrats—not even the elected politicians—who now had the power of the federal government behind them. So these functionaries could do what they had always wanted to do, and if they ran into resistance—from either a politician or a citizen— they could say, "Hey, don't blame me, I'm just following orders from Washington." It was a nifty way to pass the buck. So the politicians usually went along meekly, even heedlessly, with the new education rules; for one thing, they had more important goals to worry about—such as getting reelected.

So the pushback on all these policies, if there was to be any, would have to come from the people. Can you fight city hall? Can you fight the statehouse? And the federal government? Sure you can. It just takes a lot of work. I joined a citizens' group called the Maple River Education Coalition, and we found that together we were more than just a group, or even a team. We were a movement—a volunteer movement of concerned citizens and activists. We were a proto–Tea Party, you might say.

So I started researching the Profile, decoding the bureaucratic spin that came with it. Just as I had once studied the innards of the tax code, I was now studying the innards of our education system. It was hard work—I put in five years of my life—but it was important work.

I teamed up with another education activist, Mike Chapman, and soon we had put together a report on the Profile and then a presentation that we could show to other parents. In our presentations, Mike and I would analyze the components of the Profile, examining each part in turn, highlighting all its flaws and false assumptions. And because there was so much material, our presentations grew increasingly long and comprehensive. Yet we found that Minnesota parents, once engaged, were riveted—and then galvanized. And so our audience grew. Mike and I did all the work at our own expense—and at the sufferance of our families—because we knew that what we were doing was important. Our sessions with groups of parents, including the inevitable questions and answers, might easily stretch into two or more hours. And by the time we were done, our audience—who beforehand might have known nothing about the Profile—was ready to grab a pitchfork. They'd say, "Not with my kid, you don't!"

Soon we each traveled to various venues around the state, packing our materials in the trunk of a car, getting lost on snowy roads as we went from one living room—or auditorium or gymnasium—to another. And wherever we went, Mike and I, plus a growing number of friends and allies, learned more and more about our state's educational malpractice and malfeasance. We'd meet parents whose kids hadn't been taught multiplication tables. And interestingly, we met public-school teachers who had protested against this foolishness but had been punished by their bosses for speaking out.

Of course, we wanted to share our concerns with our elected officials, but precious few of them were interested in listening. As I have mentioned, my own state senator didn't wish to be bothered. And he was hardly alone. Our governors back then viewed us as nothing more than a nuisance. The governor at the time was a Republican, although in the years after he left office in 1999, he would go on to endorse John Kerry against George W. Bush in the 2004 presidential election and Barack Obama over John McCain in 2008.

His successor as governor turned out to be Jesse "The Body" Ventura, the ex–pro wrestler, who won in a three-way election. Ventura ran as a member of the Reform Party, and yet, for all his populist fervor, the reform we saw was lowering the tab fees for license plates. That was great, but at the same time, he also pushed the biggest government intrusion into education that the state had ever seen. Even before he was sworn in as Minnesota's thirty-eighth governor in January 1999, he was surrounded by liberal Democrats. And so despite populist hopes, the permanent St. Paul establishment seemed to continue to rule the day. And that meant, among other things, ignoring the pleas of Minnesota parents and teachers and our reform-the-schools campaign.

By now, I was active in statewide education reform. That same year, 1999, five openings came up on the local school board. I'd spent countless hours trying to inform Minnesotans about the negative impact of the Profile; now, maybe, there was an opportunity for like-minded parents to take a majority position on the school board and push for academic excellence. I let myself, in my enthusiasm, be persuaded to run for office, for a post on the local school board in Stillwater. Five political novices agreed to run as a slate—what a mistake. We tried to squeeze all five of our names onto one sign. And while we had the best of intentions, the problem was, we didn't know the first thing about running a campaign. So while our goal was to work for local control and academic excellence, the local teachers' union wanted to retain its control of the school board. Meanwhile, the big guns of Big Education, Minnesota style, were all aimed at us. Even Planned Parenthood campaigned against us. Why would a proabortion group get involved in school elections? Well, that tells you a lot, doesn't it? It's a reminder that Planned Parenthood's true intentions go far beyond legalizing abortion; in fact, the group seeks to get to kids at an early age with their vision of sexual permissiveness.

And so in November 1999, all five of us lost that school-board election. It was a chastening experience; losing an election among your friends and neighbors is no fun. As a result, I resolved not to risk embarrassing myself ever again. Yet my resolution held firm for only a few months—until that fateful rendezvous with destiny in April 2000 at the Republican district 56 convention in Mahtomedi.

CHAPTER NINE

Taking On the Establishment in St. Paul

THE 2000 state senate campaign was on. Although I wrested the Republican endorsement away from the incumbent state senator in April 2000, the senator chose not to concede. So I had to face him again in the September Republican primary.

And I had to put together a real campaign. In political terms, I was nobody from nowhere, but because of my work against the Profile of Learning, many activists already knew me. Thanks to them—and thanks to their good hearts and boundless energy—we had more than a campaign. Once again we had a movement.

For my part, I went door knocking. And as I drove around, if I saw a stray voter, I would pull over and introduce myself. It was hard work, and it forced me to spend hours, days, and weeks listening to voter after voter at the door. It was there, at the door, that I learned the voice and dreams of the people I hoped to represent. I felt that I was doing something important—something that could potentially help all the families of Minnesota. And so with more activist zeal than political skill, I won the GOP primary by more than twenty points, 61 percent to 39 percent.

Okay, I thought now, *because I'm the official Republican nominee, I will get real help from the state GOP.* But once again, I was naive. I had beaten a long-sitting member of the senate and some of the other members weren't amused.

And of course, the Minnesota senate hadn't been Republican since the early seventies. Even Ronald Reagan couldn't carry our state in 1984, even as he won the other forty-nine. Indeed, Minnesota has given its votes to the

Democrats in twelve of the last thirteen presidential elections, and 2000 was no exception—Al Gore won the Gopher State that year.

Meanwhile, my Democratic opponent in November was positioning himself as a moderate. That was typically what liberal Democrats did in Minnesota for the general election. For my part, I campaigned as a far right conservative. And if the traditional media weren't interested in reporting on that message, happily I had newer media that were eager to cover my insurgent candidacy. I was on talk radio that fall, in particular the Jason Lewis show on KSTP-AM, 1500. And so I won—by almost twelve points, in fact. The voters of the 56th state senate district had put their trust in me, and I was determined to represent them and their view. The first Minnesota Tea Partier had been elected!

So two months later, in January 2001, as a newly sworn-in member of the 82nd Minnesota legislature, I set to work on the agenda I had campaigned for—improving education, of course, and also protecting life, lowering the tax burden, reducing spending, and improving the overall business climate. I expected that the Democrats would oppose much of what I had in mind, but I had not expected blowback from fellow Republicans.

I had become familiar with St. Paul politics as an education activist. I had appeared with politicians, debated with politicians, even testified before them in the state legislature. So I knew that sometimes politicians would talk a good conservative game at home, and then play the go-along-get-along game in St. Paul, thus letting the liberals have their way. I knew that the public picture was not always the true picture.

Yet even so, once I could see legislative workings from the inside, I saw that the problem was much worse. I would introduce bills to do what Republicans should do—what they had promised to do—and I'd find that support for dismantling big government wasn't a given. I introduced bills to eliminate the state inheritance tax and the state capital gains tax; I sought to guarantee needed taxpayer protections in a formal taxpayer bill of rights. After all, Minnesota had one of the highest tax burdens in the nation, and it was hurting us. We weren't just losing jobs to countries overseas, such as Mexico or China; we were losing jobs to states next door, such as the Dakotas.

Yet for the most part, these reform efforts gained little traction, primarily because I was a fiscal and social conservative serving in an ultraliberal-dominated, Democratic-controlled state senate. I quickly noticed a pattern: The issues that some Republicans campaigned for in their districts seemed far less important to them once they got to St. Paul. And that's when I learned a basic truth: Not all Republicans wanted to fight, and even fewer were willing to take on issues that seemed "messy"—that is, issues that the liberal media championed. In the senate, stubborn and entrenched liberals were the norm, so discouragement went with the territory. Indeed, in the three decades that Republicans had been in the minority in St. Paul, for some a mind-set of passive acceptance had set in. Some would see the liberals feasting on political pork—which is to say, feasting on our tax money—and so would be careful not to upset the liberals in hope of a little project for their district. In return for such docile behavior, the liberal leadership would usually drop some little morsel onto the floor so that hungry Republicans could scamper after it. The general rule for Republicans was "Don't ever say anything bad about the Democratic leadership." Indeed, this behavior was so endemic that the minority leader of the senate Republicans actually became a Democrat. And in a few years, the Democrats made him their majority leader! In other words, in the case of some Republican members, little or no difference, philosophically, could be detected between them and the ultraleft liberals.

So a committed conservative in the state senate back then not only had to oppose the dominant liberal Democrats but also had to overcome the lethargy of prolonged service in the minority. Fortunately, we had some steadfast fighters on our side. One such fighter was state senator Warren Limmer of nearby Maple Grove. He's always been true blue—or, I should say, true red. Together we would fight the good fight, with the help of other stalwart members.

For a while I served on the Jobs, Housing and Community Development Committee. Once again, as with Goals 2000, nice-sounding names— who could be against "jobs, housing and community development"?—were used as cover for the usual bankrupt, and bankrupting, liberalism. In addition to the standard routine of waste, fraud, and abuse, I discovered that the bureaucrats we were supposed to be watching had a bookkeeping problem, not because they were corrupt but because they couldn't keep track of their money. Some bureaucrats admitted that they were off by some $75 million; they literally didn't know which number was correct. But instead of fixing the problem, the bureaucrats just asked for more money. In that committee, we routinely listened to government emissaries, all saying, let's have more spending, spending, spending. Liberal members of the committee used that time to cultivate relationships with lobbyists; a few of us just voted no and threw up our hands.

So you can see how easy it was to be swayed by the business-as-usual nature of the state legislature. If you wanted to make friends and move up, you had to do things their way.

But for some legislators, when pressure is applied, they grow stronger in their convictions. That was true for some of us on the right, and it was also true for some on the left. For example, during my first term in the state senate, I met U.S. senator Paul Wellstone. He was a firebrand leftist, but he had an honest heart. He was not cynical; he was sincere. He told you where he was coming from, and if you disagreed with him, he would respect that disagreement, and do his best to beat you. He was true to his ideology until he and his wife were tragically killed in a plane crash.

Indeed, we are all subject to fate and the forces of history. On a bright Tuesday morning in September 2001, the course of American history was changed by those nineteen evil hijackers. Nearly three thousand Americans died, and the lives of three hundred million were altered forever. I was at home on 9/11, and as the news unfolded, I thought immediately of my brother living near New York City and my stepbrother working at the Pentagon. It turned out they were both fine, thank God.

Yet we all knew that more brave Americans would die during the coming global war on terrorism. I was proud of President George W. Bush for traveling to the ruins of the World Trade Center, showing solidarity with those firefighters and rescue workers. And I was proud too when he appeared before a joint session of Congress and declared that Uncle Sam would go on the offensive against the terrorists, as well as against the regimes that harbored them. As we watched the president on TV, I said to Marcus, "There is a strong man." I saw in his eyes the resolve of a patriot committed to protecting his country. At that moment, he completely grew into his young presidency and assumed full command. America was a safer and better place because of his stout heart and conviction.

Yet at the same time, back in Minnesota, we still had our work to do. I had always opposed wasteful spending, but now, during wartime, it seemed all the more horrible that we were spending money on foolish projects. We needed that money for the military, I said to myself, or else we needed it as savings in our pockets. We needed fiscal prudence and safety, not the same old money wasting.

So I will admit I was disappointed to see President Bush work with Democratic senator Teddy Kennedy and future House Speaker John Boehner to push through the No Child Left Behind Act, which the president signed into law in early 2002. No Child Left Behind was an updated Goals 2000, imposing new mandates on all fifty states—the same federal government good intentions leading to the same downward educational results. We made progress toward the repeal of the Profile of Learning in our state, and yet in the United States as a whole, we were handing local classrooms over to the federal bureaucracy.

Still, in 2002 we scored some successes. For example, we passed the Woman's Right to Know Act, which requires that twenty-four hours before an abortion takes place the pregnant mother be given important information; she is to be told the gestational age of her unborn child, she is to learn about the medical risks associated with the abortion procedure, and she is to receive an in-depth explanation of the abortion procedure itself, including the baby's ability to feel pain during the termination of its life.

As I have often said, the one issue that we absolutely have to get right is life. As Jesus told us in Matthew 25:40, "Verily I say unto you, inasmuch as ye have done it unto one of the least of these my brethren, ye have done it unto me." And surely the least among us is an unborn child.

Enacting Woman's Right to Know was landmark progress. Yet it was still not the best response to the tragedy of abortion; the best response is a constitutional amendment protecting life as part of a renewed national reverence for the life culture. But at the same time, Right to Know was significant progress, because very few mothers, if any, truly don't want their own children. I felt gratified that we had managed to secure this protection. We pro-life activists had come a long way since the eighties, when we would stand in prolonged vigils outside St. Paul–Ramsey Medical Center in St. Paul. In those days, Marcus and I would take our little children with us, to stand out there in the cold with Pro-Life Action Ministries. They might not always have understood what was going on—at their tender age, it was probably best they didn't—but when I gazed at them and held their tiny little hands, I remembered why I was there.

Meanwhile, the liberal establishment made it clear it was aiming to get rid of me. In the wake of the 2000 census, Minnesota redistricted its legislative seats, and in 2002 I was thrown into the same senate district as a ten-year female Democratic incumbent, the chair of the powerful Environment Committee. She was a strong candidate boasting a strong fund-raising base among liberal-leaning environment and education constituencies. And of course, given my opposition to the Profile of Learning, the teachers' unions and their allies were out in force. She had money from the party and the lobbyists—the special interests. I was their foe and thus their target. Those words helped me too; I knew I would have to rely, once again, on God. For my part, I did what I always did: I worked hard. Door to door, driving around, introducing myself to folks in my new district. Yet of course, my opponent faced a challenge too—she was a liberal. For my part, I focused on commonsense conservative issues, including opposition to the Profile, and in November I won by more than nine points.

So in 2003 I was sworn in for my second term in the state senate. And we were joined by a new governor to replace Jesse Ventura; "The Body" had wisely decided not to seek reelection. The new chief executive was Republican governor Tim Pawlenty; finally, a few months later, we were able to repeal the Profile.

That same year, 2003, brought sad news. My father died in August. The word came early in the morning. It was a mile-maker moment. He had traveled a hard road in life, and sometimes he had made it harder for himself and for others, but he was my dad and I will always honor him.

Meanwhile, perhaps the biggest news to confront me in the legislature didn't come from Minnesota but from a different state altogether—Massachusetts. On November 18, 2003, the Massachusetts Supreme Judicial Court ruled that same-sex couples had a legal right to marry and the court further ordered the Massachusetts state legislature to pass a law to that effect. How dare the court order legislators to pass a law in conformity with their personal morality and opinion of a bare majority of justices—the vote was four to three—not in conformity with the majority of people in the Bay State. America had always agreed that marriage should be reserved for one man and one woman. In addition, our Constitution prefers that the courts should interpret the law, not make the law. Otherwise, legislators are irrelevant, as is the will of the people.

Of course, at the same time, I wasn't completely surprised by the Massachusetts ruling, because I knew that judges had gotten in the habit of legislating from the bench. I could see why judges might like to run the whole government; the only problem was, it's unconstitutional. Indeed, in the U.S. Constitution, the judicial branch is listed third, in Article III. Thomas Jefferson said that the courts were to be the least powerful of the three branches of government. The federal branches are equal, but at the same time, James Madison chose to enumerate the powers of the judiciary after those of the other two branches. But here we were now, confronting a whole new vista of judicial activism, and who was to say it would stop with Massachusetts? Minnesota had a "DOMA" statute, modeled after the 1996 Defense of Marriage Act that was passed with strong bipartisan support in the U.S. Congress and signed by President Clinton. But even so, I could see the possibility that the Minnesota Supreme Court could copy the Massachusetts ruling. That meant there was only one sure way to stop such a ruling: Pass a constitutional amendment in the state of Minnesota.

And so I began working on the most controversial issue of my time in the state senate. Working with my colleague Warren Limmer and other like-minded senators and house members, in January 2004 I put into the hopper a bill to start the process of amending the state constitution. Such an amendment would have to pass both houses of the state legislature and then be ratified by popular vote across the state. In other words, my proposing a marriage amendment was a first step. Yet the liberals and the left were opposed even to the hint of a move that might undo their judicial oligarchy. And so the fury against me personally was ferocious. If you can think of a bad name, I was called it—many times.

The Democratic leadership of the state senate was opposed to my amendment, and that was their right. Yet in addition, they used every possible maneuver to stop me from proceeding with the bill—and that was not right. That is, they were desperate to prevent a simple up-or-down vote, first in the committee they controlled, then in the legislative body as a whole. And when I walked into the chamber, enough Democrats would leave so that a quorum was no longer present; when I tried to speak, they would rule me out of order. Once, when I was speaking, they cut off my microphone in midspeech.

So what did my side do? We just kept working at it. We counted our votes in the senate; we built grassroots support around the state. And that's what really scared the liberal establishment. They were afraid we had the votes to pass the amendment—votes from most Republican legislators, from some of the Democratic legislators, and, most crucial, from the people of Minnesota.

For two years in a row, we conservatives had staged big rallies in front of the state capitol; the people of the state wanted a chance to vote on the bill. But the liberals were against us. Liberal dominance in the state senate prevented us from moving the bill. Seven years later, in 2010—after the Minnesota senate and house both went Republican for the first time in thirty-eight years—the bill was passed by both chambers and so will be on the ballot in 2012. After seven years of persistence, the people of Minnesota will finally get the chance to vote on an amendment stating the traditional definition of marriage. And as in thirty-three other states, I'm confident that the voters of Minnesota will define marriage as one man and one woman. The conservative profamily activists of Minnesota and their representatives deserve the credit for this achievement. It was their heart and their soul that stood strong. They persisted, and finally moved this effort toward a popular conclusion. Yet at the same time, the marriage fight reminded me of something important: Effective politics isn't just a matter of accumulating votes inside a legislative chamber. Nor is politics just a matter of building a popular movement outside a legislative chamber. Instead, effective politics is both—the inside game and the outside game. That was the model we employed on the marriage issue, and it was the model I would use again when I came to Washington, D.C.

Meanwhile, in early 2005, after I had gained clout within the state senate, I was appointed to be an assistant minority leader. Yet within a few months, my new spot in the Republican leadership put me in uncomfortable cross fire. A fight was brewing over the state budget. That fight led to a partial government shutdown, and in the resulting tumult, a compromise solution was reached that included a seventy-five-cent increase in the cigarette tax. The measure wasn't called a "tax increase," it was dubbed instead a "health impact fee." I did my best to remove the cigarette "fee" from the overall compromise, but after the tax increase was locked in, I faced an agonizing choice: The compromise legislation also contained a strong pro-life provision—recognizing fetal pain—and so the compromise had the strong support of Minnesota Citizens Concerned for Life, a key pro-life ally. In other words, to vote against the tax increase was to vote against the fetal pain provision, and I just couldn't do that. The power brokers had cleverly wired the bill so that conservatives had to choose one value or the other. I believe you can recover money, but you can't recover life; so I chose life. It was a difficult moment, but I made the right decision.

Having made that difficult vote, I immediately proposed a stand-alone bill to strip out the tax increase without affecting the important pro-life provision. But of course, the power brokers wanted nothing to do with that.

I have always told myself, my family, my colleagues, and my constituents that I would consistently vote my conscience, and that's what I did. And so, of course, that made me expendable; I was soon out of the GOP leadership.

Yet as one door was closing, another was opening. In late 2004, I was enjoying a Christmas party with the great people of my state senate district when a colleague approached me and whispered that U.S. representative Mark Kennedy, my congressman, was seriously thinking of vacating his House seat and running for the U.S. Senate the following year. Did I want to go for it? I hadn't thought about running for Congress, and, frankly, my first thoughts were negative. *Spend two years running for a seat that lasts for two years?* I shared the news with Marcus, and we talked about it, and then prayed over the possibility. After a while, we both had a confidence that I should offer my candidacy.

And so my time in the state senate was drawing to a close. In my six years in St. Paul, I had learned that some people in politics are selfless, self-sacrificing, and, above all else, will do the right thing. I thanked those wonderful colleagues for standing up and doing what's right for the people they serve. Yet I also saw some politicians who will wiggle and waffle, seeking to hide the truth about what they are doing from the people who are paying their salaries. That's the bad news. Yet the good news—and it is very good news—is that the people of Minnesota, when given all the information they need, will push those same politicians in the right direction, or they will elect new representatives who will listen to them. It is those folks who will always renew my faith in our system of governance.

CHAPTER TEN

George W. Bush, Karl Rove—and My Gloves

I announced my bid to serve the people of the 6th congressional district of Minnesota on February 14, 2006, Valentine's Day. It was a tough race in a tough year for Republicans. Perhaps most notably, the war in Iraq was not going well. President Bush had not yet launched the surge that turned the military situation around and made General David Petraeus a national hero. In addition, it's sad to say, Americans had the feeling that the Republicans then ruling Congress had grown smug and complacent—too tolerant of pork-barrel overspending and, even worse, too tolerant of bad behavior by some of their own members.

Meanwhile, in Minnesota, my opponent was a woman named Patty Wetterling. Years earlier, Patty's son Jacob had been abducted and presumably tragically murdered in St. Joseph, Minnesota. It was a shocking crime that gripped the people of our state; Patty quite rightly became a high-profile advocate for child safety. So from a political point of view, she had advantages going into the race; she enjoyed high name awareness and, of course, the prayers and sympathy of all Minnesotans. Meanwhile, I had a voting record and a history of actively working to advance conservative causes in St. Paul. I would have done it all over again, of course, but I was resigned to my opponent's large fund-raising advantage.

But what I was *not* resigned to was losing the election. This would be a battle about the future, about which one of us could best represent the views of the people of the 6th district in the halls of Congress. I believed I could best do the job.

So even as *Congressional Quarterly* handicapped the race as having "no clear favorite," I thought I would prevail if I did what I had been doing since 2000—that is, speaking out boldly while mobilizing activists and persuading the persuadable. My confidence was fortified when the national Democratic Party announced that it was targeting our 6th district specifically. I knew that if the choice could be made clear—between commonsense conservatism and the ideological liberalism of Nancy Pelosi and my opponent—well, I was confident I knew where my friends and neighbors in the 6th stood on such a choice.

Still, I had a campaign to run. Campaigning can be a chore, although it's a chore that I love. I love talking to people and getting into important issues and concerns. I believe too that every person here on earth is created in the image of God, and so it's my duty to respect all others; I try to be kind to people, to share with them, to learn from them. It's true, of course, that disputes and arguments will arise, but I try to live by the Golden Rule; in politics, that means I should disagree without being disagreeable. I like to think I can attack the policy without attacking the person. Sometimes I have fallen short of that goal, and when I do, I try to make amends, even as I resolve to do better.

Another element of campaigning, of course, is raising money. And by now, thankfully, I was receiving funding help from the National Republican Congressional Committee. In fact, during the 2006 campaign, I received a fund-raising boost from the number one Republican in the nation, President George W. Bush.

On August 22, 2006, the president came to the Twin Cities to speak at a conference on health care during the day—and to do a fund-raiser for me that night. Minnesota supporters are very generous, and my race was no exception. We held the fund-raising event at the former Pillsbury home on the shores of Lake Minnetonka, about fifteen miles west of Minneapolis; it was the perfect setting for a presidential visit.

For my part, I was confronting another question—what to wear! I figured I would just wear a business suit, but my mother was adamant: I had to look nice. And in her mind, that meant dressing like a lady would have in the 1940s or 1950s—that is, all dolled up. I listened to my mother; that's what a dutiful daughter always does. Yet even so, I figured I could look nice on the cheap. So I went to Herberger's department store and found a deeply discounted after-Easter dress and jacket. It was a pink suit, including a matching pink purse, and pink shoes. My mother insisted if I was to meet the president, I'd have to have pink gloves as well—no exceptions! And so I had the gloves, too.

Dressed to exacting motherly standards, I went off to meet the president at a suburban hotel. I was escorted into a holding room, where I met Karl Rove and other White House staffers. Then a hush fell—the president was entering the room. In these situations, there's a receiving line; in this instance, it was strictly all Republican: Governor Tim Pawlenty and Senator Norm Coleman, along with Congressman Jim Ramstad, who represented the western suburbs of Minneapolis, and Congressman Mark Kennedy, whose seat I was attempting to fill as he ran for the U.S. Senate.

The men were prepared: They were all much cannier than I about what to do when they had a moment of the president's time. They had brought along with them things for the president to sign, including cookbooks, baseballs, and photographs. I didn't think to ask for an autograph!

When the president passed by me, I had nothing to offer except a sincere handshake. I took my glove off, and he took my hand in a firm grip, saying, "I'll see you later." That is, he and I—and several hundred others—had a "date" at Lake Minnetonka that afternoon. Yet he and Karl Rove knew, and I didn't, that I would be seeing him even sooner than that.

After the receiving line, we were ushered into the hotel ballroom, heading toward a section of reserved seats in front. I was certainly interested in what the president had to say about health-care policy, but because there's always downtime during such events, I am never without a book; you never know when you can squeeze in a few moments for reading. And that day, the book I had brought with me was Doris Kearns Goodwin's *Team of Rivals*, detailing Lincoln's stormy but productive relationship with his cabinet during the Civil War. I was just diving into the historical tale when Karl Rove came up to me and said, "You have to get rid of the book."

"Why?" I asked. "It's really good."

Rove answered: "I know—I read it. But the president is going to be speaking."

Oh, I thought, *don't worry, I won't be reading when the president is speaking.* I would never be disrespectful.

He was smiling but stern: "You need to hand it over." We went back and forth, but eventually, I gave him the book. And Karl was right: If I had been photographed reading a book at any time during the event, the nuance of exactly *when* I was reading would have been lost. Some detractor would have been only too happy to "report" that I was so bored by the president that I had pulled out a book. And that would have hurt both the president and my election prospects. It was not the last helpful thing that Karl would do for me that day.

Just before the conference ended, he came back and said, "Come with me—you're going to ride with the chief in the limousine."

"You're kidding!" I said, not exactly curbing my enthusiasm. The original plan had been for Marcus and the kids to come and pick me up at the hotel in our well-used Ford Eclipse van. But now, I learned, I would be riding with the president. So as I walked with Karl to the garage where the limo waited, I called Marcus and told him I had an alternative plan, and he should meet me at the home on Lake Minnetonka.

So there I was in a big underground garage, standing in my pink suit, wearing my pink gloves, next to a giant black presidential limousine, a few Secret Service agents eyeing me coolly. I hate to risk challenging the authority of armed men, but I figured that the agents wouldn't mind if I rapped my knuckles on the thick metal, just to see what the vehicle felt like. Sure enough, it was more like a tank than a car. I circled the car a few times and thought, *What an amazing ride this will be.* It had those presidential flags on the hood, and soon I would see it from the inside.

The president strode out to the waiting car, along with the governor, Senator Coleman, and Rove. The president sat in the rear seat on the right, and Rove, using a few quick gestures, assigned the rest of us to our seats. To my surprise, Rove pointed me to the backseat to the left of the president, while Coleman and Pawlenty, along with Karl, took their places on a bench seat facing the president—and me. For a girl from Waterloo, Iowa, this was a heady experience. I kept telling myself: *Remember everything, Michele, so that you can tell the kids.* The presidential seal was embroidered into the leather seat; I thought, *This isn't as large as I thought it would be.*

The next thing I knew, we were zipping through the cordoned-off streets, part of a grand motorcade, sirens blaring. Rove reached into a compartment and handed the president a plastic bottle of water, and then one to each of the rest of us. The bottles were room temperature. The president looked at me and said, "Room temperature water is healthier." And from that day on, I have taken the lead from the commander in chief!

As we rode along, we talked first about casual topics, including dogs. The president joked that Barney, the black Scottish terrier, couldn't make the trip; the first pooch, the commander in chief kidded, was a good dog and needed to mind the store. And we all agreed that we missed Spot, the English springer spaniel who had passed a few years earlier.

The president demonstrated amazing energy despite his nearly six years in office, prosecuting the war on terror on so many fronts. He was stoic and obviously strong. And when the discussion shifted from dogs to kids and family, he grew more reflective; he recalled the moment decades before when his wife, Laura, now the first lady, had issued him an ultimatum: "It's either Jack Daniel's or me." George W. Bush chose wisely, and so he was able to begin his career in leadership.

I also saw how the president consistently thought of others. He was an eminently decent man. He made a point to look for every person he could spot along the motorcade route. People would wait for hours to get a glimpse of the car, so the president paid attention in order to wave at every person along the motorcade route that he could; he wanted them to know that he saw them and recognized them. The president was kind, affable— the opposite of egocentric. This event, and his presidency, was not about himself; it was about the people he served. In the brief time we spent together, I learned a lot about the character of the man. As an aside, several years earlier, Barbara Bush, the former first lady, had come to campaign in Minnesota for Senator Rod Grams. Barbara Bush was not only kind in person, but was also an excellent speaker and campaigner. Obviously very intelligent and possessed of a quick wit, both Barbara and former president George H. W. Bush had done a great job in parenting their children.

The president was a good listener. He paid careful attention to each of us and then responded thoughtfully. Speaking of thoughtful, he looked down at my pink-gloved hands and asked with a crinkly smile: "Why are you wearing those gloves?" I explained and he said gently, "Lose the gloves." I could see Rove agreed. I slipped the gloves off, and the conversation turned to fishing.

Then, still short of our destination, we stopped. I looked out the window and saw a popular roadside frozen-custard stand. Rove looked at me and said, "Hop out." The Secret Service already had the president out of the car as Karl continued, "We're stopping here to do a photo op—for you!"

Once again, Rove's judgment was right. Ah, yes, the leader of the free world and his friend, hopefully-to-be-congresswoman Michele Bachmann, were getting frozen custard on their way to an important event. Because of this stop, the 10:00 P.M. news story was not the president and local politicians at a fancy fund-raiser; it would be me and the president having fun with a local summertime crowd and teenage employees while enjoying a frozen treat. The fund-raiser had been no secret, of course, but now we would be in the news three times, once for custard, once for the health-care forum, and then for the fund-raising visit. And although I was still all dressed up, at least I wasn't wearing—thanks to the president's good counsel—those over-the-top gloves.

So now we were out of the car: the president, then me, all surrounded by Secret Service agents, making our way through a startled crowd of gawking custard snackers. Soon reporters, tagging along in their own vehicles, pulled up, cameras in hand. The president and I reached the order window at the same time, and we both ordered vanilla. I love chocolate, but this was not the time to risk a bad stain. I realized I didn't have any cash with me; my wallet wouldn't fit in my tiny purse, and all I had was a slim little credit card. Fortunately, the president gave me some cash, thoughtful and considerate always.

Back in the car, I handed my custard to Karl and in no time we were at the former Pillsbury mansion. We pulled up into a tent put up by the Secret Service, so that no possible sniper could have a clear line of sight at the president. That was a sobering reminder that the president was at risk wherever he went; the low-key heroes of Secret Service had the challenging task of keeping him safe.

Inside, the hosts had made just one request of me. They hoped that the president would sign their leather-bound guest book. After all, there was some Bush history to that house; decades before, the forty-third president's father, as a young man, had spent a weekend here with his then-classmate from Yale, George Pillsbury. So as everybody mixed, mingled, and air kissed, I focused on steering the POTUS, as gracefully as possible, over to that all-important guest book. Gently touching the president's elbow, I pointed to the guest book—and the president, intuitive about social niceties, leaned over and wrote something kind on the page, signing it with a flourish.

It was a wonderful event: The president was gracious in his remarks, and I was allowed to say a few words myself. My entire family joined me— Marcus, the five kids, my mother, and in-laws all rumbling onto the property in our ancient Ford high-top van, the one with a cracked headlight and a bobblehead hula girl sitting atop the dashboard. Poor Marcus. As the helpful husband in a thrifty middle-class family, raising twenty-eight kids over the years, he had grown used to arriving at fund-raisers in a comparative jalopy. He would joke to the parking valets, with a twinkle in his eye, that his other car was in the shop. For her part, my mother took one look at me and frowned when she saw that my gloves were missing. I said preemptively, "Mom, I'll explain later."

Yet another big thing also happened that night: Our two youngest children, Caroline and Sophia, had their youthful lives changed. Marcus, always thinking ahead, had said to them a few days earlier, "Let's make this event your chance to improve your social skills and your confidence." That's the way Marcus thinks; this fund-raiser with the president was one of the biggest events of our political career together—he was certainly appreciative of that—but at the same time, he was also thinking of the children. So he gently instructed the two shy girls, then twelve and fourteen, that their mission for the evening was to go up to everyone at the dinner and introduce themselves. Nobody would bite them, he promised. He even role-played the exercise with them. Caroline and Sophia were both a bit daunted at the prospect, but when they arrived at the former Pillsbury home, they went for it; sticking close together, they primly and properly extended their greeting to all the folks. The girls knew, of course, that Marcus was hovering nearby, ready to help in case of a *faux pas* emergency. And so their debut in big-time political fund-raising was a success; they had no trouble working the room. That's the way childhood ought to be: parents guiding the development of their kids, seizing every opportunity to help them grow in confidence and ability.

Meanwhile, during my 2006 campaign, other Republicans luminaries helped out as well. Vice President Dick Cheney spoke at a similar event. The vice president, of course, is no backslapper. And while he understood at the time that politics was part of the job, he knew that his main mission during those perilous years was safeguarding America. As it happened, the day he appeared with me in Minnesota was also the day the *New York Times* broke a story detailing classified American intelligence secrets. And the vice president was more than a little angry about that story. I'll always remember the scene: the vice president, with a beautiful lake in the background, a hot and intense sun in his face, speaking forcefully as he delivered an impassioned impromptu address, outlining the dangers that America was confronting every day from terrorism—and emphasizing that the *Times*'s revelations had made the danger even greater. The vice president wasn't there to win a warm-and-fuzzy contest, but he won my respect that day for his defense of American security, his intellect, and serious demeanor. As my daughter Sophia said to me later, "I would want him as my uncle."

Another champion in my 2006 campaign was the man soon to be the top Republican leader in the House, John Boehner. The Ohioan came to the city of St. Cloud, in the northwest part of my district, to help fire up the troops. Boehner was a professional, and yet he also had an easygoing charm that seemed somehow familiar. As he lit up a cigarette on the porch outside the building, I suddenly realized who he reminded me of—the TV singer and movie star Dean Martin! John was on a mission to help Republicans retain control of the House, but as summer turned to fall, Republican chances for holding their majority worsened.

Despite all the fund-raising help I received, my opponent, Patty Wetterling, had even more help; she outspent me that year by more than $1.7 million. And that was the year the Democrats, riding a nationwide electoral wave, recaptured both the U.S. House and the Senate from the GOP. My friend Mark Kennedy, a very good man and an excellent member of Congress, was swamped in that wave; he lost Minnesota, including the 6th district, his home base, to Minnesota's next U.S. senator, Democrat Amy Klobuchar.

Yet despite the Democrats' tide, I was able to win the House seat—by a solid eight points. I felt proud to be the first female Republican ever to represent Minnesota in the House.

And yes, later that night at the Lake Minnetonka fund-raiser, Karl gave me back my book—my copy of *Team of Rivals*. Whenever I see him, he won't let me live down "lose the gloves." And as for those cute pink gloves that the president wisely talked me into "losing," I still have them. I just have never worn them again in public.

CHAPTER ELEVEN

A Rebel in Speaker Pelosi's Congress

IN January 2007, Democrat Nancy Pelosi was elected Speaker of the House, to preside over the newly sworn-in 110th Congress. As she banged down her gavel, she made her intentions clear: a new San Francisco–style liberal era for the nation. I should say "progressive," because liberals don't like to be called "liberals" anymore.

The GOP had been clobbered in the last election, no doubt about that. I was one of just thirteen Republican House freshmen, while the Democrats across the aisle boasted forty-one new members. We Republicans were a smaller and humbler bunch—although for my part, I was determined to continue the good fight. We had worked very hard to win in 2006, and I wasn't about to stop that work just because I found myself in the minority. I knew the ideas of fiscal responsibility and social conservatism had not been vanquished that previous November. What had been rejected in that election was a bad brew of GOP incompetence, carelessness, and a dash of corruption. So the people threw out the Republican majority and instead handed the gavels to Nancy Pelosi in the House and Harry Reid in the Senate. I might note that Republicans were leaving power in Congress when the annual deficit was $162 billion; the next year, under Democratic congressional leadership, it soared to $455 billion, and from there, into the trillions.

In the new Congress, as a freshman in the minority I was under no illusions as to how my ideas would be received. For my part, I didn't go into politics to be part of either the minority *or* the majority. The size of the group matters less than what the group does. I went into politics to change the system, giving people more of their liberty and more of their earnings.

I am an unashamed champion of the free market. Private business is the backbone and engine of American life. And when government kills the golden goose, day by day, that's when we have to man up. As I liked to joke, having stared down five two-year-olds and twenty-eight teenagers in our home, I was ready for any kind of confrontation. And as I had learned while fighting against the federal government takeover of education, and also fighting in favor of academic excellence, the right kind of leadership could develop an effective majority. That is, an effective majority forcing genuine change. A majority that's really worth having.

Yet as a freshman in the current minority, I could see the need to choose my fights carefully. One fight I chose seemed inconsequential on the surface, but, in fact, it symbolized something very important—our right to purchase whatever product we choose, consistent with health and safety limitations. It was over those compact fluorescent lightbulbs. The CFLs, as they're called—although, of course, CFLs aren't lightbulbs at all; they're squiggly-shaped things and sort of dark even when lit. Yet while CFLs are easy to make fun of, we must also be concerned about them, because they contain mercury, a birth defect–causing toxin. If you drop one and it breaks, your home could be declared a hazmat site. So I proposed the Light Bulb Freedom of Choice Act in 2008, seeking to restore the right of Americans to choose their own lightbulbs—the kind that best suits them. My bill didn't go anywhere in Nancy Pelosi's Congress, but it sent an electric shock through the country; soon my office was getting letters and e-mails from all over, cheering on my lightbulb rebellion.

I've always enjoyed sharing ideas with a national audience, just as I enjoyed sharing ideas with individual voters. Some things need to be said, and yet they can be said while remaining both polite and fair. So even as a freshman in the political minority, I wanted to speak out. It wasn't always easy—and sometimes, as I was soon to discover, it was downright risky.

The Energy Independence and Security Act of 2007 was one of those many bills with a nice name—and a terrible impact. It worked to reduce access to American energy resources at a time when we needed to responsibly unlock those resources. Indeed, by the summer of 2008, oil prices had spiked all the way up to $145 a barrel on the world market, which meant that U.S. gasoline prices rose above $4 a gallon. Back home in Minnesota, my constituents were furious; some families in my far-flung district were forced to spend $150 a week or more on gas. People who worked at nursing homes, for example, stopped coming to work, because the price of gas made the driving to work out of reach.

Yet Speaker Pelosi and her liberal majority didn't want to do anything except attack the companies that created American energy—a clear case of blaming the messenger. After all, the oil companies weren't the problem; the problem was a worldwide surge in demand, coupled with scarcity of supply, especially in the United States, where environmental restrictions were limiting production. Indeed, that's the classic formula for higher prices. And truth to tell, I think many liberals in Congress were quietly happy about high gas prices. Why? Because they had never really liked automobiles, anyway; they preferred mass transit—or bicycles. To be sure, the former vice president and presidential candidate Al Gore never seemed far from a limousine or private jet, but as for what the elite wished for the rest of us, well, I guess we could just walk or take a bus.

For our part, we House Republicans found our voice on this potent issue. Our idea of a good energy policy could be summed up in one word: "more." That is, more of everything. We endorsed an "all of the above" approach to energy production, seeking to use more oil, more coal, more natural gas, more nuclear power—more of every kind of energy, in fact, as long as it could be justified by the rigorous workings of free-market forces. In the summer of 2008, House minority leader John Boehner arranged for some of us to travel to Alaska, so that we could see the Arctic National Wildlife Refuge—an obvious place for some "drill, baby, drill."

And that's where I first met the charming and charismatic Alaska governor, Sarah Palin. We had a wonderful discussion over a meal in Fairbanks; I shared with her how much I had enjoyed my summer in Alaska thirty-three years earlier and how that visit had permanently changed my views about Alaska's—and America's—energy potential.

Indeed, Sarah and I realized that we had a lot in common. We shared the same firm faith; we both had carved out political careers thanks to our supportive husbands. In addition, we both had five biological kids.

We even talked about speculation that she might be selected as John McCain's running mate at the upcoming Republican convention—to be held, as it happened, in my state and nearby city of St. Paul, Minnesota. She laughed at the thought: "Oh, that's not going to happen." At the time, that fateful phone call from the Arizona senator had not yet occurred. But then, just a few days later, it did.

During those summer months of 2008, I became increasingly alarmed that Barack Obama might actually win the presidency. I watched in amazement as the junior senator from Illinois rolled over Hillary Rodham Clinton to win the Democratic nomination. I didn't favor Hillary, of course, but I could see that she seemed less leftist revolutionary than Obama. And that's saying something, considering that we're talking about Hillary Clinton. Did I prefer her, and not him, answering that proverbial 3:00 A.M. phone call? Actually, I preferred John McCain to either of them, by a wide margin, but if he couldn't be in the mix I would have wanted Mrs. Clinton.

House Speaker Pelosi and her Democratic colleague in the Senate, majority leader Harry Reid, were already bad enough, I figured. But the idea that President Bush could be replaced in the White House by a man whom *National Journal* rated as the most liberal senator in the chamber—giving him the keys to the Treasury filled me with concern.

John McCain secured the Republican presidential nomination. Though he was behind in the polls through most of 2008, I believed that by election day, the American people would favorably compare McCain's lengthy record of achievement with Obama's brief record of radicalism. In the last few days before the voting, many of us hoped, the nation's support would finally shift from Obama to McCain. And I was honored to be asked to speak on McCain's behalf at the Republican National Convention, held just a skip and a jump away from our home in Stillwater.

The focus of my brief talk on that day was service, John McCain's service—as a family man, as a war hero, as a political leader. Noting that John and his delightful and stunning wife, Cindy, had adopted a child, as had millions of other bighearted Americans, I added, "Whether it's being a foster parent or being a community first responder or wearing the uniform of the United States Army, service is all American. Service isn't a political trait—though some presidential nominees certainly know more about service than others."

Then I added, "John McCain not only recognizes that personal liberty needs elbow room; he's spent a lifetime ensuring that freedom has what it needs to grow. John McCain doesn't just speak the language of service; he's lived it." And so, I concluded, "America needs John McCain's service in the White House!" That was on September 2, 2008.

The very next night, of course, from the same podium, McCain's choice for his running mate, Sarah Palin—whom I was proud to call a friend—delivered her memorable acceptance speech. It was surely an electrifying speech, energizing not only dispirited Republicans but also stirring the entire country to start wondering who Obama really was. Building on her own life story, Sarah compared her early career with Obama's early career, "I guess a small-town mayor is sort of like a 'community organizer,' except that you have actual responsibilities." Great line! The McCain-Palin ticket had now taken the lead. Perhaps the boost from the convention speech might last till election day.

But then came the shuddering economic meltdown. Suddenly, everything changed. On September 15, 2008, Lehman Brothers, the venerable New York City investment house, filed for Chapter 11 bankruptcy. The signs of economic trouble had been visible for years, of course; the political—and politically correct—government creations, Fannie Mae and Freddie Mac, had been puffing ever more air into the housing bubble since the 1990s. Indeed, bureaucrats and politicos in Washington had been delighted by the growth of Fannie and Freddie, because now they could look forward to making private-sector-level salaries while still working under the protection of the public sector. So while a few brave Cassandras — notably Peter Wallison of the American Enterprise Institute—kept warning that Fannie and Freddie were destined to blow up, much of Washington wasn't worried at all. Instead, Beltway-ites were looking to jump on the Fannie/Freddie gravy train. Yet bubbles eventually deflate, and that's what started happening in 2007. And then bubbles eventually pop, and that's what happened in 2008. Confidence worsened, and the markets plummeted. The Dow Jones Industrial Average, having hit a peak of 14,000 in October 2007, plunged only a year later to 8,000.

On September 19, 2008, four days after Lehman collapsed, Treasury secretary Hank Paulson made an extraordinary request to Congress: He asked for a vote to give him a check for $700 billion, in the form of a Troubled Asset Relief Program (TARP). That grand sum would enable him, Paulson, to bail out the big banks on Wall Street and across the country—with no strings attached. In other words, the same financial institutions that had caused the crash—having grossly overinvested in mortgage-backed securities and other "toxic trash" financial instruments—were now going to be bailed out in the wake of that crash. It was outrageous beyond belief, and I said so loudly. And people back home agreed. At my congressional office, opposition to TARP exceeded support by at least ten to one.

When Secretary Paulson came to the House to plead his case personally, I stood up and said: "We've already bailed Bear Stearns for $29 billion, and AIG for $85 billion," and then went through all the details of the bailouts, which hadn't stopped the economy's slide. Then I asked: "Where is your evidence to prove that if Congress gives you a $700 billion blank check, with no strings attached, that you'll be able to turn the economy around?" The Treasury secretary had no answer. So I told him he could not have my vote. It was a surreal moment: Many conservatives were now sounding like liberals; they couldn't wait to see the government dish out money to save Fannies—and Freddies. It seemed that weekend after weekend, back in 2008, the Treasury secretary and the Federal Reserve chairman made unprecedented loans to private businesses at never-before-seen levels of government intervention in the private marketplace. The problem, I learned, was the Federal Reserve's enabling legislation, which was so broadly written that the Fed had the power to do nearly anything it wanted. Never before had the Fed exercised this latent ability, but now it did it with breathtaking speed and with blind faith in its ability to run the economy. Bad decisions, bad precedents, indeed.

The Bush administration, which had always professed faith in the free-market system, was now reversing its course; it was embracing a kind of "bailout socialism." And Obama too supported TARP, because he and many liberals were delighted to enshrine the idea that Uncle Sam could, and should, be the lender, or bail-outer, of last resort. The only problem is, now Uncle Sam was the lender of first resort. Using our money, of course.

Yet it was painful to find out that John McCain too favored the TARP bailout. In other words, McCain had joined the bailout mantra at exactly the wrong time, and all Americans were watching. Here was no "maverick" moment. The same disappointing stance was taken by the Republican leadership in the House. John Boehner went on national television to label TARP a "crap sandwich"—and then, in the next breath, he said we should vote for it anyway.

I knew there was no way I could vote for it, because I couldn't find authority for it in the Constitution. I simply couldn't support it. So I voted no. That's where I stood, and that's where I stand. As a constitutional conservative, I put principle over party.

Meanwhile, even after the bailout, the economy continued to decline—an indicator, of course, that government spending binges simply don't work. And so as September slid into October, the McCain-Palin ticket drifted behind in the polls. The leadership of both parties had united around TARP, and yet the economic tumble had occurred, unfortunately, on Republican-appointed Hank Paulson's watch. So the American people were thinking: *Why not throw Paulson and his party out of the Treasury Department—and out of the White House?* I believe that had McCain opposed the bailout—if he had made a clean break, opposing Paulson and standing for principle at that crucial moment—he could have changed the 2008 election.

Disappointed as I was by the bailout fiasco, I hoped that somehow the GOP could pull it off. My desire to pitch in and help their campaign increased. Little did I know that I would soon be getting much the same media treatment myself.

I did work as a Team McCain "surrogate speaker"; I was delighted to do my part. I had much to say about the stark choice that Americans were facing in 2008. Yet in speaking out I nearly lost my own seat.

In the House, of course, we have to run for election every two years, and so my name was on the ballot that year, too. My Democratic opponent was a former mayor and state transportation commissioner. He was an experienced politician, and 2008 was shaping up nationwide to be another good Democratic year. Yet I had worked hard for my district, and I figured I was in good shape to win reelection.

But my campaign optimism took a sharp detour just three weeks before the election, on October 17, 2008. I was at home in Minnesota when the McCain-Palin communications office called and asked if I would appear on MSNBC's *Hardball*, a program hosted in Washington by Chris Matthews. Even though I had already done three shows that day, I was pleased to help out. I said yes, even though I had never appeared on MSNBC before, nor had I ever watched the Matthews show. I was heading back to my district when I got the call; it meant I would turn around and go back to a local TV studio in St. Paul. Yet there's one thing I've learned over the years: It's always challenging to do television by "remote." That is, if you're sitting in one studio and the host is sitting in another studio, it's hard to gauge exactly what's going on. For example, if I was a guest, the host could see me, but I couldn't see the host; there's no two-way camera in such a situation—just me staring into the dark eye of a one-way camera. In addition, depending on the quality of the audio connection, there's usually a bit of delay in the sound, so when the host asks a question, I have to wait for a moment, staring into dark glass, before I can hear the question and respond to it. Television is a marvelous medium. But that evening, as I sat down in St. Paul to do the segment with Matthews a thousand miles to the east, my own campaign was about to change.

The topic that night was Barack Obama and his long associations with Bill Ayers, the unrepentant sixties radical, and the Reverend Jeremiah Wright, the black nationalist America basher. I would have preferred to be talking about policy issues, such as economics and energy, but the options for conversation belonged to the host, not to me. And in this instance, my task as a surrogate was to bolster the argument that Obama had a curious, even suspicious, relationship with both Ayers and Wright.

During the interview, I made the point that Obama did indeed have a strange and lengthy relationship with Ayers—a man who had set off bombs as a radical "Weatherman" in the sixties, who had then gone on the lam for many years, and who had finally taken up a new life as a far-left education activist in Chicago. And it was there, in the Windy City, that he had come to know, and even mentor, a young up-and-comer named Barack Obama. Yet through the decades, Ayers had clung to his radical views. In 2001 he published a book in which he took credit for setting off bombs—in the New York City police headquarters in 1970, in the U.S. Capitol in 1971, and at the Pentagon in 1972. He was quoted in the *New York Times* as saying, "I don't regret setting bombs" and "I feel we didn't do enough." And just to make his present-day politics clear, Ayers was happy to pose for *Chicago* magazine, smirking as he stood on top of a crumpled American flag. So why was Obama friends with this man?

Obama's association with Wright was even closer. Wright was a prominent pastor on Chicago's South Side, and one of his parishioners for nearly two decades was Barack Obama. In the wake of the 9/11 tragedy, Wright had declared from his pulpit, "America's chickens are coming home to roost"—that is, the United States fully deserved what it got; the quote, of course, came from Malcolm X, speaking in an equally mean spirit about the John F. Kennedy assassination. What a horrible thing to say! And then, in case he had not made himself clear, Wright shouted, "Not God bless America. God #@!*% America." Wright has made many other derogatory statements about the United States as well. How do we know? His church sold his nasty, sometimes anti-Semitic rants in books and on cassettes. And this man was Obama's mentor for two decades? Wright had officiated too at Obama's marriage to Michelle, and he had baptized their two children. In other words, as with Ayers, many Americans found it simply inconceivable that Obama didn't know about Wright's statements over the years. And for their part, all the media sycophants could do was yawn.

So to me, Wright and Ayers met the test of being dangerously anti-American. Why was Obama so linked to them? Did he agree with any part of what they were saying? Or did he just quietly accept their support? As I said to Matthews, "If we look at the collection of friends that Barack Obama has had in his life, it calls into question what Barack Obama's true beliefs and values and thoughts are." I asked again, "What it is that Barack Obama really believes?"

Obama was perfectly free to be friendly with anybody he wanted, of course, and he was equally free to believe anything he wanted. But it seemed that the media had a startling lack of curiosity about both Obama's background and the individuals he looked to as mentors.

As I said to Matthews on the show, if John McCain had entertained such sinister associations in his past, the media would have been all over them—and him. But because it was Obama, the liberal-leaning media kept quiet. All you could hear were crickets, as my kids would say. That was the Main Stream Media double standard, no news flash there.

Clearly, the MSNBC host Matthews was an unabashed Obama fan; earlier in the 2008 campaign, he had said that when he heard Obama speak, "I felt this thrill going up my leg . . . and that is an objective assessment." Matthews then moved from Obama to members of Congress. He wanted to know if I thought members of Congress were anti-American. I responded, "It isn't for me to say whether members of Congress are pro-America or anti-America." Instead, I argued, "the news media should do a penetrating exposé and take a look. I wish they would. I wish the American media would take a great look at the views of the people in Congress and find out, are they pro-America or anti-America? I think the

American people would love to see an exposé like that." Matthews knew that he had caught me in something potentially exploitable, and so he brought the interview to a quick conclusion. And that was it.

Walking out of the studio in St. Paul, I was concerned about the segment. But I didn't know how much trouble I was in until I was at home with Marcus and our son Lucas called to tell us that a firestorm was breaking. He added, the MSNBC liberal lineup was in a feeding frenzy—as was seemingly every other liberal commentator in the country. I was used to being attacked by liberals, that was nothing new, but our son was now warning me: This time it would be different. And he was right.

The rest of the liberal media went into a rage. A headline in *the Huffington Post* was typical: "MICHELE BACHMANN CHANNELS MCCARTHY: OBAMA 'VERY ANTI-AMERICAN,' CONGRESSIONAL WITCH HUNT NEEDED." That was Friday night.

A few days later, House Speaker Pelosi flew into Minneapolis, held a press conference and announced that the Democratic Congressional Campaign Committee would be allocating an additional one million dollars to my opponent's campaign. Donors from Manhattan to Santa Monica were writing big checks to the Democrat in the 6th in order to beat me! And for a while, their efforts were working: My poll numbers went from being up by thirteen points to being down by four points—a dizzying seventeen-point drop in less than a week, fueled by a tidal wave of pro-Obama support.

Supportive calls and campaign funds came in from colleagues, including Roy Blunt, Virginia Foxx, Jeb Hensarling, Steve King, Jack Kingston, and Marilyn Musgrave.

Then, just in the nick of time, the cavalry came over the hill. Conservatives in the media began sticking up for me, especially the Talk Radio Brigade. The first hero was the Great One, Mark Levin, followed by Rush Limbaugh and Sean Hannity. Then Bill Bennett, Mike Gallagher, Roger Hedgecock, Laura Ingraham, Jason Lewis, Michael Medved, and Michael Reagan. So at least I still had some airspeed at the national level.

Back in my own district, my campaign advisers said I had to do a *mea culpa* TV spot to deal with the serious damage. I agreed. But when I arrived at the house where the commercial would be taped, I looked at the script they'd written for me. It was, "I'm sorry, I was wrong, I promise I'll never do it again." I thought, I may not have used the right phrasing on

Hardball—but how could I honestly say I was wrong for a) expressing concerns about Obama's views, and b) that it's not for me to say who has pro-America or anti-America views—that's the media's job? So I went upstairs, sat in an empty bedroom, prayed, and thought about what I wanted to say. Then I pulled out a BIC pen, wrote my script, and then went back downstairs. "Here's what I want to say," I told my aides. They started to argue, but I was firm. So here are my words as they appeared on TV:

> Once again, our nation is at a crossroads, and it's a time for choosing. We could embrace government as the answer to our problems or we can choose freedom and liberty. I may not always get my words right, but I know that my heart is right. Because my heart is for you, for your children, and for the blessings of liberty to remain for our great country.

And then I gave the disclaimer, "I'm Michele Bachmann, and I approved this message." I wanted to express that I understood there was a firestorm of controversy, and yet I wanted to express my concern that Obama would take the country down the wrong path. As Ronald Reagan so famously said once, this is a time for choosing. Well, this, too, was a time for choosing. Also, I realized that the national mood had changed; it was clear by then that the Obama-Biden ticket was going to win the White House. I needed to reassure my supporters that I would remain the congresswoman with core principles in opposing the coming reign of liberalism in Washington. Minnesota voters now knew one thing for sure: If they reelected Bachmann, they would have a fighter in Washington, a determined warrior who would always stand firmly and decisively against the Obama agenda.

The year 2008, of course, turned out to be another bad year for Republicans. Not only did the McCain-Palin ticket lose, but the Republicans lost a net twenty-one seats in the House. And my friend Norm Coleman, our state's Republican U.S. senator, would ultimately lose—in a much-contested, much-recounted election, complete with fishy ballots that reportedly came from someone's car trunk—to the ultraliberal Al Franken.

Yet in my own race, I ended up winning reelection by three points. Not a landslide, to be sure, but thanks to the people of my district, I was reelected. At our election-night party at a local hotel ballroom, my friend

Barbara Harper—a key ally ever since she had gone to that counting room at Mahtomedi High School six years earlier—held up a sign proclaiming, "NICE TRY, CHRIS MATTHEWS!"

From this close-call experience I learned some valuable lessons. As I have said, in politics I wanted to be able to disagree with opponents without being disagreeable or disrespectful. Yet in the stormy years to come, many more hardballs would come—they come with the territory of politics. But the 2008 campaign gave me an opportunity to learn to do better.

My first birthday, at 210 East 9th Street, in Waterloo, Iowa.

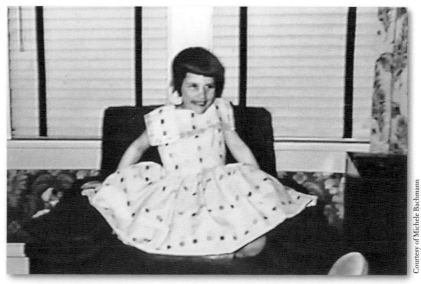

Easter 1962 in Waterloo. My republican grandmother Amble sewed my Easter dress.

At age three, I was already working the phones

I spent a summer in Anoka, Minnesota, working as a babysitter for the Lee and Karen Carlson family. Young Gretchen is now featured on *Fox & Friends*.

Me in eighth grade in the middle of my Cher period.

Marcus and me in our 1978 engagement photo.

Marcus and I married on September 10, 1978, in Montana, Wisconsin. It was 90 degrees and Marcus wore a navy velour suit!

My graduation from William & Mary Marshall-Wythe School of Law in 1988. I had just received my master of law degree. Marcus had just received his master's in counseling the week before from Regent University.

On the White House lawn right after my interview with the Treasury Department office of the chief counsel in the spring of 1988. I'm holding Harrison, with big brother, Lucas, peeking out around the sign.

A young Bachmann family photo. From left to right: Harrison, Caroline, Marcus, Lucas, me, and Elisa. Baby Sophia is in my lap.

Sophia and Caroline with me while I was part of an education reform movement working for academic excellence in Minnesota schools and while running for the Minnesota state senate seat.

My father's grave at Ft. Snelling Cemetery, Minnesota. He served honorably in the U.S. Air Force and died in 2003.

Our family in 2011.

President Bush and I stopped for frozen custard on the way to a fund-raiser for my 2006 congressioinal campaign. I'm wearing my pink suit, but—thanks to his intervention—not my over-the-top pink gloves.

During the first New Hampshire Republican presidential debate at St. Anselm College in Manchester.

MICHELE
BACHMANN
★ FOR PRESIDENT ★

On June 27, 2011, I went back to my Waterloo birthplace and, joined by my family and friends, I announced my candidacy for president of the United States.

CHAPTER TWELVE

Gangster Government

SO Barack Obama was elected to be our forty-fourth president. He didn't have my vote, but he had my prayers. So much of what he said on the campaign trail was nonsensical platitudes—just meaningless phrases, seemingly produced in a focus-group factory. But he did make one very specific pledge that I took seriously; he called for universal health care—another euphemism for the government control of, and ultimate takeover of, our health-care system.

An early warning sign came in November 2008, right after the election, when Obama announced that Timothy Geithner was his choice for Treasury secretary. As president of the Federal Reserve Bank of New York, Geithner had been a key player in the Bush-era bailouts, all of which I had opposed. I opposed them because I don't believe taxpayer money should bail out private businesses, period. I also believe government must not pick winners and losers. I don't vilify Wall Street; America needs a dynamic and thriving capital-markets system. But I also think that if Wall Street makes bad bets, well, that should be their problem, not the taxpayers'. Those bailouts had been shrouded in secrecy, and I had opposed the secrecy as well. Transparency is vital in any government operation other than one involving national security, and Geithner and the Fed had been anything but transparent. Behind the scenes, out of the public eye, they had been dishing out billions of dollars to favored banks here in the United States and around the world, and to private American companies as well.

As an aside, I can say that this problem is much bigger than just Geithner. It goes also to the leadership of Federal Reserve chairman Ben Bernanke and to the nature of the Federal Reserve system itself. Interestingly, critics of the Fed across the political spectrum have agreed on the necessity of aboveboard accountability and transparency. On the libertarian right, it's been my House colleague Ron Paul of Texas, and on the self-declared socialist left, it's been Senator Bernie Sanders of Vermont. All of us might not agree on much, but we agree on this: Let's audit the entire Federal Reserve system and pull away the unnecessary veneer of secrecy.

But in fact, the huge bailouts and shocking lack of transparency were matters of official public policy. It was government policy to allow bailouts, and it was government policy to keep the bailouts secret—so as not to upset or panic the markets, for one reason. I believed, however, that the better public policy was no bailouts at all, as well as complete and total transparency. But my immediate problem with Geithner was more than just policy; it was the problem of integrity. We soon learned that Geithner—the man who would be leading the Treasury Department—hadn't paid his taxes, the taxes he legally owed to the same U.S. Treasury. And until he was named to the high post—as a successor to the great Alexander Hamilton—he had been perfectly happy to skate away from his personal financial obligations.

So I was disturbed to read that Geithner—during all the time he had been working in Washington for the International Monetary Fund—had failed to pay $35,000 in taxes for the years 2001-2004. The IRS finally caught up with him during a 2006 audit, assessing him for almost $15,000 in additional taxes for the years 2003 and 2004. But that was only part of his shortfall; for the years 2001 and 2002, the statute of limitations had expired, and so he chose not to pay those amounts also due. In other words, Geithner had gotten away with tax evasion; he had beaten the tax man—and that was fine with him.

But then President Obama nominated him for the Treasury post. It was then, only then, that he figured he needed to fix the "optics" of his nonpayment, and he finally, belatedly, paid in full. And now this man was going to oversee the Treasury? And the IRS? A proven tax scofflaw?

Some will say, of course, that an ethics-challenged cabinet secretary is a small thing. What about a *big* thing—the 2009 "stimulus" package, which ultimately totaled $787 billion, before adding interest costs. If interest costs are included, the total cost to the taxpayers rises to well over $1 trillion. We all remember the stimulus. Its premise was simple: Because we had spent so much money and run the economy off a cliff, we should spend even *more* money. It was perfectly straightforward—and perfectly wrong. Just what would this spending do? What would it accomplish? In January 2009, the chairwoman of Obama's Council of Economic Advisers, Christina Romer, made a bold and optimistic prediction: If the near-trillion-dollar stimulus bill was enacted, she declared, unemployment would never reach as high as 8 percent. At the time, the rate was 7.8 percent. So Romer's prediction sounded soothing. But then the stimulus bill passed—and the unemployment rate went up. It went up *above* 8 percent, and it stayed that way. In fact, it went as high as 10.1 percent. As of this writing, the unemployment rate has been above 8 percent for more than two and a half years, the longest such period since the 1930s.

Meanwhile, during the debate over stimulus legislation, I gained some insight into the president's thought process. Early in 2009 Obama came to Capitol Hill to try to persuade Republicans to vote for the stimulus. He is a good speechmaker, less a persuader. Still, during our brief question-and-answer session, he shocked me with one of his responses. When asked how important winning the stimulus vote was to him—how it might rank in comparison to other priorities—he gave a revealing answer. He said he would prefer to pass his agenda and be a one-term president, rather than *not* pass his agenda and enjoy two terms. *Well, if he means it,* I told myself, *and it sure sounds as if he means it, I know he is firmly committed to his ideology.* He's a genuine left-wing true believer, and so conservatives had better fight to defend his agenda while we have the chance.

I was against the stimulus all along, of course. Or I should say, I was against Obama's kind of stimulus. I would gladly have voted for a package of incentive-improving tax cuts, along with a program of deregulation and expanded energy production. But Obama and the liberals had their own ideas. And they had the votes: In late January 2009, Speaker Pelosi rammed the stimulus package through the House. I'm proud to say that this misbegotten pile of pork didn't win the vote of a single one of my House Republican colleagues. It was one of our finest hours; we Republicans were fighting back.

Meanwhile, the whole nation was coming to learn that the "stimulus" was even more bogus than people had thought. Let me recall now this bit of stimulus folly: In March 2009 President Obama "deputized" Vice President Biden with a new responsibility: overseeing the proper spending of that $787 billion package. Obama announced, "To you, he's Mr. Vice

President, but around the White House, we call him the Sheriff, because if you're misusing taxpayer money, you'll have to answer to him." Then, evidently believing his own bravado, Obama went even further: "I'm also deputizing every single American to visit a new website called recovery.gov so you can see where your tax dollars are going and hold us accountable for results." All that sounded great—and yet when Americans went to the recovery.gov site, they discovered, to their bewilderment, that billions were listed as having been spent in places that did not in fact exist. For example, recovery.gov listed a "15th congressional district" of Arizona, giving the good news that thirty jobs had been saved or created in that district, thanks to $761,420 in federal stimulus spending. But there was just one catch: There is no 15th congressional district in Arizona. The Grand Canyon State at the time had only eight congressional districts. And, by the way, what is a "saved" job and how does the government define a "saved" job? Answer: the same way they computed that Arizona had fifteen districts. Similarly, the recovery.gov site bragged that in Connecticut's "42nd congressional district," the stimulus had created twenty-five jobs. And once again, there is no 42nd congressional district in Connecticut.

So what were the Obama people thinking? How could they make mistakes like this—and then publish them? I can think of two possible answers: First, the Obama administration was so addled by Keynesian theorizing—that is, the notion that you can spend yourself rich—that the ideologues really didn't care where the money was being spent, just as long as it was being spent. Billions, trillions, the more the merrier. As I have often said, nobody should dare tell the president what number comes after "trillion." The second possible answer is a more cynical version of the first: Those in the Obama administration didn't care where the stimulus money was going, geographically, because what really mattered was spreading money to their friends and political allies—the big-city liberal mayors, the Saul Alinsky nostalgists, the ACORN activists, the taxpayer-subsidy-dependent green-jobs propagandists, and all the other moochers, hustlers, and rent seekers demanding "a place at the table" when liberals control the White House.

So liberals raided the Treasury and spent money in early 2009, and the rest of us paid for it. They were almost giddy as they pushed money out the door by the bushel basketful. It was as though they didn't care where the money went: "Just spend more!" was the motto. This was more than foolish; it was darn near criminal. Moreover, one thing soon became apparent: Obama and the political types surrounding him had no idea how real jobs were actually created. Articles appeared in the media noting the lack of private-sector experience in the president's cabinet—and this was one time when I believed exactly what I was reading. And so, of course, the stimulus was a flop.

The reality of job creation is simple: It comes from hardworking human action, not from borrowing and printing money. The employer, or prospective employer, is convinced that it's better to use his or her capital to hire someone to do something than simply to leave that capital in the bank. The act of hiring is a matter of faith—faith in possibilities, faith in the future. Indeed, that's how Marcus and I started our business; we believed that if we opened our doors and hired people, clients would come, and we'd be able to cover our fixed costs, pay our employees, and, we hoped, even keep a little bit for ourselves. That's the profit motive, and it's a good thing.

Yet when regulators, litigators, and tax collectors come along, employers often end up *not* being employers after all. They are hamstrung, tied up, red taped, restricted, legislated against—and thus no longer able to hire people and keep the economy going. And once a business fears the hydra-headed modern American government, it tends *not* to stay in business. Over the past three years, hundreds of employers, big and small, have told me that it's fear of the government—specifically, fear of the Obama administration—that has killed millions of potential jobs. Or as Steve Wynn, the famous casino owner in Las Vegas, said not long ago, the Obama administration is "the greatest wet blanket to business, and progress, and job creation in my lifetime."

But of course, jobs were being created in Washington—at least for limousine drivers. According to a 2011 report from the Center for Public Integrity, the number of limousines owned by the federal government rose by 73 percent during the first two years of President Obama's administration. What an amazing statistic! Just think: All those well-kept bureaucrats in their long black cars! Yet despite the increase in nicely uniformed chauffeurs, it was hardly an example of the administration looking out for the little guy. It was, rather, a symbol of Beltway arrogance, economic incompetence, and, of course, the self-indulgence of the ruling class.

And by the way, the same holds true for federal salaries. According to *USA Today*, in December 2007 precisely one employee at the Department of Transportation earned a salary of $170,000 or more. Eighteen months later, 1,690 employees enjoyed salaries above $170,000. In other words, good times at the DOT. It's possible to come up with diverging explanations for these huge increases in federal perks and pay. But it's impossible to deny that the gap between how Washington thinks and acts and how the rest of the country thinks and acts is growing wider.

Moreover, we can't say that all these excesses were the fault only of liberal Democrats; the imperializing of the capital city has often been bipartisan. All the clichés about Washington, D.C., readily apply to the bright young things in both parties: They come to Washington to do good, and they end up doing pretty well for themselves. Still, it was clear that the Obama administration all by itself was adding new layers of venality and corruption.

Back to cars. In the spring of 2009 the Obama administration seized control of the Chrysler bankruptcy, putting into this private company the sum of $4.5 billion of our money. Actually, we should note, 40 percent of the money was borrowed, so we taxpayers paid to borrow the money, only to "lend" it to private companies! If they were such a good credit risk or a worthy investment, why didn't they get their own loans? Why wouldn't the United Auto Workers lend them the money?

In the final settlement, the White House decreed that Chrysler bondholders, those holding secured debt—that is, those with the first legal claim on Chrysler assets—would receive only thirty-three cents on the dollar, while United Auto Workers retirees, holding unsecured debt, would receive fifty cents on the dollar. Yet it's a fact: Under the law, secured creditors are entitled to one hundred cents on the dollar, if the money is there; only then, if there is any money left, are the unsecured creditors entitled to anything.

In other words, the politically connected UAW muscled its way to the front of the payout line, barging ahead of the less well-connected bondholders. Bankruptcy, of course, is always a wrenching and painful procedure, but that's never an argument for breaking the rules of law. We might note that these shunted-aside bondholders included not only individual retirees but also the pension funds that are relied on by average Americans. So to all the financial victims whose private property interests were denied and then given to others, the Obama administration was saying, in effect, "That's it. Tough luck. What are you going to do about it?"

Am I putting words in the mouth of the Obama administration? Not at all. Indeed, the truth about the administration's behavior is worse than that: The administration not only stiffed legitimate creditors but also threatened them if they complained. Here's what bankruptcy lawyer Tom Lauria, representing the secured creditors, told a Detroit radio station at the time: "One of my clients was directly threatened by the White House and in essence compelled to withdraw its opposition to the deal under threat that the full force of the White House press corps would destroy its reputation if it continued to fight." Those words of threat and intimidation were recorded by Michael Barone in the pages of the *Washington Examiner*. In May 2009 Michael wrote: "We have just seen an episode of Gangster Government." He added: "It is likely to be a continuing series." And Michael was right. The estimate of the total cost of all the auto bailouts—covering General Motors as well as Chrysler—has since risen to $14.3 billion. Again, that's our tax money they're playing with. The rule of law was steamrolled. If contracting parties can't rely on the rule of law and the sanctity of contracts, then smart people will prefer to do business where the terms of their contracts *will* be recognized and upheld—in other words, not in America.

Yet $14.3 billion is peanuts compared with the cost of bailing out Fannie Mae and Freddie Mac. In June 2011 the Congressional Budget Office estimated that the total cost of those subprime-mortgage-lender bailouts came to $317 billion. As I mentioned earlier, the problem of Fannie and Freddie goes way back, back to the days when Uncle Sam was convinced that it was a good idea to pump air into the housing bubble. And both parties were complicit in a further devious practice: paying private-sector-level salaries and private-sector-level lobbying fees to people working on behalf of what were ultimately public-sector institutions holding a claim on the public treasury. You've heard the phrase "private gains, public losses"? Well, that was the story of Fannie and Freddie. If their employees made money, they got to keep it. If they lost money, they stuck the federal government with the bill. It was as simple as that. What private business could compete with a government-backed competitor? They couldn't. And soon, Fannie and Freddie effectively controlled the secondary lending market for home mortgages in the United States.

As a member of the Oversight Subcommittee of the Financial Services Committee, I saw firsthand all the shenanigans as they were happening, and I sounded the alarm. In hearings I raised my voice, demanding more testimony, more documents, more information. And yet the establishment culture of Washington resisted any change in its cushy business as usual; Committee chairman Democrat Barney Frank, for instance, bullied and blustered committee members on both sides of the aisle, telling all of us that we didn't know what we were talking about, that everything was fine. In other words, he told us to shut up so that his friends and allies at Fannie and Freddie could continue to rake in millions during this ongoing scam.

Little did we know at the time that Frank had already conducted his own personal business as usual. Years earlier, he had pressured Fannie Mae into hiring his romantic partner, a man who would go on to receive a nice, comfortable salary. *New York Times* reporter Gretchen Morgenson, coauthor of a highly regarded 2011 book about Fannie, *Reckless Endangerment: How Outsized Ambition, Greed, and Corruption Led to Economic Armageddon,* recalled these goings-on in a recent interview; she said that in 1991 Frank "actually called up the company and asked them to hire his companion." She added, "Of course the company was happy to provide a job for his companion and rolled out the red carpet in a series of interviews with a variety of executives, and it ultimately did hire the man." The obvious question: What did Fannie get in return for this hire? The answer: It got Frank's powerful help in repelling scrutiny of the organization's dubious activities. According to Morgenson, Frank was "very aggressive" when the director of the Congressional Budget Office looked into Fannie's suspicious dealings—that is, when the CBO director "was trying to call for increased capital requirements and to call for a focus on safety and soundness at Fannie Mae." So what happened to the director? What happened, as Morgenson describes, was that "Frank really took him apart in testimony." In other words, Frank did Fannie a favor in return for the favor that Fannie had previously done for Frank. Fannie and Frank: not so perfect together. This incident occurred well before Obama came to Washington, and yet it speaks to the culture of Fannie and Freddie—and to the ongoing reality of "gangster government."

For his part, Obama came to fit right in with the D.C. culture. Perhaps the corrupt ways of Washington reminded him fondly of Chicago's legendarily corrupt ways—you know, Obama's once good friend Tony Rezko, and all the rest. It was obvious that Obama wasn't fighting for real change or reform; he was simply going along with what the liberals in his administration—and the liberals in Congress—wanted him to do. The president seemed happiest making speeches about mythical economics, holding fund-raisers, hobnobbing with Hollywood celebrities, and hanging out at Martha's Vineyard.

Yet in Washington, whenever there's a problem, there's always a way, it seems, for politicians to make it worse. And that's how America got saddled with the Dodd-Frank financial "reform" bill, engineered by Frank and then-senator Chris Dodd of Connecticut. The latter, incidentally, chose not to seek reelection after public revelations that he had received a discounted mortgage from one of the banks he was supposed to be regulating. Meanwhile, the two of them, Dodd and Frank, teamed up in 2010 to enact the not-so-modestly titled "Dodd-Frank Wall Street Reform and Consumer Protection Act." I might add that the "Dodd-Frank" at the beginning isn't just shorthand; those are the first two words in the formal name of Public Law 111-203.

Obama happily signed the bill into law on July 21, 2010, saying, "For the last year, Chairmen Barney Frank and Chris Dodd have worked day and night . . . to bring about this reform. And I am profoundly grateful to them." Yet what, exactly, was Obama grateful for? What did this legislation actually do?

The purpose of the legislation, as stated in the preamble, is "to promote the financial stability of the United States by improving accountability and transparency in the financial system, to end 'too big to fail,' to protect the American taxpayer by ending bailouts, to protect consumers from abusive financial services practices, and for other purposes." One rule of thumb that works pretty well is this: Whatever the stated name of a bill is—especially if it's authored by a liberal—the *real* purpose is almost always the exact opposite of the stated purpose. But all that fancy wording was, in reality, simply spin-doctored happy speak—the financial equivalent of the failed Goals 2000. Or, to use George Orwell's term for the deliberate inversion of truth, an update of Newspeak.

The nearly two thousand pages of Dodd-Frank proved to be just another mosh pit for lobbyists, allowing them to jump around from loophole to bailout to special carve-out. Indeed, Dodd-Frank represents yet another explosive expansion of the regulatory state that will continue to cost the U.S. economy trillions, as banks try to cope with new layers of uncertainty, confusion, costs, and court cases. As I have noted, hiring and job creation are functions of business confidence—faith in the future. Yet Dodd-Frank is just the opposite; it's an old-style haunted house of arbitrary bureaucratic horror. Included among its provisions is a dubious legal hybrid, the Bureau of Consumer Financial Protection, the brainchild of liberal activist Elizabeth Warren. The idea of a "proconsumer" federal regulatory body, of course, has been a goal of nanny-state Naderites for decades; now, finally, they have their prize. Yet believe it or not, the new bureau is to reside at the Federal Reserve; in other words, an allegedly protransparency outfit will be nestled amid the shadows and fog of the Fed. Isn't that's special? Who says Washington politicos don't have a sense of humor?

C. Boyden Gray, former counsel to Vice President and then President George H. W. Bush and an expert in regulatory matters, makes a further critique; he argues that Dodd-Frank is unconstitutional. As he wrote in 2010, the bill creates "a structure of almost unlimited, unreviewable and sometimes secret bureaucratic discretion, with no constraints on concentration—a breakdown of the separation of powers, which were created to guard against the exercise of arbitrary authority." Yes, Boyden is right: Dodd-Frank is unconstitutional, and if Congress refuses to repeal the bill, it should be struck down by the courts.

In June 2011, Thomas Boyle, vice-chairman of State Bank of Countryside, in Countryside, Illinois, shared too his grave concerns about Dodd-Frank, testifying before the House Small Business Committee:

> I am deeply concerned that this [Dodd-Frank] model will collapse under the massive weight of new rules and regulations. The vast majority of banks never made an exotic mortgage loan or took on excessive risks. They had nothing to do with the events that led to the financial crisis and are as much victims of the devastation as the rest of the economy. We are the survivors of the problems, yet we are the ones that pay the price for the mess that others created. Banks are working every day to make credit and financial services available. Those efforts, however, are made more difficult by regulatory costs and second-guessing by bank examiners. Combined with hundreds of new regulations expected from the Dodd-Frank Act, these pressures are slowly but surely strangling traditional community banks, handicapping our ability to meet the credit needs of our communities.

In other words, as Dodd-Frank plays out in real-world America, it will wrap red tape around banks that had nothing to do with the crisis in the first place. It will throttle credit to small businesses; it will keep unemployment high. That's the bad news. Meanwhile, the legislation will make Beltway lobbyists rich. But that's not good news. That's not good news at all.

In my own House committee, I opposed Dodd-Frank as it made its way through the committee. I opposed it once more as it went through the House as a whole; I voted against its final passage, and I immediately introduced a bill to repeal Dodd-Frank.

Okay, now let's turn to the Obama environmental policy. Here we see, as always, the usual green liberalism. But underneath it all, we see something more—corruption through government connections. As an example, I'll repeat what everyone knows: The Obama administration has declared war on carbon dioxide. Its "experts" say we need to block CO_2 in order to save the penguins. I might note, of course, that CO_2 is what makes plants grow, so surely it can't be all bad. Moreover, the whole science of "climate change" is ultimately unknown, scarcely even knowable—as well as riddled with its own academic corruption, as in the "climate-gate" fiasco. And so it would be supremely foolish to legislate caps on carbon. Let's ask ourselves this question: If the problem is too much carbon, then why is the answer taxing ourselves to give more money to the givernment?

Yet in 2009, as the economy worsened, the Obama administration chose to push its "cap-and-trade" plan. It was touted as a way to save penguins and polar bears, but what it really would have done, if put in place and enforced, is create a new Enron-like carbon-speculation scheme, to the delight of insider wheeler-dealers. Like all bubbles puffed up by the government, the system would have blown up eventually, as did Enron, but the smartest sharpies in the room would have taken out their gains first; too much potential exists for corrupt market manipulation—and that's why they loved the whole scheme. Cap-and-trade managed to pass the Nancy Pelosi House—without my vote, of course—but it was so awful that even the Harry Reid Senate wouldn't vote for it.

So what happened then? What did the Obama green bureaucrats do when Congress wouldn't do as they wished? They went ahead and tried to regulate carbon emissions anyway, blithely ignoring Congress's constitutional prerogative. That's why the Environmental Protection Agency should be renamed the Job Killing Agency of America.

So this is the Obama pattern. It's a pattern of gangster government. And it has spread widely, its malefic stain infiltrating the entire federal establishment. It follows four basic rules, I might add.

First: "Never let a crisis go to waste." Such are the famous words of Obama's first White House chief of staff, Rahm Emanuel. What they mean is that leaders should intimidate the populace so as to achieve political ends. That is, they should stoke a sense of crisis, so that the panicked population will gratefully bow down to Washington bureaucrats, hailing its beneficent rescuers. And often the tactic works; examples include the "stimulus," the auto bailout, Obamacare, and Dodd-Frank. That's also what Obama managed to accomplish in the summer of 2011, when, in the midst of the showdown with Congress over the debt ceiling, he struck fear into the hearts of senior citizens: *Well, you know,* he told them, *I'm not sure that people will get their Social Security checks.* That created a real scare. It was pure political gangsterism, of course.

Second: Make legislation so complicated that ordinary Americans can't understand it. That's why we see all these multithousand-page bills, unintelligible in their bureaucratic jargon—the bureaucrats and lobbyists know exactly what they are doing when they write them all in "bureauglyphics." And here's the corollary: When they fail in their understanding, they'll give up and submit to the state. Or those who are more resourceful will hire a lobbyist to explain it to them; most likely, of course, the lobbyist will be part of the same D.C. gang, so even more money will stay in "the family." That's the way that the IRS has always operated, and it works— I've seen it firsthand. And the same money-milking model extends to the rest of the federal leviathan. The root of all this is the level of disrespect that the administration displays toward the American people. When bills are indecipherable, when money and terms are hidden in subsequent rules and regulations, such actions trample on the consent of the governed. That is to say, on us! How can we consent to the laws that we live under if the president and other top leaders willfully hide their meaning from us?

Third: Assume that laws are only for "little people," not for Beltway types. As we have seen, Treasury Secretary Geithner was happily playing that double game. By the way, we can add: The fun of being an Obama "czar" is that they can do whatever they want.

Fourth: Even when the country and Congress say no, go ahead and do it anyway. Yes, damn the Constitution, full speed ahead. That rule has worked consistently for the EPA, and someday, if the greens get their wish, we'll be reduced to a third world lifestyle.

From border security to homeland security to national security we can see the administration's gangster tactics. All I can say is that the founders gave us a glorious Constitution, replete with careful checks and balances, and they gave it to us for good and sensible reasons. In Federalist No. 51, James Madison outlined one particular of the Constitution, the separation of governmental powers, protecting us against undue concentration of power in any one branch:

> The great security against a gradual concentration of the several powers in the same department, consists in giving to those who administer each department the necessary constitutional means and personal motives to resist encroachments of the others.

In other words, each federal branch checks the power of the other two federal branches. That's the only way to preserve our constitutional freedoms, to limit the arbitrary and abusive power of Big Government. Thus each generation, in turn, must remain ever vigilant.

The stakes today are high, because the Obama administration has launched a wide-ranging assault on our constitutional system. Yet throughout our history, the stakes have often been high. As a very young Abraham Lincoln said in 1838, speaking to the Lyceum in Springfield, Illinois: "At what point then is the approach of danger to be expected? I answer, if it ever reach us, it must spring up amongst us. It cannot come from abroad. If destruction be our lot, we must ourselves be its author and finisher."

The future sixteenth president was right. Although I pray every day for the safety of our great nation—and I am sure many Americans do the same—I share Lincoln's concern that the destruction of America is most likely to come from within.

And so I oppose gangster government and vigorously fought it on the House floor.

CHAPTER THIRTEEN

Obamacare

PERHAPS no other Obama law is more emblematic of big government than Obamacare. Although as we shall see, big government also has gangsterish characteristics.

Politicians such as the late Ted Kennedy, and, more recently, Bill and Hillary Clinton, have been in favor of national health insurance for decades, and Obama had talked constantly about universal health-care "reform" during his presidential campaign. Yet even so, once he was inaugurated in 2009, I wondered which part of his agenda the president would launch first—cap and trade or health care? After all, with the economy still declining, it didn't make a lot of sense to enact a new entitlement program that would cause the economy to decline even further.

In addition, I wondered if congressional Democrats really had their hearts in the idea of national health insurance. Back during the first years of the Clinton administration, Democrats had pushed hard for "Hillarycare" and, for their trouble, had been punished by voters; they lost their majority in both houses of Congress in the 1994 midterms. So now, a decade and a half later, was "Obamacare" really going to be a better bet for them? If the White House had to worry about a weak economy—and if congressional Democrats had to worry about losing their majority—maybe they would look to political self-preservation and so lean against pushing for a giant expansion of government. Just when baby boomers were joining the ranks of Social Security and Medicare recipients, pushing both of those programs toward an insolvency horizon, now came dedicated members of Team Obama, convinced that their win gave them the right to implement a giant left turn for America. And so they rejected any such sensible thinking. Fired by ideological fervor, they went doggedly, dog-matically ahead with their plans.

So in full array, Obama, Pelosi, and Reid led the Democratic major-ities in both chambers to storm up health-care hill, ready to fight for a bill that few, if any, of them would read before they voted for it. And once again the country was reminded that the Obama-era Democrats were firmly wedded to their liberal-left ideology—and, as a new addition, to Chicago-style politicking as well. As for the nonworkable-in-the-real-world ivory-tower ideology, the intelligentsia seemed genuinely convinced that the American people needed the government's help in health care from cradle to grave; that was their dominant impulse—finally to build socialized medicine, the crown jewel of socialism, here in America. Yet at the same time, the Obama/Pelosi/Reid leadership did not hesitate to use Chicago "boss"-style politics. That is, if Americans could be enrolled in a big new giveaway program, they would soon be hooked; having then grown depen-dent on the government, they would vote forever to maintain their right to "free health care." And so for both ideological and political reasons, the leadership of the Democratic Party united around one overarching idea: Even in the middle of a recession, America needed higher taxes, more regulation, and increased bureaucratic control. And it was all so we could save money! President Obama insisted that we had to *hurry, hurry, hurry* and pass it—the quicker we did, the more money we would save! Why, the average household would save twenty-five hundred dollars a year in health-care premiums, he insisted. Hurry! Hurry! Hurry! What was the rush? The liberals were afraid of exactly what happened: People would start reading the bill and see what was in it. And then the people would demand a full stop, rejecting the bill.

Obamacare, as it emerged in 2009, was a throwback to the sort of central-planning schemes that Friedrich Hayek, Ludwig von Mises, and Milton Friedman had long warned against. Experts were to decide everything—aided, of course, by lobbyists and liberal pressure groups. So Obamacare would seek to reshape the insurance market, mandating that insurance policies cover an agenda full of politically correct possibilities—this, that, and everything else. It sounds nice to think that health insurance is "comprehensive," but as is often said, economics is about the allocation of scarce resources—and money is always scarce. The reality is that if the government mandates something, then somebody—maybe you—has to pay for the whole thing. And even if you prefer to buy pieces of health insurance, strictly on an as-needed basis, the government can order you to buy the whole bundle. That is, instead of ordering *à la carte*, you have to buy the *prix fixe*—as determined by the government.

So the costs of insurance mandates can add up quickly. In a 2008 study, the Council for Affordable Health Insurance counted some two thousand mandates already required across the various fifty states, including coverage for acupuncture, marriage counseling, athletic training, social work, and massage therapy; these are mandates that individual states require of every private health-insurance policy. Meanwhile, Dr. Scott Gottlieb, a health-care expert at the American Enterprise Institute, has crunched the data and found that the nationwide cost of these state mandates can run as high as 50 percent of the cost of a policy, up to four thousand dollars in high-mandate New Jersey. Merrill Matthews, of the Institute for Policy Innovation, observes, "You could lease a Ferrari for the price you're paying for your health insurance in New Jersey." So is that what we need? Do we need Ferrari coverage—at Ferrari prices? Of course not. Ferrari pricing is one reason why so many Americans have chosen, in past years, to go without any coverage at all. As with any product, if the price goes up, fewer people buy it.

But really, no health insurance at all? And more uninsured Americans? Doesn't that go against the whole point of national health insurance? Of course it does. So the medicine socializers have an answer: Mandate that each American buy health insurance; make it an absolute requirement. And if you don't buy it, the health police (also known as the IRS) will take your money, maybe even throw you in jail. But what if you don't have the money to buy it? No problem at all, says the government—we'll give you the money, because everyone knows that the government has money to give away.

But what if you simply don't *wish* to have health insurance? What if, for whatever reason, you simply prefer to spend your money on something else? Well, here's where the nice-guy government "giving" you everything morphs into the tough-guy government telling you what to do. It's called the "individual mandate." The government simply decrees that everyone must have government-approved health insurance, simply because you are a citizen of the USA. Does that sound like an infringement on personal freedom? Indeed, I would say it's an *unconstitutional* infringement on personal freedom—as in, the government can't do it. So here's where I differed not only with Barack Obama, but also with state laws that have mandated the purchase of health insurance as a condition of state citizenship. David Axelrod, President Obama's chief political strategist, pointed to the 2006 Massachusetts requirement for the purchase of health insurance as a template for Obamacare. The Massachusetts requirement has left the people of the Bay State with the highest health-care premiums in the country; Massachusetts law also mandates funding of abortions, as does, of course, Obamacare.

Obamacare, as well as the failed trillion-dollar stimulus, will be central to the 2012 presidential election. Then we will see the proponents of bureaucratic control lined up on one side and the proponents of personal freedom lined up on the other side.

If Republicans wish to take advantage of the opportunity to offer a sharp contrast to Obama, the GOP presidential nominee must not only be committed to Obamacare's full repeal; in addition, the nominee will have to lead the repeal fight. Waiting in the White House for Congress to pass the full repeal through the House and Senate will not get the job done. Too many special interests are invested in Obamacare; so with a passive presidential effort, socialized medicine that is both expensive and deficient will prevail. Defeat of Obamacare will take active presidential heavy lifting—as well as conservative majorities in both chambers. I also underscore that we will only have one shot in 2012 to get this job done, because after that, Obamacare will have metastasized into state and local government such that we'll likely never get rid of it.

The insurance mandate speaks to a profound violation of every American's constitutional rights as well as to a basic misreading of the American people, misinterpreting what Americans really hope for in their lives. For one thing, they desire the opportunity for liberty and have a desire for greater personal choice, and they know that health-care decisions are no exception. Furthermore, Americans instinctively understand that the enduring issue in health care is health itself, not health insurance. It's *health* that counts. Let me explain.

In the twenty-first century, freedom-loving Americans are not looking for bureaucratic solutions—that is, solutions or pseudosolutions lingering from the midtwentieth century. In the era of the Internet and the iPhone, we have access to more information than ever before; we are able to make more decisions on our own, and we are taking on more personal responsibility. It's often said that information wants to be free; well, the corollary is that information itself is freeing—information frees all of us. For instance, I know that if I can go to WebMD for a solid answer to a medical question, I am far less dependent on any expert or authority. I revere the medical profession, but even the most saintly doctor doesn't necessarily want to hear from a patient at 2:00 A.M. with a quick question. Happily, the Internet is always awake.

So back in 2009, when the new administration was talking its bait-and-switch version of health-care "reform," I understood that the health care that America really needed was a serious injection of market forces, followed by a booster shot of empowered freedom. We needed to be knowledgeable and active consumers surveying an open marketplace. In that marketplace we would see health-care providers and health insurers of all kinds coming to us, competing for our interest—and our dollars. The consumer would be sovereign. Could the government help in some cases? Could the government help the poor, or those who might not be able to make clearheaded decisions? The government is already purchasing the bulk of health care in the country, and yet often when it comes to government, it's a struggle to distinguish between a helping hand and a heavy hand. And let's always remember where the government is getting its money—from us.

I also understood that changes to our $2.5 trillion health system should not impose a further burden, weighing down local hospitals, for example, with more uncompensated care; that is, people who receive treatment, but never pay. A system this complex is only made more so, to the point of illegibility, by another tranche of bureaucracy, laying on still more red tape. I recalled the famous quote from the great eighteenth-century conservative Edmund Burke: "The nature of man is intricate; the objects of society are of the greatest possible complexity; and therefore no simple disposition of direction of power can be suitable either to man's nature or to the quality of his affairs." A little official humility, in other words, is in order. And if the issue is reforming American health care, a careful, cautious transition is needed. We should have the governmental equivalent of the Hippocratic Oath: "First, do no harm." But Obama clearly did harm to America's current Medicare recipients when he chose to take over $500 billion away from Medicare just at the moment when more Americans are entering into the program. Undoubtedly we can find better ways to deliver quality health care to America's seniors, but if taking $500 billion away from them is Obama's first prescription, I don't think seniors will be eager to hear what his second prescription might be.

Then there's the issue of health itself. In Washington, D.C., terminology, discussions of "health care" inevitably turn into discussions of "health-care *finance*." That is, the emphasis is put on health insurance, health subsidies, and payment schemes. Yet with a moment's reflection, we can see that health-care finance is not the same as health itself. For one thing, health-care finance does not automatically give access to cures and healing; cures and healing are not always available to us. For instance, if you go to the doctor with a broken arm, the doctor can fix it, but if you go to the doctor with, say, Alzheimer's disease, he or she can give you little hope—and certainly no cure. Financing schemes can't fix that ailment; they are financial, not medical. Cures are achieved not by health insurance but by diligent medical researchers working in the highest realms of scientific endeavor.

Universal coverage, in other words, no matter how complete—no matter how many mandates are imposed—won't do what only medical science can do. Today, nearly six million Americans suffer from Alzheimer's, at an annual cost, according to the Alzheimer's Association, of $172 billion a year. And as our population ages, those numbers will only increase exponentially; the number of Alzheimer's victims is projected to quadruple in the next forty years, and the cumulative cost of caring for those patients is expected to reach $20 trillion by 2050. That's a huge moral and psychic burden on all of us, not to mention a colossal expense. And yet if people are sick and need help, we will, of course, give them that help. That's who we are as Americans. No doubt the free market and the private sector, properly monitored, could provide better care at lower cost than a bureaucracy—but the fact remains that some medical conditions, such as dementia, are inherently costly.

In other words, all the brave Obama talk about "bending the curve" on health-care costs is bending the curve *up,* not down. Adding coverage for thirty million to fifty million more Americans will mean either higher costs or fewer services. So the ones already paying now will pay more and get less. And those paying nothing will still likely pay nothing in the future. The one certainty is that Obamacare will move us toward a darkening twilight of rationed delivery and fewer medical breakthroughs. And so the free market that gave us the finest health care in the world will be just a dwindling memory.

From the beginning, it was obvious that if Obama managed to get his legislation through Congress, he still wasn't going to make health care any cheaper. Instead, as Newt Gingrich said, all that Obama was going to do was put a bureaucrat between you and your doctor. As always, the real driver of health costs is illness itself. Illness is what costs money, and so the most effective way to reduce health costs is to make illness cheaper. And illness can be made cheaper only by prevention and cure.

An example of how illness has been made cheaper in recent years can be found in the category of heart disease. Over the last five decades, heart disease has become far less deadly and far less costly than it once was; these days, patients are avoiding costly heart surgery by receiving outpatient angioplasties and stents or by taking drugs called statins. Or even by simply taking over-the-counter aspirin; as our knowledge of heart disease has improved, we have been able to identify inexpensive chemicals that can save a trip to the hospital—or save a life. Heart disease is still a huge killer, of course, but the advance of medical science has greatly improved heart-disease survivability, not only lowering costs but also, as an extra benefit, increasing the nation's workforce output. And as always, this progress is the result of scientists making discoveries, not bureaucrats issuing rules.

The president has made another error of incalculable proportions by adding a layer of bureaucracy on top of the health-care system. Bureaucracy is very expensive and not very responsive; nobody asked to have more hassles in health care. If we thought fighting with private insurance companies over payment for services was a pain, wait until Big Brother becomes your insurance company—and there's no right of appeal. Under bureaucratic control, the only way to lower costs is by rationing—that is, by imposing arbitrary limits on medical care. And who wants that? Examples of rationing would be limiting the prescription of costly drugs or limiting the use of surgery or other costly treatments. And such practices are, of course, exactly what Obamacare envisions; among other control-freak committees, the legislation has created an Independent Payment Advisory Board made up of fifteen political appointees who, beginning in 2015, will have the fiat power to adjust Medicare expenditures. This is the sort of elite mechanism that imposes increasingly severe systemwide rationing, as in, say, the United Kingdom, where documented cases abound not only of treatment cutoffs but also of assisted suicide and euthanasia. That's one nation's way to save money. Indeed, it's heartless, but true: Rationing treatment and promoting suicide of the gravely ill—or the merely inconveniently ill—would lower government's costs at the expense, of course, of our lives and well-being. Most Americans, of course, fully agree that all such schemes are repugnant and unthinkable. But the chilling truth is that Obamacare is the law of the land today; unless we elect a new president with a clear mandate, and a fierce commitment, to seeing its full repeal. Otherwise, government rationing will become the new normal for all of us.

As a kid growing up in Waterloo, I remember adults talking with reverence and awe about Dr. Jonas Salk, the great scientist who had developed the polio vaccine in 1955. His vaccine not only saved lives but also changed the medical climate of American society, offering relief and freedom from fear—and it also saved money. Indeed, it saved a lot of money. According to one study I read, in the early fifties, before anyone knew about the vaccine, economists had estimated that if present polio trends continued, the United States would be spending one hundred billion dollars a year on treating the disease and its painful, often permanent, aftermath conditions. A large part of that money would be spent on wheelchairs, iron lungs, and all the equipment necessitated by the ravages of the disease. Of course, one hundred billion dollars back then, adjusted for inflation, would be an enormous sum today. But instead, how much money are we spending today on polio? How much are we spending today on his once-dreaded scourge of playgrounds and swimming pools? Virtually nothing. The scourge is long gone, at least in the United States. That's because the vaccine made the disease disappear.

So I thought to myself, *Surely that's a better way to "bend the curve" on health-care costs—to tackle certain costly diseases head-on.* And I knew we didn't need a giant government program; Salk developed the polio vaccine while working for the March of Dimes, a private charity. What we needed, I realized, was leadership—leadership that would mobilize private charity and philanthropy, energizing a new commitment to cures. And that leadership would carry out other tasks as well; not only would it streamline various regulatory procedures, including those of the Food and Drug Administration, but it would also, equally important, push back the power of the trial lawyers. Trial lawyers? How are they relevant here? Well, it's trial lawyers who regularly take billions of dollars out of the medical sector, who often engineer grotesque, out-of-proportion settlements in dubious medical lawsuits. Real victims, of course, should be compensated for their real losses, although only for their actual losses; the John Edwards–type tort lawyers should be barred from extracting outrageous sums from juries that don't necessarily correlate damage awards with either hikes in health-care costs or declines in medical innovation. If we want more medical cures, if we want researchers and scientists to pursue breakthroughs in cures and healing, we must shield these healers and their efforts from excessive damages that enrich the tort bar and scare away innovation.

With the right kind of leadership, we might make real progress toward better treatments and cures. That could be a game changer in health care. To return to the Alzheimer's example: If we could push back the onset of the disease by even a few years, we could dramatically reduce the costs of maintenance and care. If we can be healthier, if we can work longer, and if we can retire later, the nation thereby saves vast sums of entitlement money.

Regarding another aspect of medical progress: the invention of medical devices that can save and improve lives. As it happens, my home state boasts a number of high-tech medical device companies, including Medtronic, Boston Scientific, and St. Jude Medical. Earl Bakken, cofounder of Medtronic, is a Minnesota version of Thomas Edison; in 1957, working in his garage, Earl invented that breakthrough medical device, the heart pacemaker. As a result of his vision and the entrepreneurship he shared with his cofounder, Palmer Hermundslie, Earl is responsible for saving or prolonging countless lives. We Minnesotans are truly proud of him. In addition, his invention led to the creation of new jobs as well as to a valuable export industry. And if Medtronic shareholders made money, that helps the creation of the next generation of medical devices. Enticing another generation of inventors and investors into the field of improving our health—that's Adam Smith's "invisible hand" in action: making money, saving lives.

Better health, more wealth—isn't that what we want? Yet strangely, the Obama administration hasn't seemed to care. In fact, the administration has actually seemed hostile to this wondrous vista of medical and economic opportunity. As part of the Obamacare plan, for instance—as part of an assurance to the public that the plan "would be fully paid for"—the White House sought to impose a forty-billion-dollar tax, over ten years, on medical equipment makers. The last thing we should seek are extra taxes on medical field Thomas Edisons! Minnesota's two liberal Democratic senators, Amy Klobuchar and Al Franken, sought to reduce that new tax to "only" twenty billion dollars, and they then happily voted for it—that is, voted for a huge tax imposed on some of their most creative and productive constituents. Klobuchar and Franken even claimed credit for "cutting" the tax by twenty billion dollars. That's Washington for you: Reducing a giant tax increase to a half-giant tax increase is seen as doing your constituents a favor. We have already seen, in fact, multiple layoffs across the medical device sector and new manufacturing ventures going offshore. Causing a medical recession within a recession is no laughing matter.

For his part, Obama didn't seem to notice. He just read his teleprompter speeches, sublimely content to speak at, not to, his audiences; even his talks in front of schoolchildren required what wits have since dubbed TOTUS—the teleprompter of the United States. Meanwhile, in Capitol Hill back rooms, Speaker Pelosi and her Democratic majority struggled to assemble their bill, a legislative leviathan over two thousand pages long—not including, of course, the many thousands of extra pages of regulations, which will never truly finish being written, required to "implement" the bill. According to one estimate, Obamacare would create 159 new boards and commissions, and the wording of the bill included some seven hundred repetitions of the phrase "the Secretary shall." That's the secretary of health and human services, thus effectively promoted to "czar" status.

As with the "stimulus," as with cap-and-trade, as with Dodd-Frank, we have learned that there's a cynical good reason why politicians favor these behemoth bills: They can hide the goodies inside bigger governmental bureaucracies, hoping that no one will notice. And yet the resulting paper piles are so complex that even the politicians lose track; as Pelosi once said of Obamacare, "We have to pass the bill so that you can find out what is in it."

Even the government says that Obamacare would cost a trillion dollars over ten years—and you know what that means in terms of cost overruns. And at the same time, the legislation, according to a Congressional Budget Office estimate, would result in the loss of 800,000 jobs? And that, according to one study, Obamacare could cost 114 million Americans their private health insurance?

None of us should be shocked, of course; the government has a dreary history of overpromising, and underdelivering. And so Obamacare, too, will be seen as that sort of failure; a bill that was touted as saving money as well as expanding health insurance is actually going to shrink insurance. And here are two reasons why:

First of all, the Left's long-standing goal is not just government supervision of the insurance market, including all those mandates. Genuine lefty ideologues don't want to *regulate* the private medical sector; they want to *eliminate* the private medical sector. That's the definition of the so-called single-payer system: The government is the single payer. And, of course, the government is the big taxer too, in order to pay for it all. So over time, all of us—except for those able to buy their way out—are swallowed into the government maw. That's "social justice," George Soros style. All Americans will have something the government will call "health insurance," of course, in the sense that they have a piece of paper telling them that they are "insured." And so as they wait in line for an indeterminate amount of time to see a doctor, they can comfort themselves with the thought that they have "full coverage"; the only catch is that they will have to wait till the government is good and ready to give it to them.

Second, as the government is herding us down the road to serfdom, there's the issue of Medicare. I was in a meeting at the White House and heard firsthand from President Obama in an unguarded moment what the plan is for Medicare. In that meeting, the issue of Medicare insolvency came up. As mentioned earlier, the Obamacare proposal included a $500 billion slash in Medicare. So the president was asked not once, but three times, did he have a plan for keeping Medicare solvent? Obama's answer astonished me. He answered no, he had no plan for keeping Medicare solvent, because if the program went insolvent, seniors could just go into Obamacare. Although of course, he didn't call it Obamacare. The formal name for the legislation, as passed, is the Patient Protection and Affordable Care Act—pronounced, of course, "Obamacare." But the president's meaning was unmistakable: The long-term plan is to collapse Medicare and Medicaid into Obamacare. So then we will all—young, old, and in between—be assigned to one giant single-payer system for everyone, just as in the United Kingdom. The question is, How soon will it be before access to private care will be restricted or even outlawed? After all, government doesn't like competition.

Now you know why I did everything within my human capacity to rally Amercians to oppose Obamacare's passage. And nearly to a person, my Republican colleagues were against it too. But of course, the Democrats had the votes. And so it would be high noon on Capitol Hill.

CHAPTER FOURTEEN

Tea Party!

BUT then something miraculous happened. The American people woke up.

In early 2009 many Americans recoiled from what they were seeing in Washington. They said, "Not with my country, you don't." It was one of those moments when something snapped, and suddenly you knew things had changed—everything had changed. The spell had been broken; time had slipped from one epoch to another. And now, in the new light of the moment, the world looked different. Indeed, the world *was* different. The American people have come to see that Obamacare isn't just bad health-care policy and bad economics. It isn't just unconstitutional. In a deep way, in addition to all its other flaws, Obamacare is *immoral*.

That is, Obamacare is an affront to the animating principles of the American tradition of self-reliance and individualism. We might rely on one another for help from time to time, and we might work hard all our lives to save for a dignified old age, but there's something deeply wrong when a portion of the population—the productive portion—is subsidizing everyone else. We've all heard the phrase "robbing Peter to pay Paul." Well, in America today, we have Peter writing a check to the government, then the government skims off a share and writes a check to Paul, and then Paul writes a check back to the government, which then skims off another share before sending a check back to Peter. In 2011 Fox News reported that the entire federal government sends out some 212 million checks a month. Here's a better idea: Why don't we start cutting out the middleman, which is the government, and just have each of us keep more of our money?

These doleful trends have been evident for some time in America—just as the damage done to our society has been evident and growing for some time. It has to stop. And that point is now. This is *our* rendezvous with destiny.

In recent years, even Americans who never paid much attention to U.S. history in school were suddenly becoming avid readers. They knew that our own don't-tread-on-me history would provide useful lessons for the present day. And so we were reminded of the language of our own sacred Declaration of Independence, in which the founders itemized the "repeated injuries and usurpations" that were causing them to rebel. One of those items from 1776 struck a particular chord in 2009: "He has erected a multitude of New Offices, and sent hither swarms of Officers to harass our people and eat out their substance."

And so something was coming. The elements of a new kind of rebellion were brewing. Tea Party! Only this time, the Tea Party was televised—and then YouTubed. For example, on February 19, 2009, we saw Rick Santelli's famous rant on the floor of the Chicago Board of Trade, denouncing the stimulus not only as bad economics but also as immoral. It was profoundly unfair, Santelli said, that some people had to work to carry the water, while others could simply do nothing and drink the water. That is, if we create a system in which unproductive people live permanently at the expense of the others, well, that's a lousy system. The American people are generous, but they are not suckers. The next thing we knew, the folks on the trading floor were clapping and cheering.

That's how the Tea Party gained critical mass. Ordinary Americans woke up and said, "I've had enough!" They could see President Obama's attempt to transform America into something unrecognizable: one part European-style socialism, one part trendy playground of multiculturalism, one part laboratory for progressive relativism, and one part lawless war zone of governmental gangsterism. And so they reached back into their history to find ways to show their opposition. For me, it was a flashback to my days as an education activist in Minnesota back in the nineties, when I would show parents what the liberals were up to—at which point parents would brace themselves for the necessary fight and ask, "Where's my pitchfork?" That's the moral spirit—and it's the fighting spirit.

We all remember the congressional town-hall meetings in the summer of 2009—those exuberant, colorful, sometimes even rowdy moments when the independent spirits of Americans erupted. "No to Obamacare!" they shouted. The mainstream media often tried to ignore those displays, but the new media were now bypassing the old-media blockade. So the protests, driven by the new technologies, went viral. You could see the shocked expressions on the face of liberal politicians as they were confronted by their own angry constituents. *I am here from the government,* they were saying, *and I am here to help you. What? You don't want my help?* No doubt George III was equally perplexed when he heard the news from across the Atlantic back in 1776.

Once again, if the main objective of the Obama/Pelosi/Reid forces had been to do the will of the people, they would have pulled back. But they proved instead that they didn't care what the people wanted; they cared about what they wanted. And yet, as I saw over and over again during this period, the Democratic leadership was more ideologically driven than politically pragmatic. They were liberals, even leftists—and they meant it. They had no intention of turning back.

By the end of October 2009, Speaker Pelosi and her House majority finally had their health-care bill—their legislative Frankenstein. Knowing that the public was increasingly fearful—the townspeople now had torches as well as pitchforks—Drs. Pelosi and Reid stitched and bolted their monstrous bill together, hoping it could stagger its way to completion.

Meanwhile, outside the dark castle, House Republicans met to discuss our counterstrategy. It had became clear to us, unfortunately, that even as the people made louder and louder noises of opposition, the GOP leadership was resigned to defeat. The Republican leadership was going to vote no—even hell, no—but that wasn't good enough; the Democrats had the votes in Congress. In other words, the Republicans would oppose the bill, and then, in defeated resignation, they'd watch it go through the House and the Senate, then on to the president for his signature. And that would be that. End of story.

Well, that wasn't good enough. People across the country wanted to see their leaders fight back. I am a fighter, and I fight to win. And besides, socialized medicine in the United States was the tectonic battle of our age—we needed a miracle. I came to Washington, D.C., for the same reason I went to St. Paul: not just to fight Big Government, nor even to contain Big Government, but actually to defeat Big Government and reverse its damage. So I stood up. Now was no time for a white flag. And as the town-hall meetings had shown us, our own people wanted us to fight. Some Republicans said to me, *That's nice you're voting no, but it's too late—the Democrats have us licked.* I had heard that sort of resignation before, from some, in my days in the Minnesota state senate. But now, as I listened to the outcry of the American people, I knew what the people wanted us to do.

I thought to myself, *We don't have to accept things as they are. We can change things—we just need to be creative. We might be losing the inside game of vote counts in Congress, but we can still win the outside game of the country's wishes as a whole—and the outside game is bigger and more important. Most legislators do the best they can inside their own legislative chamber, and that's often the extent of their actions. But if they see a new reality outside— that is, masses of people demanding something different—they might think again about what to do. They might realize that for every voter who makes the effort to come to the capital, there are probably a hundred or a thousand voters back home holding the same opinions.* The battle is ultimately the larger battle, I realized—the battle for the heart and soul of America. And that's the battle we must all join.

So here was my idea. If Washington wouldn't listen to America, I would invite America to come to Washington—and speak even more loudly, forcing Washington to listen. And if enough noisy Americans came to Capitol Hill, perhaps we could stop this lumbering monster before it trampled our health and our liberty. That way, Republicans wouldn't just be voting no on the bill and losing; they would be voting no and winning the hearts and minds of voters outside the Beltway.

Fortunately, I had allies. When you stand true for something, you always have allies—and good allies at that. We immediately started planning: phone calls, e-mails, talk radio. And, of course, television.

On Friday, October 30, 2009, I went on Sean Hannity's Fox News show. He was in New York, and I was in Minnesota. Sean is that rare combination: a passionate public advocate for conservative principles and a perfectly nice and pleasant fellow in private. For the show Sean had done his job as a journalist; he had dug through the bill, which sat in a pile next to him, and told his audience that of the two thousand pages of legislative folderol, only five pages truly mattered. And then he held up those five pages, hitting the key points that every American needed to know: Yes, the bill funded abortions. Yes, it was a government takeover of the health-insurance market. Yes, it meant higher taxes. Yes, it cut $500 billion from Medicare. And yes, it included "death panels."

That day, we had gotten our "final copy" of the health-care bill, and I also kept a copy of the bill on my lap—all twenty pounds of it. In the hectic days to come, I would be lugging that heap of legislative language around to many different places. Meanwhile, I agreed with every one of Sean's points, adding that the bill was not only "the crown jewel of socialism" but also unconstitutional.

Then I launched my pitch. I said to Sean and his audience, "We need to pay a 'House' call on Nancy Pelosi." I was asking the American people, in other words, to come to D.C. by the carload. Meet me at high noon next Thursday, I said, right in front of the Capitol. We'd have a press conference and then the people could walk through the halls of the House—the Cannon, Longworth, and Rayburn buildings, plus the Capitol itself, seeking out members of Congress. When they saw them, they could look into the whites of their members' eyes and say, politely but firmly, "Don't take away my health care." Thinking then of the Great One, talk radio giant Mark Levin, author of the bestselling book *Liberty and Tyranny: A Conservative Manifesto*, I added to Sean and his audience, "This is a 'liberty and tyranny' moment." As indeed it was.

Now I had crossed the political Rubicon. All that weekend and into the next week, I worked with more leaders—conservative, libertarian, Tea Party, and just plain not-going-to-take-it-anymore people—to pull a press conference together. Mark Levin was key, as was Erick Erickson of Redstate.com. And so was Jon Voight, the Academy Award–winning actor, and John Ratzenberger, the immortal Cliff Clavin from the sitcom *Cheers;* both came out to join us. We joked that we were holding the "Super Bowl of Freedom," and that name stuck.

Our big press conference was held the following Thursday, on November 5, 2009. We welcomed what turned out to be tens of thousands of Tea Partiers: "You came to your House, you came for an emergency house call! Are they going to listen? Oh yeah, they're going to listen!" I continued, "Thomas Jefferson said a revolution every now and then is a good thing." That's a peaceful revolution, of course, just as we are launching here and now. Then I recalled the question that Abigail Adams wrote to her husband, John Adams, one of our great founders and our second president. After all that we've done, Abigail wondered, will generations unborn know what was done for them? The answer was yes, of course. And now people will remember this day as well. We, in our time, are a privileged generation, because we have been summoned by destiny to do something great—to reclaim freedom.

I could see the reporters' heads spinning: All those ordinary Americans with non–politically correct views? Daring to defy the great Obama? So the mainstream media attacked, of course, using its favorite weapons, snark and ridicule. The *Washington Post* ran a bizarre headline: "NO ONE SAID FREEDOM WAS PRETTY." I thought, *Whoa, that's a low view of freedom-loving Americans.* To me, and to the vast majority of Americans, freedom is indeed pretty—it's beautiful, in fact. Period. Needless to say, the *Huffington Post* chimed in too, headlining: "A DAY AT THE FREAK SHOW." You get the idea.

Yet the power of the Main Stream Media was not what it once was. The American people now had other sources of information—as well as, of course, their own common sense. And so despite MSM cheerleading, opposition to Obamacare ballooned, from just 28 percent in April 2009, according to an AP-GfK poll, up to 46 percent by the time of the "Super Bowl of Freedom." All other polls showed a similar upward movement; by 2010 opposition to Obamacare was clearly the majority position—in reality, the big-majority position.

Yet the liberal Democrats formed an ungallant light brigade and charged onward. On November 7, 2009, Speaker Pelosi forced her House Democrats to cast their votes for the bill. Or rather, most of her House Democrats; some had been spooked by the rising opposition. In the end she won the assent of only 219 Democrats; 38 others voted "no"—some out of a sense of principle, some out of a sense of survival. The Republican ranks were more solid: 177 of us in opposition, with just one going over to the other side. The final vote: 220–215.

Yet by now, in late 2009, the Democrats were starting to worry. In the home state of the original 1773 Tea Party, Massachusetts, Republican Scott Brown won a historic U.S. Senate election, breaking the Kennedy family's six-decade grip on the seat. But for the Democrats, there was no turning back; they were now sailing forward blindly on the political equivalent of the *Titanic*. Captain Obama stood serenely at the wheel, telling his Democratic passengers to ignore reports of icebergs in the next election. So Obamacare passed the Senate on December 24, 2009; months later, in late March 2010, after a second confirming House vote, Democrats finally pushed the deadweight of Obamacare across the finish line.

Obamacare was a victory for left-wing ideologues, and it was also a victory for governmental gangsters. As soon as the bill was enacted, the administration started issuing waivers for the provisions of the bill; that is, it began opening up loopholes that would, for example, allow an insurance plan to spend more on administrative overhead than the new law allowed. In other words, the Obama administration was admitting what critics had been saying all along—that the bill was unworkable and unaffordable. And yet it was making this admission only to a select few. So who got these waivers? Well, it helped if you were a well-connected labor union or a well-heeled donor or the client of a wired-in lobbyist. Within a year of Obamacare's passage, the number of waivers granted had risen to over a thousand; it was becoming embarrassing to Democrats. So the administration announced that it would no longer be granting waivers; the dubious process was making Obamacare look bad. Yet conservative blogger Michelle Malkin, who had been tracking the story since the beginning, wasn't buying that new spin. She wrote in June 2011, "Expect a resurrection of the waivers in some other name or form. . . . I guarantee you: Unions, Democrat lobbying groups, and liberal execs will find a way to get their exemptions—and the White House will find a way to distribute their crony waivers by another name." Is Malkin a cynic? No, she is prescient. She is simply onto the reality of gangster government.

If Washington, D.C., was hopelessly in the grip of liberal gangsters, I could see that there was only one recourse—to win the next election. Indeed, the 2010 midterm elections were coming, and so the battle lines had to be drawn. In that year, I crisscrossed the country, speaking up for like-minded candidates. I would sum up the Tea Party movement as "TEA." That is, Taxed Enough Already.

Yet in fact there was much more to talk about. We Republicans, reinforced by the Tea Party and everyone else who could see that Obama-style liberalism was a disaster, spoke strongly on many crucial matters. We were against Obamacare and the bureaucratic takeover of our health-care system. We were against bailing out Wall Street. (Not every Republican but, by now, most.) We were against the "stimulus"—which actually, of course, was a destimulus. We were against the government running the auto industry. We were against cap-and-trade's strange mix of repression and profiteering. We were against green energy fantasies.

That's a lot of "against." So what were we *for*? What constituted our positive, twenty-first-century conservative vision of limited government? We were for lower taxes. We were for individuals making their own health-care decisions. We were for the freedom to reduce unemployment by not taxing investment money away from job-creating businesspeople. We were for a constitutional vision of personal liberty. We were for a strong America, confident in its essential values. We were for standing up for our treasured allies. In other words, we needed GOP—Government Of the People. The American people are always the solution.

On July 15, 2010, I filed the paperwork to establish the Tea Party Caucus as a formal component of Congress. As I said at the time:

> The American people are speaking out loud and clear. They have had enough of the spending, the bureaucracy, and the government knows best mentality running rampant today throughout the halls of Congress. This caucus will espouse the timeless principles of our founding, principles that all Members of Congress have sworn to uphold. The American people are doing their part and making their voices heard and this caucus will prove that there are some here in Washington willing to listen.

The Democrats and their media allies mocked Republicans and Tea Partiers. They painted us as toothless hillbillies coming down from the hills, wearing red-white-and-blue bib overalls. But I could see that despite these attacks—and maybe, in fact, because of these attacks—we were winning. Why? Because the more Obama and the Main Stream Media attacked us, the more ordinary voters could see that we were really something different, that we were boldly proclaiming an important new message. If we had been just the same business-as-usual, go-along-get-along Republicans, liberals would have left us alone, maybe even thrown us some crumbs off the table. But because we were fresh and different, bringing vital new energy to the political scene, we were a genuine threat.

And at the same time, what were the Democrats offering? Here's a partial list of policies that needed to be unmasked: Unbridled spending. Unsustainable debt. Undermined currency. Unfundable liabilities. Unfathomable taxation. Unrestrained regulation. Underwater mortgages. Unleashed energy inflation. Unguarded borders. Unsettled families. Unending unemployment and underemployment. And unknown, unprecedented, and seemingly unstoppable stealth appropriations. Taken together, all those "uns" added up to the undoing of the Democrats' grip on the country.

Of course, not everything in 2009–2010 was Obamacare and Tea Party. As the proud servant of the people of the 6th congressional district of Minnesota, I had a duty to help constituents. Much of the work of a member of Congress might be considered routine, but it is still important. When people lose their passport just before a foreign trip or can't get a Social Security check or can't get an answer to a crucial question—our office was there to help. It would be nice, of course, if the federal bureaucracy could respond in a timely manner, but if a phone call from me or my staff could nudge things along, we were glad to do it.

One such example was the case of Ronald Kane of Woodbury, Minnesota. Ron served in the army during the Vietnam War, and yet he never received proper honor for his extraordinary heroism. Back on July 11, 1969, he and his unit were patrolling in the A Shau Valley when they were ambushed by the enemy; Ron, showing no fear for his own safety, rallied his men to repulse the attack, then led them to safety. At the time, he was told he would receive a medal for his heroism, and he believed it would all be taken care of. Like so many returning veterans, he had a civilian life to pick up again; he assumed that his medal would eventually be sent to him. Well, the decades piled up, and finally, in 2002, he realized that his medal had never arrived. So he contacted the Pentagon and waited. And waited. At one point, Ron even drove to the National Personnel Records Center in St. Louis to see if he could track down his military records—all, once again, to no avail. He also contacted other federal officials and received no help. Finally, in 2007, he contacted my office, and we were able to help him receive what he had earned nearly four decades earlier—a Silver Star. I felt privileged to speak at an award ceremony for Ron on Memorial Day 2010, as he finally received his due, forty years later, from a grateful nation. His whole family was with him, as well as admiring neighbors, but Ron remained modest about his heroism: "I just did it to save my men." True heroes are always like that—modest, even as their heroism is recalled. They simply did what they needed to do. As for the rest of us, it's our duty to honor them appropriately.

Also in 2010, I faced my own biennial election. I had plenty of friends but also foes. Given my relatively close call in 2008, the national Democrats thought that this time maybe they could defeat me. My opponent was a community activist, Democratic Party official, and state senator; I knew she would have plenty of money. So I did what I have always done: I worked hard. I raised more money than any member of Congress in the history of the institution—although I might note that my average donation was just forty-five dollars; I will never be the candidate of the limousines, in either party. In the end, I won the election by thirteen points.

On election night 2010, I appeared again on MSNBC's *Hardball*. Once again Matthews was in Washington, while I was in Minnesota—only this time I wasn't in a studio, but amid an election-night party of friends and supporters at the Sheraton Hotel in Bloomington, which served as the Republican Party headquarters that victorious night. But some things never change: Matthews once again had an agenda. Noting that Republicans had taken back the majority in the House, as well as the new investigative authority that comes with it, Matthews led off by asking, "Will you use the subpoena power to investigate the Democratic members of Congress for un-American activities?" So I answered—struggling to hear his questions over an ecstatic crowd—that my goal was to make sure that taxes didn't go up. Matthews asked the "anti-American" question again, and in my response I reminded Matthews that the Bush tax cuts were scheduled to expire less than two months in the future, on December 31, 2010; such an expiration, I warned, would mean a "dramatic increase in taxes," just what the economy did not need. That was my agenda, and so, as always, I was declaring it firmly and staying true to it.

So then Matthews said, "Congresswoman Bachmann, are you hypnotized tonight? Has someone hypnotized you? Because no matter what I ask you, you give the same answer. Are you hypnotized? Has someone put you under a trance tonight? That you give me the same answer no matter what question I put to you?" *Actually*, people in that Bloomington ballroom—as well as TV viewers—may well have thought to themselves, *it's Matthews who seemed to be hypnotized, because when he didn't get the answer he wanted, he repeated the same question.* But, of course, Matthews was playing to his crowd, including those in the studio with him; I could hear his cohosts chortling. I said, "I think the American people are the ones that are finally speaking tonight. We're coming out of our trance." And I added, "I think people are thrilled tonight. I imagine that thrill is probably maybe quite not so tingly on your leg anymore."

On November 2, 2010, the American people began taking their country back. Republicans won control of the House, winning a total of sixty-three seats, the greatest gain for a party in a midterm election in more than seven decades.

I was at the tip of the spear in the 2010 elections. I might not be an insider's insider—I never wanted to be—but I tried to get things done on the larger national stage. I am a fighter because I believe I was sent to Washington to actively uphold the Constitution. I listen to people and communicate with them. That's how you build a movement, and then establish a governing coalition, and then change the country. Do what you promised people you would do.

One sad note: David Meyer, the husband of my lifelong friend Barbara, passed away on December 2, 2010. Married for thirty-two years, Mr. and Mrs. Meyer had enjoyed a great life together in northern California, raising two wonderful children. But then David was stricken with pancreatic cancer; he was a brave battler for two and a half years, but doctors could not save him. We visited several times during his struggle, and Barbara and I talked on the phone even more often than usual during that period, exchanging prayers and other words of encouragement.

When Barbara called me to say that David had only a few more hours to live, I left my office on Capitol Hill just as we were voting and jumped on an airplane and flew to San Francisco, to the airport nearest to where they lived. Agonizingly, my plane was late; when I finally landed at 11:00 P.M., I called Barbara, who told me the sad news that David had passed away while I was in the air. David died at home, surrounded by family, true and faithful and good spirited to the end. Barbara suggested that I find a hotel room near the airport and get at least part of a night's sleep, but I wanted to be with her and her kids in their time of need. She would have done the exact same thing for me. So I drove the three and a half hours to be with Barbara, Christy, and Daniel, and to pray with them. I thought of Paul's epistle to the Thessalonians: "For if we believe that Jesus died and rose again, even so them also which sleep in Jesus will God bring with him." And then Paul instructs us: "Comfort one another with these words."

Later that same day, I had to get back on an airplane and fly back to Washington for more votes. Nine days later I flew out to Ukiah a second time, where I was privileged to deliver the eulogy for David. Barbara has always been and always will be a sister to me. I thank God for my family and for these dear lifelong friends.

Yet at the same time, I could see that I was being called to serve on a larger scale. I have thanked God many times for giving me the opportunity to serve on the national level. Now the work I had begun needed to be continued. The question of America's future was at stake, and I had the resolve to continue the fight to save it.

CHAPTER FIFTEEN

Called to Serve: Seeking the Presidency

IN late 2010, friends and constituents began suggesting that I run for president. Folks credited me with playing a leading role in energizing the Republican vote in the 2010 midterm elections. They told me that I had a solid conservative record, that I was an articulate spokeswoman for all the key conservative beliefs, and that I had been right to oppose the 2008 bailouts initiated by Democrats and Republicans and continued by Democrats, as well as the big-spending foolishness perpetrated by President Obama. America needed that sort of conservative, they told me, the kind of leader who puts principle ahead of party. They also said that through my plain speaking I had helped bring disaffected swing voters over to the GOP. They also mentioned that I had an intriguing résumé. And so, they said, I should get into the race for the 2012 Republican nomination.

At first I dismissed the idea. I was happy in the House; I felt that I had a voice and a clear role to play.

But then I began to see that there was a lot more work to be done. The 2010 election had broken the power of the Obama presidency—but Obama was still president. The elections had brought Republican victory in the House but not in the Senate. The country was hurting, and the voters were watching; if the GOP were to slip into bad habits, it could be pitched out of power just as quickly as it had gained the majority. The real point of having power, I believed, was to follow the Constitution—that would make America a better place.

Meanwhile, the Obama administration was at it again. Earlier, I described the many components of liberal government—and of gangster government. I described the increased spending and the increased regulating—and even the tax cheating. I decried Obamacare and the administration's thuggish handling of the Chrysler bailout. I mentioned its handling of Fannie, Freddie, and Dodd-Frank. All of these represent the dysfunctional Beltway business-as-usual practices that shocked the conscience, and drained the wallet, of ordinary Americans.

Yet even after his policies were repudiated by the voters in 2010, the president was still working his will through the under-the-radar bureaucracy. And to me, two incidents proved to be the two last straws. The last straws, that is, convincing me that the absolute maximum effort was needed to stop Obama-style liberalism—and gangsterism—in its tracks.

The first straw came in February 2011. That's when I learned from Ernest Istook, a former Oklahoma congressman turned budget watcher at the Heritage Foundation, that the Obama administration had hidden $105 billion to begin implementation of Obamacare, $105,464,000,000, to be precise, in a series of postdated checks in funding to be paid out between 2011 and 2019.

Usually legislation to create a program such as Obamacare only *authorizes* the spending of funds; it takes separate legislation actually to appropriate—that is, spend—the money. But not this time. This time the liberals couldn't wait for the familiar workings of Congress; they wanted to start spending money right away—and with "the fierce urgency of now," as Obama always said during the 2008 campaign.

President Obama knew the American people wouldn't like his bill, so he didn't want to take any chances that a 2010 election could mean the repudiation of Democratic majorities (which it did in the House), that is why he, Pelosi, and Reid prefunded Obamacare, but conveniently forgot to tell most everyone in Congress. Do a Google or even a Lexis/Nexis search on Obamacare funding—you won't find many articles, if any, on Obamacare and $105,464,000,000 in funding. Even by Washington's standards, that's a lot of money. Every member of Congress who voted for Obamacare should have to answer two questions for their constituents. First, did they read the bill before voting for it? And second, did they know they were voting to spend that $105,464,000,000?

And if they did, where were they getting the money from? The Democrats all prided themselves on the so-called "pay-go" rules, meaning they had to show they had a legitimate source to pay for their $105 billion in spending.

So the normally required sequence—first authorization, then appropriation—was bypassed; federal money, it turned out, was already being spent to set in place the fabled crown jewel of socialism. This is the federal government we're talking about, and so if Uncle Sam is already spending close to $4 trillion a year, despite taking in only about $2.2 trillion a year, Obama could simply borrow another $105 billion. Here's an example: Section 1311[a] of Obamacare allows the secretary of health and human services to provide $16 billion in grants to the states to start setting up "exchanges" for the sale of Obama-approved, and-mandated, health insurance. That is, $16 billion to *begin* setting up a federal program; that is, to hire the consultants, rent the office space, and hold the all-important retreats at swanky resorts. It's the good life in D.C., and the rest of us are paying for it. So we are reminded, once again, why Washington enjoys the highest median household income of any metropolitan area in the nation. I know that I'm getting pretty deep in the weeds here, but the liberal big spenders have been deep in these weeds for decades—that's one reason that we're in financial bankruptcy. For Republicans to be effective in countering this big-government weed patch, tough talk won't get the job done. Instead, they are going to need, first, the ability to understand the nature of this expensive federal shrubbery, and second, of course, they are going to need the strength to mow it down.

Moreover, in this instance, we saw the recurrence of a baleful pattern: The feds began "giving" grants to the states to set up their own satellite programs—and only too late did the states wake up and realize that not only did they have a bad program on their hands, but they were spending more to run it than they were actually getting from the feds. That total of $105 billion, to put it in perspective, was enough to fund the entire operation of the state of Minnesota for three years or the state of Iowa for seventeen years.

So in regard to this stealth $105 billion, I was livid and thought the world should know what most members of Congress should know. When twelve-digit sums get spent with virutally no knowledge of those doing the voting, that's gangsterism on steroids. On March 6, 2011, I went on NBC's *Meet the Press*, holding up a sign reading "$105,464,000,000"; I explained, as best I could in a few moments, the outrageousness of this latest scam. So many outrages occur every day in Washington that to many members of Congress it seemed just too complicated, too much trouble to worry about. I thought, *Our team needed to fight over that $105 billion in non-transparent spending. Otherwise, what's to stop Obama from doing it again? For more? And what if Republicans had slipped in $105 billion into the largest piece of legislation to come along in a generation, and we had failed to disclose this material term to the Democrats? The Democrats would have gone ballistic, and rightly so. And the media would have gone equally ballistic.* But instead, our side just let it go.

The second straw came in May 2011. That's when the National Labor Relations Board (NLRB) issued a complaint against the Boeing Company aimed at stopping the opening of a new airplane plant that Boeing had built—at a cost of some $750 million—in South Carolina. The plant was built to expand production of Boeing's new 787 "Dreamliner" passenger jet, creating four thousand new jobs. Yet the NLRB, fired up by new Obama appointees, filed suit to stop the production, accusing Boeing of engaging in an "unfair labor practice" by opening a plant in right-to-work South Carolina as opposed to prounion Washington State. It was an unprecedented legal argument from the NLRB and threatened grave damage not only to Boeing but also to South Carolina. The Palmetto State's charismatic new governor, Nikki Haley, denounced the action: "This is a direct assault on everything we know America to be." She was right. Diana Furchtgott-Roth, a former chief economist at the Labor Department, noted a further absurdity: the NLRB's saying that Boeing was taking assets away from Washington State. After all, Boeing was continuing to make 787s at a unionized plant in Everett; it was simply planning on building more 787s at the second plant in North Charleston. And because Boeing currently had backlogged orders of some 850 planes, both plants had many years of full-capacity production to look forward to. I asked myself: *What's the problem here? And why would the Obama administration, operating through the cat's paw of the NLRB, seek to shut down production and jobs? Is this the Obama economic plan—at a time of staggeringly high unemployment? Is this his big idea, to take a company that is winning in the world competitive marketplace—and clobber it?*

It was another gangster move. According to two legal experts at the Heritage Foundation, Hans von Spakovsky and James Sherk, the NLRB's action was "an unbridled, unauthorized, and unlawful expansion of the regulatory power of an executive agency." That is, the NLRB was operating as a rogue agency, pushing beyond its authorized functions, pushing beyond liberalism, beyond activism, all the way to "unlawful."

Furthermore, the two Heritage experts noted the likely dire consequences: "If allowed to stand, [the NLRB's] actions threaten business investment and job creation as well as the employment of both unionized and nonunion workers." In other words, the NLRB was threatening employment for all Americans, both union and nonunion. It was adding yet another threat to America's already endangered job market.

And it was worse than that. The NLRB, created in 1935, is nominally an independent agency, charged with monitoring unions and union elections. And yet during the last few years, the Obama administration has taken extraordinary steps to increase the agency's influence and reach. The NLRB is authorized to have five board members, all confirmed by the U.S. Senate; in early 2011, when it had only three members, Obama nominated a fourth prospective member, Craig Becker, a well-known union activist, most recently associate general counsel to the Service Employees International Union. Yet Becker was seen as so outspokenly liberal that the Senate refused to confirm him. So Obama appointed him anyway, using a legal but dubious maneuver called a "recess appointment"; the purpose of a recess appointment is to fill a gap, but now, instead, the Obama administration was using the recess-appointment process to advance a specific liberal agenda. This appointment enabled Becker to sit as a voting member of the NLRB through the end of 2012. In addition, Obama appointed a second liberal, prounion ideologue, Lafe Solomon, to be the general counsel of the NLRB; this position entails extensive agenda-setting powers within the agency, including the setting of board policy. Yet for Solomon too the Senate would not give confirmation, and so the Obama administration blithely named him *acting* general counsel.

One might think, of course, that both Becker and Solomon would feel chastened by their failure to gain the advice and consent of the U.S. Senate and that, as a result, they would feel somewhat constrained in their actions. But instead, both men seemed to take their temporary status as an incentive to get as much done for the prounion cause as they could in the time available. So now, under the impetus of Becker and Solomon, the NLRB was attacking Boeing and, by extension, all of American business.

Those two incidents—the $105 billion Obamacare slush fund and the

NLRB attack on Boeing—reminded me that while Republicans had won much in 2010, they needed to win much more in 2012. We needed a real sweep for Republican reformers, not just nominal wins for Republican time servers.

So I began to look around to see, who would have the backbone to stop these abuses? Who is going to possess the insight and the energy to reach into the innards of the executive branch and put the clamp on these violations of custom and law? Moreover, who would take the case to the people? Who would be an effective champion of transparency and good government as well as, of course, limited constitutional government? We needed to stop $105 billion slush funds. We needed to stop left-wing activists from honeycombing into regulatory agencies. We needed to take our country back.

I knew that the next president needed to do more than manage the problem; the next president would have to *dismantle* the problem. The next president couldn't just continue piling up debt. Nor impose an unconstitutional health plan that costs too much and provides little value. Nor allow political correctness to stand in the way of jobs. Nor appoint liberal judges to advance antifamily policies. Nor fail to secure the border. Nor fail to lead overseas.

Marcus and I had to face the hard question: Was I the right person to reverse Obama's policies? Was I the right person to bring about reform and change? People were looking to me. And so, of course, Marcus and I prayed. As Proverbs tells us, we can make our own plans, but the Lord gives the right answer. Some politicos, of course, said that it was too late for me to announce, that other candidates had been running for months, even years, and were too far ahead in organization and fund-raising. Then I sensed an answer. I knew what I was being directed to do. I was called to serve.

I announced my bid for the White House on June 27, 2011. I went back to my Waterloo birthplace, joined by my family and friends. "It's great to be in Iowa," I declared. Yes, Iowa. Home to all those Ambles and Munsons and Johnsons and Thompsons—all those hardworking folks who since the 1850s had made the Hawkeye State into the breadbasket of the world, who had raised patriotic families as well. "And even better to be in Waterloo where I was born." Yes, I could think back to my happy childhood, when I learned so much from my parents, grandparents, and relatives and when I learned also about the Sullivan brothers, who enlisted to fight for their country and for freedom. As one of Sullivans wrote, "We will make a team together that can't be beat."

I continued:

I stand here today in front of many friends and family to formally announce my candidacy for President of the United States. I do so because I am grateful for the blessings God and this country have given to me, and not because of the position of the office, but because I am determined that every American deserves these blessings and that together we can once again strengthen America and restore the promise of the future.

And I closed with:

Together, we can do this. Together we can rein in all the corruption and waste that has become Washington and instead leave a better America for future generations.

Together we can make a team that can't be beat!

Together we can secure the promise of the future.

Together we can —and together we will!

God bless you and God bless the United States of America!

That was my announcement speech. So now, what is my campaign plan? How do I plan to win the Republican nomination? And then the White House?

My campaign plan is simple. I am going to say true things. I love these words from Paul's epistle to the Philippians: "Whatsoever things are true, whatsoever things are honest, whatsoever things are just, whatsoever things are pure, whatsoever things are lovely, whatsoever things are of good report; if there be any virtue, and if there be any praise, think on these things." Those are important words for faith, for life—and even for politics.

So here's what I think, in four parts.

First: I am a national-security conservative. I believe that a president's most important role is to be commander in chief. I believe in peace through strength. That is, I believe in defending America, defending our allies—

and defeating terrorism. Sitting as I do on the House Permanent Select Committee on Intelligence, I am reminded that every day, some people around the world wake up thinking about how they're going to destroy the United States. Many of these America haters work in the Iranian government. Indeed, they run the Iranian government. So when I learn more about President Mahmoud Ahmadinejad's nuclear ambitions and his declared determination to destroy Israel and the United States, I take him seriously. If history has taught us anything, it is that when a madman speaks, you listen, and then you work to defeat him. At the same time, of course, we must obey the Constitution, and that means that the president must seek authorization from Congress for military action.

And as we oppose our enemies, we will stand by our friends. So I will reverse the Obama administration's pressure on Israel, which seeks to force Israel back to its indefensible 1967 borders. Obama's policy threatens Israel's security, even as it encourages Israel's enemies to think that they can use terror, and the threat of terror, to extract dangerous concessions.

Meanwhile, we will defend the homeland. We will have no more politically correct nonsense about terrorism; we will keep Guantánamo open, and we will use it to lock up terrorists who seek to kill Americans. We will defend our southern border—and all our borders and coastlines.

Overall, I emphatically believe that America has been the greatest force for good in world history. I believe we should continue to be a city upon a hill, a light unto nations. That vision is often associated with Ronald Reagan—the greatest president of my lifetime and one of the greats of American history—but in fact, others shared the same vision. John F. Kennedy also spoke of America as a city upon a hill, back in 1961. And both Ronald Reagan and JFK, of course, were quoting the Puritan leader John Winthrop, who in 1630 set great goals for the new land called America—goals I believe we have reached. So while I admire Winthrop's idealism, I also admire the realism of those who put his vision into practice across so many centuries. The original inspiration for Winthrop came from the Book of Matthew, in which Christ proclaimed from the mount, "Ye are the light of the world. A city that is set on an hill cannot be hid." Two thousand years later, I have faith that we can yet again, through our hands and feet, be that shining city.

Second: As I am a foreign-policy conservative, so I am also an economic conservative. I believe in defending freedom and free enterprise from all opponents, foreign and domestic. If only one word could describe my political goals, it would be *"liberty."* That's what inspires me and motivates me more than anything here on earth. Economic liberty, religious liberty, financial liberty—they are all connected. You can't truly have one without the rest. I always recall the words of the Muskego manifesto, the words that inspired my forebears to come to America from Norway: Here in America, they wrote, is a land "where freedom and equality prevail in civil and religious affairs, and without any special permission we can enter almost any profession and make an honest living. This we consider more wonderful than riches." *More wonderful than riches.* That's the way I feel too.

Yet with freedom comes responsibility. And in the past our leaders have been irresponsible. When I came into Congress, the national debt was $8.67 trillion. Now it's headed up to $16.7 trillion, with no end in sight. In other words, it took 219 years for it to get this high, and now, in just five more years, it's almost doubled. No wonder America's AAA bond rating has been downgraded.

As president, I will consider it a duty to cut federal spending. Not only because the economy needs relief from overspending but because the government itself needs relief from overspending. So I won't just put an end to Obamacare; I will put an end to all the spending that has made our government simultaneously painfully gargantuan and hideously ineffectual. That is, so fat and bloated that it can't do anything, even as it suffocates the economy. I'm not against government; I think our current government is a mortal threat to America—just as, in its morbid obesity, it's a mortal threat to itself. But I think that some government is necessary. I am essentially a libertarian on pure market questions, but I know that we need a government to ensure domestic tranquility. I simply want to restore government to the sort of flinty integrity it had when the good citizens of Black Hawk County, Iowa, back in 1853, knew exactly where every cent of that $873.08 was going. And today, thanks to the Internet, we could again have that sort of to-the-penny awareness of where our tax money is going.

So yes, I will control federal spending and bring it into balance—we have to or we won't survive. But in doing so, I will never endanger our security. And if we have another government spending crisis—and I am sure we will—I will continue to defend defense. I will make sure that our men and women in uniform get their paychecks. I have had five biological children and twenty-three foster children, but I feel a special awe toward all the men and women of our armed forces. And I know that the American people feel the same way. We will always support them as they keep us safe.

Yet even as we cut public spending, we are going to foster growth in the private economy. I have specific plans for cutting spending, cutting taxes, and cutting regulation—and for increasing exports, increasing investment, and increasing innovation.

As for the tax code in particular, I know what a disaster it is. I have seen it from the inside. As president, I will examine various approaches to tax reform, as well as tax reduction. Flat, fair, or hybrid—I'll consider whatever tax system we need to unleash the entrepreneurial, transformative potential of the U.S. economy. Under a Bachmann presidency, every young person with a good idea and a lot of stamina will know that America is the best place in the world to start a dream, and start a business.

Third, I am a social conservative—and I mean it. I haven't just talked the talk when it suits me politically—I have walked the walk. Consistently. I have been strongly pro-life since the early 1970s, and I have been active in the right-to-life movement since the eighties. In the Minnesota state senate, I was at the forefront of the effort to enact the Woman's Right to Know Act. And in Washington, I have been involved in every piece of pro-life legislation that Congress has considered.

On profamily education policy, I bucked my own party to lead the fight against a liberal, paternalistic, secular education agenda beginning in the nineties, ultimately securing the repeal of Minnesota's Profile of Learning in 2003. Also in 2003, I was at the forefront in pushing for a traditional-marriage constitutional amendment in Minnesota, which, I'm proud to say, will go before the voters of my state in 2012.

I believe we must remember the work of the biblical Nehemiah, who rebuilt the sturdy walls of Jerusalem. That is, today we must reinforce the sort of ethical framework—for most of us, the framework provided by the Judeo-Christian tradition—that protects liberty from anarchy.

So that's the "three-legged stool" that Republicans often talk about—that is, the peace-through-strength conservatives, the economic conservatives and libertarians, and the social "values voters" conservatives. A majority of Americans associate themselves with one or more of these categories. So in other words, a candidate who can coalesce these three groups can win a national election. That's what Ronald Reagan did—twice. And so did George W. Bush.

But in addition, there's a new source of political energy in America today: the Tea Party, or should I say tea parties, because there are so many of them, each proud of its own autonomy and independence. I once said that the Tea Party represents 90 percent of Americans. I now realize that I misspoke. I should have said 100 percent, because I believe that nearly all Americans retain faith in the ordered liberty that the Constitution offers. Americans have rebelled against autocrats in the past; today they have no wish to see czars reigning on imperial thrones.

Tea partiers are also sometimes called constitutional conservatives, because we put so much emphasis, and rightly so, on the Constitution as the basic source of legitimate governmental authority. As I asked of Treasury Secretary Tim Geithner: Show me in the Constitution where you have the authority to give a $700 billion blank check to whomever you choose. And of course he couldn't do it. Too many Washington power brokers haven't much cared what the Constitution stipulates—unless, of course, the issue is accused criminals and terrorists, in which case they tease out exaggerated theories of procedure to hamstring authorities. But constitutional conservatives *do* care.

Tea partiers and constitutionalists speak up for the common sense of ordinary Americans, who are instinctively suspicious of concentrated power and yet at the same time expect the government to be able to do a few things well, rather than a lot of things badly. You don't need to be a constitutional expert to see the need for due process and fair play when it comes to dealing with the IRS or the EPA or OSHA.

In the political center of this country stands a huge group—Democratic commentator Pat Caddell calls them the "radical middle"—of practical-minded Americans who may never have been political a day in their lives but who are now simply fed up with the faltering status quo. They are disaffected Democrats, independents, libertarians, and those who would reject any political label, and yet they all share the same realization: The current system is an insult to American ideals. And when I say that it's "gangster government," they smile and nod their heads. Finally, they think to themselves, there's a leader who gets it.

So these four groupings—foreign policy, economic, social, and Tea

Party/constitutional—represent a powerful coalition in the making. Actually, it was already made in the 2010 elections; it just needs to be revived again in 2012. And then it needs to become the governing coalition of a reformist, center-right leadership that keeps its promises.

So I have described the building blocks of my candidacy. But of course, building blocks have to build. To win the White House in 2012— to make Obama a one-term president—we need a compelling narrative that shows how we can make a team that can't be beat.

I believe that a conventional, play-it-safe campaign will ensure that America has to endure another four years of Barack Obama and his wrecking-crew policies. That is, if the Republican presidential nominee fails to energize key constituencies, or worse, if the nominee is seen as insincere, then we will lose. So we need a fresh effort deriving its strength from the common sense of the American people, from their commitment to the nation's founding values and to the knowledge that the country must rest on a secure moral foundation that puts common sense ahead of trendy theorizing. It must reach out to the whole nation, inspiring disparate groups ranging from churchgoers to homeschoolers to alienated rec room youth searching for something to believe in; it must reach out to Americans, rallying citizens and patriots of all parties.

And my plan is already working. Just seven weeks after I entered the race, after a lot of hard work, I was honored to win the Ames, Iowa, straw poll on August 13. That night I thanked my supporters, reminding them that with their continued efforts, we could restore that next link of liberty, connecting our glorious past to an even more glorious future.

Together, we can do this. I was born to parents in humble circumstances, but out of that, my husband and I helped to build a big family and then a job-creating business. We have cared for unwed mothers and foster children. I know the pain that ordinary people go through, and yet I also know the rules for success. I was forty-four years old when I first ran for office. I am a small woman, but my heart for the animating principles and values of America is great. I love this country as much as it has loved me.

Yes, the presidential campaign will be tough. I am ready. I like to joke that I have a titanium spine. And I am inspired by the words of John F. Kennedy at the 1963 national prayer breakfast in Washington: "Do not pray for tasks equal to your powers," said JFK as Billy Graham nodded in approval. "Pray for powers equal to your tasks." That's my prayer, too.

And so I will drive a freedom-and-prosperity train from all parts of the nation to Washington. I will call it the Liberty Express. Conservatives will be on board, of course. Then we will stop and invite soccer moms to join us, and the women concerned about their children and families. And then men without jobs or who are worried about their jobs. We will include the hardworking, sometimes neglected singles, because they are vital and welcome in the family of community and country. We will stop too for African Americans, who share our vision of faith and family, who are seeking true hope. And Hispanics as well, hardworking values voters who will also want to come aboard. And Asian Americans and all the minorities in this ethnically diverse country of ours, all those who look with a hope for the day when a change will come. Get ready: Better days are ahead. Even before we get to Washington, we'll set our job-creating/economic-growing/government-reforming agenda in motion.

Together we can do this. We can come together and stick together as we renew our nation. A plan for America's renewal. As the great Daniel Webster declared as he commemorated the fiftieth anniversary of the battle of Bunker Hill, we must always be "one cause, one country, one heart."

And of course, we will pray. As Abraham Lincoln said, the issue isn't whether God is on our side; the issue is that we are on God's side. That's my prayerful hope. And so, in the spirit of our great president, I have faith that right makes might. And in that faith I will, to the very end, dare to do my duty for God and country.

ACKNOWLEDGMENTS

I would first like to thank Marcus, who has been with me every step of the way, over thirty-three wonderful years. And I would like to thank my five biological children and my twenty-three foster children. I love you all. You have given me both joy and strength. It's been said that love can be divided endlessly and yet still not diminish. That's certainly been true for me.

I would also like to thank my parents and my grandparents, all of whom worked so hard, gave me so much—and asked for so little in return. Their example, their work ethic, and their wisdom forged the core of conviction that guides me to this day. And I thank my siblings, who have always been friends as well as beloved family. I must also express gratitude to my ancestors, including the Munsons, whose story has provided inspiration to me, more than 150 years after they first came to Iowa from Norway. I may never know the stories of others in my family, but I realize that they all contributed, in their way, to weaving the fabric of this country—a fabric both durable and wondrous.

I also thank God for the many generations who built our nation, beginning with the founding men and women who gave us this land of liberty and opportunity. It is their example over the centuries—from brilliant vision to heroic sacrifice to quiet duty—that inspires me to fight in my own time for a return to greatness under the Declaration of Independence, the U.S. Constitution, and the Bill of Rights.

I would also like to thank my friends and colleagues, my co-workers and co-laborers—all those whom I have been blessed enough to know and to work with. So many of you have helped me, and mentored me, on causes great and small. I have listened to your voices, I have read your writings, and I have derived strength from your deeds. From campaigns to capitals, I have been proud to know you—and you have contributed greatly. And, of course, I must thank the people who have trusted me with their votes and their support. I am honored and humbled, as well as grateful, and will strive always to earn your continued trust and confidence.

And thanks also to Alex Hoyt and Adrian Zackheim, who first saw I had ideas that I could share with the nation. So thanks also to the whole team at Sentinel, Emily Angell, Jackie Burke, Tricia Conley, Susan Petersen Kennedy, Tiffany Liao, Noirin Lucas, Allison McLean, Eric Meyers, Joe Perez, David Shanks, and Will Weisser.

And thanks also to my research and writing partner, Jim Pinkerton, who helped me put onto these pages my memories, my reflections, and my goals.

But I must return once again to acknowledge and honor our country—to give thanks to this beacon of hope, these United States of America, this sanctuary for so many who have yearned to breathe free. A long time ago, in a little corner of the heartland, some sturdy pioneers spoke for all of us when they described the young nation as "this fertile land, where freedom and equality prevail in civil and religious affairs." In counting their blessings as more wonderful than riches, they were inspired and motivated to help build the American Story.

With God's grace, may it always be so.

APPENDIX:
Goals 2000 in the Context of a Global Power Grab

As discussed in chapter 8, the origins of Goals 2000 and other similar U.S. legislation can be seen in international agreements, such as "The World Declaration on Education for All," proclaimed at a 1990 United Nations conference in Jomtien, Thailand. That document, building on numerous previous documents generated by myriad UN conclaves—and augmented by myriad more documents since—is open in its declared ambition to remake the nations of the world on a vast scale. Few Americans know about this world government "mission creep"—the federal government certainly hasn't told them—but as we shall see, the influence of the international education bureaucracy is reshaping American public schools.

For example, Article VIII of the UN's "Education for All" tells us that education, by itself, isn't good enough; society, too, has to change: "Supportive policies in the social, cultural, and economic sectors are required in order to realize the full provision and utilization of basic education for individual and societal improvement." In other words, society has to be remade to meet bureaucratic specifications—and not just those of national bureaucrats, but those of international bureaucrats as well. Moreover, Article IX puts some mobilizing muscle behind these goals: "If the basic learning needs of all are to be met through a much broader scope of action than in the past, it will be essential to mobilize existing and new financial and human resources, public, private and voluntary." Now here's an oxymoron for you: *mobilize voluntary resources.* Well, what if those "resources"—that is, you and me and everyone else—don't volunteer to be "mobilized" by some nascent world government? And what do you do when you are "mobilized" anyway? Think about it: It's hard enough to fight city hall. It's even harder to fight your state capital. And harder still

to fight Washington, D.C. So how are you going to fight some ruling bureaucracy in another country, a far-away institution that might not even
acknowledge your legal standing to put up a fight? By now, we are starting
to see more clearly that "education" is just the thin edge of the wedge for a
remaking of the world. And here's another one: Article X, "Strengthening
International Solidarity"; the first lines of this article read, "Meeting basic
learning needs constitutes a common and universal human responsibility.
It requires international solidarity and equitable and fair economic relations in order to redress existing economic disparities." In other words,
"education for all" isn't really about education; it's about establishing
a new international world economic order to fix "existing economic disparities."

Some will say, of course, that these are just words—word castles
erected by expense-accounted bureaucrats with too much time on their
hands, living out a fantasy life of jargon as they junket their way around
the globe. But actually, no; these ideas have big consequences. Amid all
this word piling, we can see the antecedents to the Goals 2000 legislation
that was, in fact, enacted by the U.S. Congress just four years after the
Jomtien conference. That is, in both the UN document and the U.S. document, we see the same bureaucratic exhortation, the same commitment to
greater government funding, and the same commitment to government
power at the expense of local autonomy. (The National Education Goals
[Section 102] of Goals 2000 is included at the end of this appendix.) The
added twist, of course, is that once the decision-making power goes international, codified in obscure agreements and treaties, it is then beyond the
reach of Americans, who are never consulted in these decisions and would
certainly never approve of them if they were. There's a term for this phenomenon: "democracy deficit." That is, the bureaucrats in distant institutions make unaccountable decisions, and citizens and taxpayers find out
about them only later. This phenomenon has been happening in Europe
under the European Union for years as central planners gather power into
Brussels and then seek to impose liberal secular homogenization upon the
Continent as a whole. As a most flagrant recent example, people across
Europe have awakened to discover that some minister in Frankfurt has just
written a huge check to bail out some wastrel government.

This democracy deficit is evident here in the United States, too:
American judges now freely cite foreign law in their decisions, and the

Environmental Protection Agency—joined by an archipelago of other bureaucratic entities scattered across the federal government—seeks to bend America to rules written by international environmental authorities, most egregiously, in the area of climate change. These legal precedents are ominous to American sovereignty—but that's not an accident, that's the goal. And what if America's legal sovereignty and economic viability are crushed under the weight of international rule making? A small price to pay, the bureaucrats will answer, for global justice. And besides, we know full well that the bureaucrats always seem to flourish, no matter what the state of the economy.

One expert who saw early on this larger context for education policy was my fellow Minnesotan Allen Quist. Decades ago, Allen saw that the true global source of trendy new education policy lay in the centralplanning mind-set of international bureaucrats. He asked: "Are we doing what's right for kids? Or are we doing what's right for central planners? Who is calling the shots? Is it school boards, cities, states, federal government, or international bodies? The struggle has never been about good education—it's been all about power." The good fight against the international central planning of education had to start somewhere, and I am proud to say that we in Minnesota were at the forefront. After five years, we finally beat back the Profile of Learning, which was just one of many efforts to regiment children, and parents, according to the dictates of bureaucratic utopians.

Yet even so, as we have seen in the "No Child Left Behind" legislation of 2001, the same top-down education mind-set persists. And as Allen says, the "top" isn't Washington, D.C.; the top is actually international institutions, including the UN. So that's a fight that must continue into the future. It's a fight on behalf of all those who wish to see children educated in a properly structured school environment, guided under the leadership of parents and teachers, not bureaucrats.

Please take a look at the "National Education Goals" within Goals 2000 listed below. I think you will see the same ponderous bureaucratic style as in the international "Education for All" document—and the same ponderous bureaucratic mind-set. That is, children are, in effect, resources or inputs who must comport to a politically correct list of requirements, even as governments at all levels grow larger and stronger to "implement" these goals. I believe that if the American people knew where so much federal education "reform" was coming from, they would rise up and reject these bureaucratic dictates, reclaiming decision-making authority and restoring it to where it belongs—to taxpayers, parents, and students.

Section 102. National Education Goals

The Congress declares that the national
education goals are the following:

(1) School Readiness.
    (A) By the year 2000, all children in America will start school ready to learn.
    (B) The objectives for this goal are that—
        (i) all children will have access to high-quality and developmentally appropriate preschool programs that help prepare children for school;
        (ii) every parent in the United States will be a child's first teacher and devote time each day to helping such parent's preschool child learn, and parents will have access to the training and support parents need; and
        (iii) children will receive the nutrition, physical activity experiences, and health care needed to arrive at school with healthy minds and bodies, and to maintain the mental alertness necessary to be prepared to learn, and the number of low-birthweight babies will be significantly reduced through enhanced prenatal health systems.

(2) School Completion.
    (A) By the year 2000, the high school graduation rate will increase to at least 90 percent.
    (B) The objectives for this goal are that—
        (i) the Nation must dramatically reduce its school dropout rate, and 75 percent of the students who do drop out will successfully complete a high school degree or its equivalent; and
        (ii) the gap in high school graduation rates between Amer-

---

ican students from minority backgrounds and their non-minority counterparts will be eliminated.

(3) Student Achievement and Citizenship.
   (A) By the year 2000, all students will leave grades 4, 8, and 12 having demonstrated competency over challenging subject matter including English, mathematics, science, foreign languages, civics and government, economics, arts, history, and geography, and every school in America will ensure that all students learn to use their minds well, so they may be prepared for responsible citizenship, further learning, and productive employment in our Nation's modern economy.
   (B) The objectives for this goal are that—
      (i)   the academic performance of all students at the elementary and secondary level will increase significantly in every quartile, and the distribution of minority students in each quartile will more closely reflect the student population as a whole;
      (ii) the percentage of all students who demonstrate the ability to reason, solve problems, apply knowledge, and write and communicate effectively will increase substantially;
      (iii) all students will be involved in activities that promote and demonstrate good citizenship, good health, community service, and personal responsibility;
      (iv) all students will have access to physical education and health education to ensure they are healthy and fit;
      (v)   the percentage of all students who are competent in more than one language will substantially increase; and
      (vi) all students will be knowledgeable about the diverse cultural heritage of this Nation and about the world community.

(4) Teacher Education and Professional Development.
   (A) By the year 2000, the Nation's teaching force will have ac-

cess to programs for the continued improvement of their professional skills and the opportunity to acquire the knowledge and skills needed to instruct and prepare all American students for the next century.

(B) The objectives for this goal are that—

    (i) all teachers will have access to preservice teacher education and continuing professional development activities that will provide such teachers with the knowledge and skills needed to teach to an increasingly diverse student population with a variety of educational, social, and health needs;

    (ii) all teachers will have continuing opportunities to acquire additional knowledge and skills needed to teach challenging subject matter and to use emerging new methods, forms of assessment, and technologies;

    (iii) States and school districts will create integrated strategies to attract, recruit, prepare, retrain, and support the continued professional development of teachers, administrators, and other educators, so that there is a highly talented work force of professional educators to teach challenging subject matter; and

    (iv) partnerships will be established, whenever possible, among local educational agencies, institutions of higher education, parents, and local labor, business, and professional associations to provide and support programs for the professional development of educators.

(5) Mathematics and Science.

  (A) By the year 2000, United States students will be first in the world in mathematics and science achievement.

  (B) The objectives for this goal are that—

    (i) mathematics and science education, including the metric system of measurement, will be strengthened throughout the system, especially in the early grades;

    (ii) the number of teachers with a substantive background in mathematics and science, including the metric system of measurement, will increase by 50 percent; and

(iii) the number of United States undergraduate and graduate students, especially women and minorities, who complete degrees in mathematics, science, and engineering will increase significantly.

(6) Adult Literacy and Lifelong Learning.
  (A) By the year 2000, every adult American will be literate and will possess the knowledge and skills necessary to compete in a global economy and exercise the rights and responsibilities of citizenship.
  (B) The objectives for this goal are that—
    (i) every major American business will be involved in strengthening the connection between education and work;
    (ii) all workers will have the opportunity to acquire the knowledge and skills, from basic to highly technical, needed to adapt to emerging new technologies, work methods, and markets through public and private educational, vocational, technical, workplace, or other programs;
    (iii) the number of quality programs, including those at libraries, that are designed to serve more effectively the needs of the growing number of part-time and midcareer students will increase substantially;
    (iv) the proportion of the qualified students, especially minorities, who enter college, who complete at least two years, and who complete their degree programs will increase substantially;
    (v) the proportion of college graduates who demonstrate an advanced ability to think critically, communicate effectively, and solve problems will increase substantially; and
    (vi) schools, in implementing comprehensive parent involvement programs, will offer more adult literacy, parent training and life-long learning opportunities to improve the ties between home and school, and enhance parents' work and home lives.

(7) Safe, Disciplined, and Alcohol- and Drug-Free Schools.
    (A) By the year 2000, every school in the United States will be free of drugs, violence, and the unauthorized presence of firearms and alcohol and will offer a disciplined environment conducive to learning.
    (B) The objectives for this goal are that—
        (i) every school will implement a firm and fair policy on use, possession, and distribution of drugs and alcohol;
        (ii) parents, businesses, governmental and community organizations will work together to ensure the rights of students to study in a safe and secure environment that is free of drugs and crime, and that schools provide a healthy environment and are a safe haven for all children;
        (iii) every local educational agency will develop and implement a policy to ensure that all schools are free of violence and the unauthorized presence of weapons;
        (iv) every local educational agency will develop a sequential, comprehensive kindergarten through twelfth grade drug and alcohol prevention education program;
        (v) drug and alcohol curriculum should be taught as an integral part of sequential, comprehensive health education;
        (vi) community-based teams should be organized to provide students and teachers with needed support; and
        (vii) every school should work to eliminate sexual harassment.

(8) Parental Participation.
    (A) By the year 2000, every school will promote partnerships that will increase parental involvement and participation in promoting the social, emotional, and academic growth of children.
    (B) The objectives for this Goal are that—
        (i) every State will develop policies to assist local schools and local educational agencies to establish programs for increasing partnerships that respond to the varying

needs of parents and the home, including parents of children who are disadvantaged or bilingual, or parents of children with disabilities;

(ii) every school will actively engage parents and families in a partnership which supports the academic work of children at home and shared educational decisionmaking at school; and

(iii) parents and families will help to ensure that schools are adequately supported and will hold schools and teachers to high standards of accountability.